The Jew

The Jew

Novel Based on a True Story

Dominik Poleski

Library of Congress Control Number:		2017902144
ISBN:	Hardcover	978-1-5245-8307-1
	Softcover	978-1-5245-8308-8
	eBook	978-1-5245-8309-5

KJV
Scripture taken from The Holy Bible, King James Version. Cambridge Edition: 1769; King James Bible Online, 2016. www.kingjamesbibleonline.org.

Print information available on the last page.

Rev. date: 06/01/2017

To order additional copies of this book, contact:
Xlibris
1-888-795-4274
www.Xlibris.com
Orders@Xlibris.com
754817

1

THE DAY, LIKE any other day, seemed typical, uneventful and quiet. It was the end of September; and the gloomy weather announced fast approach of a different season, and that was to be expected. Several large patches of heavy, dark clouds hung low, as if just above the rooftops, only to be dispersed from time to time by a sudden gust of cold, easterly wind, which seemed to nag at them to move on, and carried with it scarce drops of rain, with falling colorful autumn leaves, swirling down in a familiar, perennial pattern and slowly lying down to rest on the wet ground below.

The slim, black silhouette of Alek was clearly and unmistakably recognizable even from a considerable distance—the characteristic lanky, bent-forward figure, the long arms swaying alongside his disproportionately long legs, giving an impression of utter awkwardness. He walked quickly, as if trying to avoid being seen, seemingly oblivious of the passers-by and few onlookers, and only occasionally lifting his head up to check the path in front of him. Once satisfied, he bowed his head again and surged forward.

Alek had a habit, or possibly out of necessity, wearing what seemed like the same clothes day in and day out. Baggy black trousers and a white shirt with sleeves rolled up to his elbows on a sunny day; but on a day like this, a dark well-worn jacket over the shirt, and of a color that was rather hard to identify. On his feet was a pair of always the same, old leather shoes, that were black once. From time to time, he walked right into a puddle left by the rain in the cracked and uneven surface of the concrete tiled sidewalk. That didn't disturb him; his pale face didn't seem to betray any emotions—if anything at all, just an intense concentration.

Rarely a passerby would notice a faint, barely discernable smile on his face when, for a second or two, he lifted it reluctantly to look ahead. He was in a hurry, intent on doing his usual errands as quickly as possible, and getting back home without incident.

Alek usually stopped at one or two stores in the commercial part of town, for he always knew exactly what he wanted. He didn't say much, seldom spoke more than a few words besides the customary greeting, and only asked for whatever he came for. Those were just the usual household necessities, like bread, milk, or grits, and again quickly lowering his head, he would wait for the products to arrive on the counter. He would then nervously put the money down, take the change, or sometimes even without waiting for it, and just as quickly turn around and leave the store. Although it wouldn't be the first time, it would leave the clerk bewildered and shaking her head, and then letting out a deep sigh.

Alek didn't waste time going back home, his humped figure moving swiftly, measuring out those familiar long strides along the gray, uneven pavement. His mother was anxiously waiting for him at home. She took a day off work due to a cold she had suddenly caught. It had become a frequent occurrence after a backbreaking toil at a local fruit processing plant, constantly bending down, lifting, moving, and pacing the wet concrete floor, between the unheated, damp concrete-block walls of the main hall, filled with the stifling air smelling of rotting fruits and vegetables.

Alek passed the commercial section of town and continued on till the scenery changed to that of a straight row of dilapidated residential housing on both sides. Then he turned into a narrow cobblestone side street. He momentarily stiffened and hesitated, and then quickened his pace, since it seemed deserted and a little darker here. He had barely made some forty or fifty steps when a sudden violent jolt, an unexpected brutal force threw him against a wall, almost knocking him down. A pair of strange hands, tightly clenching the shirt around his neck, shook him, and repeatedly thrashed his frail body against the building.

"Watch where you're going, you idiot. Can't you see? Are you blind?" growled the angry young man, pinning him to the wall.

"I'm sorry, I'm really sorry…I didn't mean to…I didn't see you," Alek began to plead with the stranger, pale with fear and trembling. He thought he must have accidentally run into a pedestrian, which wouldn't be the first time, but it was all just a misunderstanding.

He soon realized that the man had no intention of letting him go just yet, when he bellowed, "Hey guys, did you hear this? Just listen to him. He didn't see me…Try keeping your head up, stupid," said the man, pushing against Alek's chest with his clenched fist. Alek let out a low groan, as he caught a glimpse of two other teenage boys, about fifteen or sixteen years old coming out from just around the corner of the house. They approached slowly, looking at him intently, with characteristic disdainful smirks on their faces, and took positions on both sides, forming a semicircle with him in the middle, up against the wall. He was trapped.

A paralyzing fear engulfed Alek's frail body, and his legs began to shake uncontrollably, making it difficult to stay standing. There was no way out and no one around to help; the street was deserted. The young man, perhaps no older than seventeen, held Alek's shirt with his right hand tight under his chin, now grinning with the confidence of someone who had been waiting for this moment for a long, long time, and wasn't about to let his prey get away easily.

"You're a fucking Jew, aren't you?" one of them, who seemed to be the oldest, asked with visible contempt, stepping up even closer to Alek, pushing him harder against the wall, while the eldest was still holding him by the shirt. They didn't expect an answer; they all knew very well who Alek was. They'd all seen him many times before, walking the same streets, never looking sideways, and ignoring them. They didn't like being ignored, not by someone like him.

Alek, stricken with an overwhelming fear, with his back clinging to the wall, couldn't say a word. His lips trembled, his dark eyes began to swell with tears, and each second seemed like an hour.

"Didn't you know you couldn't walk this way? This area is off-limits for suckers like you. Didn't you know that?"

"No, I didn't. I'm sorry…I didn't mean it. I'll never do it again," Alek began to plead as panic was setting in.

"What's your name?" asked one of the younger boys.

"It's Alek. Please let me go…I'm really sorry. I was just on my way home… Please, I promise, you'll never see me here again," he said in a low voice, with a painful grimace of complete helplessness on his pale face.

"So, Jew, what do you have in that bag you're carrying?" asked the oldest member.

Alek didn't say a word, just opened his hand and dropped the bag to the ground. The boys looked down. The contents were clearly visible as the canvas bag opened up. They were not interested in what was there; there was nothing they could use, or was of value to them.

"Do you have any money?" asked the leader.

"No, I don't have any left, just a few small coins, nothing really" answered Alek, his voice barely audible, his lips trembling, and his thin frame slightly curled up inward, as if protecting itself against the attackers.

"So, you don't have money, and are walking where you're not supposed to walk, and saying that you didn't know, and now you just want to go home, right? Did you hear this, guys?" said the eldest, and slapped Alek on the side of his head.

"Give it to him, what are you waiting for?" intervened one of the others and grabbed Alek by a fistful of his hair.

Alek gave out a faint cry of pain and began sliding down the wall, as if looking for protection in the ground below, or hoping it would part beneath them and swallow up his tormentors. The attackers took it as a sign to spring into action, and any reservations they still had were dropped at once. The three of them started to slap and punch Alek wherever they could.

Alek tried to shield his face instinctively, waving his arms awkwardly, as if attempting to drive off a swarm of bees, but with little success. From his mouth, strange sounds were pouring out, as if from an animal being slaughtered and about to give out its last breath. It was a shrill wail, the sound of unbelievable anguish and sheer terror, while few more punches landed on his head and body.

Somewhere from a distance, a sudden scream and yelling rang out: "Stop! Stop! Stop it right now, you hooligans! You bandits!"

The attackers turned in the direction where the menacing yells were coming from. There was a stout elderly woman running toward them, quickly closing the distance, swaying heavily from side to side, waving her arms with a black purse flying in her hand. The boys sensed the fury of the oncoming woman and didn't want to take any chances.

"Let's split, men. That's the old hag Pavloska. She's crazy!" shouted one of them. They all looked at each other for a split second, as they knew what to do, as if they had it all rehearsed many times before. Before the old woman even got near the place, they all dispersed in different directions and, like ghosts, disappeared in between the gray buildings.

The old woman, now barely moving her feet forward, breathing heavily, and gasping for air reached Alek, who was covering his face, crouching by the wall and sobbing uncontrollably. Pavloska tried to say something, holding her left hand on her rising chest, taking deep breaths, as if in the midst of a heart attack. She bent over Alek with considerable effort and, trying to regain her composure, muttered, "Are you hurt? Don't be afraid, my dear…those bandits are gone. Poor boy… nobody deserves this." She reached with her hand to take Alek under his arm, but he forcefully shrugged it off, knocking it backward.

"Are you all right? Are you hurt?" Pavloska desperately asked again.

Suddenly, from that curled-up, thin body, a most horrific cry came out. It was a choked-up, wailing squeal one could only hear at a slaughterhouse. Frightened, the old woman took a step back.

"Are you all right, child?" she asked again, and added, "They must have done something terrible to him, oh God…what is this world coming to? They must have hurt him badly, those bandits!"

Alek was still crouching down, now sobbing quietly, face hidden in between his arms and the bag, the loaf of bread, and a paper package of grits lying scattered on the wet ground nearby.

"I promise you, this thing will not go unpunished as long as I live. You don't have to be afraid now, everything will be all right. I'll walk you home, come with me," continued Pavloska.

Alek slowly lifted his head and looked around, bewildered. A narrow streak of blood from his nose was making its way into his swollen, trembling lips. His tearful deep-set black eyes still betrayed his pain and obvious fear and were also badly bruised all around.

Pavloska put her hand under Alek's left arm, and, pulling gently, tried to encourage him to get up. Alek resisted at first, but then started to stretch his legs slowly, and slid upward with his back still against the wall.

"That's good, my dear. That's good…You're such a fine young man. Don't be afraid now. As long as I'm here, nothing will happen to you. You can be sure of that," said the old woman as she continued to pull Alek gently up.

"Leave me alone, please," Alek snapped, shrugging off her hand, already standing on his feet, although still somewhat dazed and confused. An occasional spasmodic sob escaped his swollen, bloodied lips, but he was slowly regaining his composure, and he clearly had no interest in talking to Pavloska. She looked at him with great concern, as if he were her own child, but was lost for words, and tried not to impose on his fragile state, waiting for Alek to make the next move. He looked slowly at the ground around him, at the few scattered belongings, and forward to the main street that he came from not long ago, barely fifty paces away, clearly visible at the end of this dingy secluded alley. There at the entrance, he noticed a boy of about twelve or thirteen years old, just standing there and looking with interest at the whole scene unfolding.

Alek had a sense he had seen him somewhere before, as their eyes met for a split second. He then reluctantly glanced at Pavloska, and made a few shaky steps in the direction of the street, followed by several quick long strides, and then started to run with his characteristic adolescent awkwardness, fully stretching his thin long legs up front and then back, as if momentarily leaving them behind.

The old woman barely had time to react, made a few steps to follow him, but just as quickly gave up, pleading, "Stop, please stop! Wait a second, wait for me!"

Alek ran—ran as fast as he could, without looking back, occasionally swerving sharply to avoid a rare passerby or a puddle, and continued to run through mostly deserted streets leading to his home. He soon reached the familiar courtyard and burst through the front door.

2

MRS. BRODSKI SEEMED to sense that something awful happened long before he appeared at the door, since he was out much longer than usual. She stood waiting just inside, in the small hallway leading to the kitchen, and literally threw herself at him as soon as he appeared and cried out with horror, "Oh my God! What happened to you? What happened?"

"Nothing, Mom. Nothing, really. I'm fine...I mean, I'll be all right, don't worry." Alek quickly freed himself for his mother's gentle embrace, and in a few strides crossed the kitchen toward the living room. When he reached the sofa, he sank into it, or rather, dropped with the full impact of his weight. His mother followed right behind and sat next to him, clenching his thin, blood-smeared hands.

"Alek, who did this to you? Please tell me right now, what happened?"

"Oh, it's nothing...Please, just leave me alone. I need to be alone, Mom."

"Don't tell me it's nothing. I can see what happened. Who did this to you? I knew it. I just knew this was bound to happen. Alek, for god's sake tell me, what happened?"

"Mom, I'll be all right. I need some rest. Just leave me alone, please."

"I won't leave you alone. Tell me everything that happened, I want to know. I'm your mother, and I love you, son."

Alek sat there silently with his head down, unable to utter a word. His mother, powerless to extract any information, just looked at him with profound sadness and despair, as bitter tears started streaming down her cheeks. She tried hard to maintain her composure, to keep it all together, to not show her weakness. There were just the two of them, a family of two in this house, in this neighborhood, in this town, and this whole country. They had no one else they could rely on without family or close friends, only the neighbors they hardly knew, and each other.

Mrs. Brodski, exasperated, looked at her son with a heavy heart, taking deep breaths and sighing, then looking around the room for no apparent reason, as if looking for solace, hope, or even faint traces of life other than the two of them. There was nothing, only the old, solitary wooden clock on the wall, which seemed to tick louder and louder, faster and faster the more she looked at it. In the silence that engulfed the room, the sound of the clock was becoming unnerving, racing like the palpitations of a sick heart in its last throes, before bursting open, spilling all its parts onto the floor below, unable to go on as if nothing happened; and the time stood still. If there was ever a time for the Almighty to reveal himself having failed so miserably just over two decades before, it was now.

The family of two, mother and son, just sat there impassively, with sullen faces, their heads down, each unable to utter a word, overcome with emotions, surrounded by soothing silence.

Mrs. Brodski temporarily lost in thought; aftererward, she quietly got up, went into the kitchen, poured warm water into a large porcelain bowl, took out a small towel, and came right back into the living room. Alek was still sitting there on the sofa, engrossed in his thoughts, staring down at the well-worn wooden floor with the narrow longitudinal planks covered with dark old varnish spanning in the direction of the longer side of the rectangular room. The entire house consisted of a short corridor from the outside entrance door to the kitchen, a small bathroom, and one bigger room, which served both as a living room and a common bedroom. The kitchen was quite spacious, although badly outdated, with a single window out onto the gray wooden fence dividing the two adjacent courtyards. The main fixtures of the kitchen were a large cast iron stove; burning coal and wood; and an old white cupboard that was also used as storage for pots and pans and a pantry, lined up against the longest wall but seeming to permanently lean backward; and a small wooden table near the window, with three simple wooden chairs. The fogged-up, single-pane window had double small curtains, parting in the middle, stretched on a thin rope across the window frame, about two-thirds of the height up. The feeble, worn-out fabric with flowery, mostly pale blue and red pattern showed all the signs of age, just like the surrounding off-white walls, with patches of bulging and peeling paint over uneven plaster, and a few yellowish stains, crossing over from the ceiling above. Like all the floors in this communal apartment, it was covered with long, wooden planks with several cracks, small holes and indentations filled with grime as a result of continued usage over decades, and color of which by now was impossible to accurately determine.

The living room gave the impression of being crammed with old furniture, without any particular order or style, accumulated over a long time. Besides the sofa, it contained a single bed in the farthest corner of the room, by the only small window; then a rectangular wooden table closer to the center of the room, with six matching chairs and a big area rug under them, in a myriad of faded colors vaguely resembling those in the famed Persian rugs. Along one of the walls stood a rather large brown wooden drawer chest with a brass menorah on top of it; and a little farther to the side, a dark-brown armoire. Along the other wall stood a brown, wooden bookshelf with neatly stacked rows and rows of books—mostly in Polish, but also some Russian classics.

The furnishings were completed by two odd night tables, one by the sofa, and one by the single bed. Three of the walls were sparsely decorated with framed black-and-white family photographs. The biggest and most prominent picture was a rather large wedding photograph of Jakub and Zofia Brodski. The walls themselves were white once, now faded and stained, especially below the ceiling, with obvious signs of leaking roof and a few patches of discolored, peeling paint.

Mrs. Brodski placed the bowl of water on a chair beside the sofa, sat down near Alek, and began to gently wipe away any traces of dried-up blood off his visibly bruised face. His lips were cut and swollen, and there was a small cut above his black-ringed and swollen left eye. Alek's head jerked backward or sideways, a grimace of pain on his face as he gave out a long and hissing sound every time his mother touched one of the cuts with the water-soaked towel.

"Sit still, please," whispered his mom.

"But it hurts," Alek snapped.

"I know it does. I'm trying to be as gentle as I can. I think we might have to go to the clinic and have the doctor look at it"

"No, Mom, I'm not going anywhere. I'll get over it, I'll be fine…"

"I'm not so sure about that, my son. We'll see. It's quite a distance to walk, especially for you in this condition. I can't count on the neighbors, you know. They all don't seem to be very happy about us living here. Some resent us for whatever reason. I think we're the only Jewish family in this town, if one can call us a family."

"No, Mom, they hate us here, I know it."

"That's what I just said. Some resent us," Mrs. Brodski corrected him. "Now tell me, who did this to you? Were they the same boys who pushed you around and taunted you before?"

"Yeah, the same three. I know that one of them, the eldest, is a son of the chief policeman," said Alek.

"How do you know that, are you sure?" asked his mom in disbelief.

"I've seen him before a couple of times with his dad walking with his arm around his shoulder, and he is a policeman."

"Alek, are you sure?"

"Yes, Mom, I'm sure."

"Well then, in that case, I might have to pay him a visit at the police station, tomorrow," she said angrily, as if she had already made up her mind.

"I don't want you to go, Mom. I don't want any trouble."

"There will be no trouble, son. Enough is enough! I have my own reasons to complain too I haven't told you about. It has not been easy for me either, the way I've been treated here around the town."

"I didn't know that, Mom."

"I didn't tell you, Alek, because I didn't want you to worry, but that's not a big deal. What they did to you is just too much for me, and is not going to get any better, I'm convinced. We have to put an end to it. We can't live like this, and doing nothing is not an option any longer. After all, we've been doing nothing for the past few years now."

"Do you want me to go with you, Mom?"

"No, not this time. I'd rather you stay home and rest. I don't know what's going to happen, and at any rate, I don't want you to go through more aggravation. It might turn out you'll have to go there with me eventually. Only time will tell. Son, has anyone else seen this? I mean, were there any witnesses?"

"Yes, Mom. There was this old woman who showed up and chased them off, and later stayed with me. I don't know her, but I think she is local. There was also a boy, standing and staring at me. I'm sure I've seen him before. He was just looking at me for no reason."

"Good, that's good, Alek. At least we have witnesses."

3

THE BUILDING HOUSING the local police, or Citizens' Militia, as it was officially called in the new Socialist Polish People's Republic, was located in an old two-story concrete building near the town's center. It was actually part of one long row of buildings spanning two entire blocks, home to many shops and small government businesses. The police station was located on the second floor, at the eastern end of this dilapidated, crumbling, and gray concrete structure. The slightly ajar wooden double doors led into the building's vestibule, ending with a steep staircase to the upper floor. Everything around this place, right from the entrance, was in a condition of total neglect and disrepair. Peeling paint, rotting wood, rusting metal balustrades and iron bars in the few small windows were the norm everywhere.

Once inside, walking down the dimly lit and cold, main floor entrance hall, one was struck by the unbearable stench of urine and human excrement. If anyone was to venture a little closer, just out of curiosity, they would see there were other colorful adornments; and on full display, like on a sumptuous platter, a stray patron's vegetable salad, given back unwillingly for no other reason than assimilation problems. Puddles of urine and feces were still clearly visible in the darkened corners, most likely the aftermath of a typical rowdy night at the local popular drinking hangout, about a hundred meters to the west, in the same row of buildings.

After hours, late at night, the police station vestibule had a dual purpose: a handy and quick convenience outlet when everything else was closed, and, of course, a place to express utter contempt for the uniformed authority on the way back home. All this went on with almost assured impunity, while the officers preferred the relative comfort of the second-floor office, and rarely ventured downstairs, especially on any cold and rainy day. Whoever ventured in here on a legitimate business, was also struck by the unusual, and quite original, mural artwork in the corners of the filthy concrete walls, left there by drunken "artists," who obviously were not expected to carry a roll of toilet paper and used their fingers as a paintbrush, and the excrement as an artistic medium. This whole place emanated the most repulsive and creepy feeling; and many visitors, once inside, had a change of heart, turned around, and just as quickly left the building, never looking back.

The common perception in town was, that the personnel of this proud law enforcement unit in the name of the People's Republic of Poland had little more than elementary school education. Education was not the most desirable attribute to possess, certainly not for this job; but rather; your average police force member ideally had to be big, strong, and stupid. Conformity was an indispensable virtue for the lawmen, and the law was first of all what the unit commandant said, then the local secretary of the Polish United Workers' Party—and so it went up the party ranks right to the first secretary, Comrade Vladyslav Gomulka. The country was in the party's iron grip, and the police was its faithful arm, its extension. All the men in uniforms went through a basic indoctrination course in socialist ideology, carefully tailored to their comprehensive abilities, with periodic follow-ups. Not enough of socialism was deemed dangerous, since it could encourage independent thinking to make up for the gaps in proper understanding; and too much could inflict an unnecessary strain on the poor fellow's mental capacity and confuse him completely.

Mrs. Brodski stood in front of the double entrance door, hesitating briefly, then looked up at the red-and-white metal name plaque on the wall above and, gripping the handle pushed the heavy door in with considerable effort. Once inside, she slowly approached the staircase, looking around, up and down. The smell and what she had just seen after scaling just a few steps must have taken away whatever courage she had. She paused and looked back, holding the handrail tightly. The door was now closed behind her. Profound feeling of fear and nausea gripped her body as she dragged her leaden legs behind her, and momentarily, she wanted to turn back.

Loud banging and raspy screams of agony from above reached the bottom of the stairs, which only magnified Mrs. Brodski's fright and hesitation; but she kept climbing, and slowly made it to the first landing. There were two intermediate landings to the second-floor militia headquarters. She mumbled something to herself, invoking God's mercy as the banging became louder and louder with each step she took. It seemed to be coming from a jail cell adjacent to the main quarters.

The main police office was quite spacious, with a long counter just past the front door, then behind it three cluttered desks, several chairs, some cabinets, a wooden coat hanger, two black telephones, and a radio. High up on the main wall, directly across the entrance door, hung three portraits—a standard feature of all government offices. The first one to the left was of a bold, oversized head of the first secretary of the United Workers' Party, Comrade Vladislav Gomulka, peering down at all below. Then in the middle, just slightly higher, hung the portrait of a white eagle on a red background, Poland's national symbol. The portrait to the right, at the same height as Gomulka's, was an equally bold likeness of the second communist in command, Comrade Jozef Cyrankiewicz, the country's prime minister.

The air inside was stifling and reeked of tobacco, sweat, grime, and, unmistakably, of cheap Russian cologne in various proportions, and only added to the whole unsettling atmosphere. There were two policemen on duty in the office at this time, one of them of medium height but obviously a fat specimen; and the other was exactly the opposite, tall and skinny. Both had a characteristic small mustache, as if it were a code requirement, and both were absorbed doing some paperwork, undoubtedly a very important task in the daily routine, and didn't even notice Mrs. Brodski standing there behind the counter.

"Good morning," she said again with particular emphasis.

Few seconds later, but what seemed more like minutes, the fat one sitting behind a desk slowly raised his head, looking perplexed or annoyed, but didn't utter a word. The other cop went about his business, looking for something in the filing cabinet, and then, without even a glance in the direction of the counter, said rather loudly, "Kovaluk, there is a woman standing at the front. Go and see what she wants."

The fat one awoke suddenly, looked up, rolled his eyes, and lifted his heavy arse slowly, then unceremoniously walked over to the front counter with his eyes fixed on Mrs. Brodski. There was an unmistakable aura of importance on his greasy red and ugly face.

"What can we do for you, madame," asked officer Kovaluk.

Mrs. Brodski hesitated and couldn't utter a word. She just stood there, paralyzed by the overwhelming fear and uncertainty. She seemed disoriented and completely lost. Her mind raced through, unable to recover any traces of rational thought, as if she was unsure where she was, or why. She wanted to say something, moved her lips, but no words came out. The policeman, visibly impatient, repeated, "Mrs., what can we do for you?"

Mrs. Brodski shuddered, looked back at the entrance door, and back again at the burly man in front of her. Slowly, it all began to fall into focus. She snapped out of the brief amnesia and the overwhelming fear of this office, the seat of the omnipotent authority.

"Oh, yes, yes…I'm sorry. I wasn't sure, you see…I'm actually not sure if I'm at the right place."

"What seems to be the problem?" asked the cop, irritated.

"I'd like to see the commandant, if I may," she said, finally regaining some of her lost composure.

"I'm afraid that's impossible. He's busy. I'm sure I can take care of this," Officer Kovaluk snapped back.

"I think, it'd be better if I talk to the commandant myself," she continued.

At that moment, the other policeman in the back of the room lifted his head and looked sternly in the direction of Mrs. Brodski. Their eyes met for a split second, but she lowered her gaze just as quickly and looked back again at Officer Kovaluk standing impatiently in front of her, behind the counter.

"So, what is it, madame?"

"My name is…," Mrs. Brodski started, but was quickly interrupted.

DOMINIK POLESKI

"We know who you are. Everybody in town knows who you are. The question is, what did you come here for? What do you want? You either tell me now, or don't waste our time."

"I'm sorry for all the trouble I'm causing you. I came here to file a complaint," she said shyly.

"A complaint?" asked Kovaluk, as if taken completely by surprise, and then added impatiently and with agitation, "Against whom?"

"You see, sir, my son, Alek, was beaten up by some hooligans on the street."

"Mrs. Brodski, things like these happen all the time. It is nothing serious, just child's play. We don't deal with matters of this nature. You came to the wrong place. You should talk to their parents, or go to their school—maybe talk to his teachers, not us."

"I'm afraid it's more serious than that. Alek sustained some injuries to his face, chest, and arms. He was roughed up and pushed around by the same bunch on a few previous occasions. Things have been escalating for some time now. We need to put an end to it. We cannot live like this any longer. Alek told me that one of the young men is the son of—" She abruptly stopped and lowered her head.

"Whose son is he? Please tell me, don't be afraid," asked the policeman sarcastically, with a faint smile on his face.

Mrs. Brodski stood there in silence, looking helplessly at Officer Kovaluk with her big, frightened black eyes.

"Well, are you going to tell me, or are you just going to stand there and waste my precious time?"

"Alek said that he recognized one of the attackers. He is the son of Mr. Commandant," she finally uttered it out.

"What? Are you out of your mind, Mrs.? That's a serious accusation. For your sake, I hope you know what you're saying," said the policeman with dismissive smile and obvious contempt. Then he turned around and asked the other policeman, "Edward, did you hear what she just said?"

"No, I didn't, what did she say?"

"She said that your son, with his friends, beat up her boy, Alek Brodski."

"She must be crazy. She doesn't know what she's talking about," the station commandant snapped as he approached the counter.

There was a moment of silence as the three of them looked at each other, in turns incredulously. Captain Sokolowski's facial expression and abrupt gestures with his long, thin hands left no doubt that he didn't take Mrs. Brodski's statement lightly, and was more than just visibly irritated. In this border town, he was the omnipotent authority, he was the law, and anyone who dared to question or oppose that would be met with the full force of his wrath.

He had come to this town with his family just over two years before, with the task of introducing exactly that—law and order, "to clean up" this place. At forty-five, he was the youngest in the detachment of four, and the most educated, with a middle school diploma and the energy of a maniacal zealot, giving him a feeling of invincibility as he embarked on his mission. The common perception was that Sokolowski was virtually incorruptible, and those who tried regretted it dearly.

"So, you're saying my boy, Adam, assaulted your son, is that right?" The captain turned to Mrs. Brodski with a cynical, derisive tone in his voice, and a particularly cold and penetrating look in his eyes, both of which by now had become his well-known trademarks. Mrs. Brodski once again hesitated, looked sideways, and down at the front counter, rather than face the obvious annoyance in Sokolowski's shallow eyes and those narrow lips of his, twisted in contemptuous, vengeful grimace, which seemed to be permanently affixed to his facial expression.

"Did I hear it right, Mrs.? My son and some others assaulted your son, or am I delusional?" repeated the commandant with increasing agitation.

"Yes," said Mrs. Brodski in a barely audible, soft voice.

"When did it happen?"

"Yesterday afternoon."

"Where?"

"On a small side street, just off the Red Army street, and few blocks away from the center."

"Were there any witnesses?

"Yes, my son said there was an old woman who intervened and chased those hooligans away, and a boy standing nearby, who just happened to be there."

"Names?"

"I'm afraid I don't know their names."

"So, no names, but there were witnesses. That's interesting..."

"You see, Officer, we hardly know anybody here."

"Why didn't you come here yesterday?" the captain continued his interrogation.

"I wasn't sure what to do," Mrs. Brodski answered politely.

"What is your son's name?"

"Aleksander Brodski."

"I think I've heard this name before. How old is your son?"

"He is fifteen years old."

"Where is your son now?"

"At home. I didn't let him go to school today. I'm afraid he's not well."

The commandant was writing it all down on a piece of paper. Then he stopped and looked at it for what seemed like several minutes. A deep silence engulfed the room. The three of them stood there as if frozen, giving the mood an inhospitable and strangely surreal feeling. There was the sudden outburst of banging coming from adjacent jail cell, accompanied by somewhat muted cries for help. A persistent series of *Thud...thud...thud...* at equal intervals against the heavy steel door sent a cascading echo bouncing off the thick concrete walls.

"Help, help, help me!" cried out the man inside, and then again after a brief intermission: *Thud...thud...thud...*

Commandant Sokolowki abruptly lifted his head in an obvious gesture that he had finally lost his patience, and shouted to his subordinate, "Kovaluk, go and shut that son of a bitch up, once and for all!"

"Not a problem, Chief," said the policeman with an air of authority and confidence, and, with a quick, instinctive movement of his plump hands, checked if his gun and baton were still at his waist. Then with a few rapid strides, he stepped out the door. What followed shortly after, somewhere on the other side of the door and still quite audible, was a barrage of the most obscene and incomprehensible tirade one could imagine. Then a menacing avalanche of threats to top it off, in what seemed like a well-rehearsed and frequently applied repertoire of abundant but less known vocabulary of at least three akin Slavic languages. It had its desired effect, and must have stunned the poor soul behind the bars like an electric jolt, which left him numb and silent.

Kovaluk rushed back into the office and slammed the door behind him. Then with his hand still shaking, he pulled out a package of cigarettes from his side uniform pocket, took one out and rolled it between his fingers twice. He lit it up, inhaled deeply, and then nervously exhaled, blowing out the thick white smoke up in the air. His normally red cheeks were now pale, as the smoke rose into the air above their heads, but an overwhelming sense of pride and accomplishment he could barely contain was written all over his face. Sokolowski looked at him with pity and then, without saying a word, let out a strange growl; then a faint, sarcastic smirk flashed across his faced.

Mrs. Brodski felt trapped, helpless; and all she could think about was getting out of this place and going back home, where Alek was waiting, and where within their small, crammed living quarters, they could still find peace and tranquility. Her apprehension before coming here now appeared to be fully justified, for she could not have anticipated a rather malicious interrogation at the hands of the guardians of law and order. The commandant turned to Mrs. Brodski again.

"You were saying that my son and some others assaulted your son, Alek. Normally, I wouldn't bother with things of this nature, but since you're making this rather serious accusation, I will look into it. I will investigate this thoroughly. I'll talk to my son. You must understand, we deal here with matters of vital importance, not some child's play gone wrong. Like that drunkard in the cell, you know what he's done? Let me tell you, last night he got drunk out of his mind, and started publicly yelling out all those profanities and slanders against our first secretary of the Party, Comrade Gomulka, our prime minister Cyrankiewicz, the Party, and against our friend and neighbor, the Soviet Union. I can understand someone can have, on occasion, too much to drink—in all honesty, we all do—but to shoot your mouth off like that, and in public for all to hear—that's crossing the boundary, and must be dealt with accordingly and decisively. We won't tolerate open contempt, subversion of the worst kind; and enemies of the state will be eliminated. Apparently, it wasn't the first time he had done that. Besides, lately, we've had reports of intensified spying activities along the border nearby. These are dangerous times we live in, Mrs. Brodski. The enemy never sleeps, trying to undermine our socialist motherland. We have to be vigilant and always ready to defend ourselves against the evil forces of Western imperialism."

Mrs. Brodski had difficulty listening to the commandant's tirade, most likely taken right out of some provincial party's indoctrination session, an obligatory curriculum for all those in position of authority. Socialism, imperialism, spying, subversion were such fantastic and irrelevant concepts to her now that they only magnified her feeling of frustration and helplessness. She almost broke down, barely maintaining her composure; although the temptation to lash out and relieve the mounting anger was hard to restrain. She turned to Sokolowski and, looking him straight in the eyes, said, "I'm sorry for taking up your valuable time, sir. I know you have more important things to do, so I'll just go now."

"I assure you, I'm all for the rule of law. I will talk to my son, and one way or another, we'll let you know," said the commandant with a dismissive tone.

Mrs. Brodski left the station as quickly as only she could, all the way down the steep concrete steps, holding tight to the handrail. The whole experience left her in such emotional distress that she could not control herself any longer, and bitter tears trickled down her face. In a state of almost complete emotional despair, but with unwavering determination, she stepped onto the sidewalk, temporarily blinded by the daylight. Without as much as a glance at her surroundings, she hurried back home. But she had no regrets, not in the least.

As soon as she stepped through the threshold, knowing well that Alek was waiting anxiously, she conveyed some of the carefully chosen details of the events at the police station to him; but more so, she tried to reassure him of her boundless motherly resourcefulness, strength, and protective instincts, and at the same time sparing him any new emotional burden.

Alek remained in a pensive and reflective mood for most of the day. He barely uttered a few words, didn't eat much, didn't do much, just lay down on the sofa, then got back up and sat there, and then lay down again, walked into the kitchen or bathroom a few times, and looked out the window from time to time.

An unexpected knock on the door early in the evening a few days later spoiled the silence, just when things were slowly getting back to normal. Maria Pavloska stood there unannounced, introduced herself with a smile, and asked if she could come in, she'd like to talk.

Mrs. Brodski greeted her warmly, happy to see her. She recognized in the old woman a kind and gentle spirit, a good-natured demeanor, and a humility that seemed to emanate from her.

Pavloska had brought with her a small package of coffee beans as a gift. Her husband, Stanislav, although close to retirement, was working for the National Railways on freight trains and traveled frequently to the Soviet Union. Many staples there were readily available, although quite scarce in this part of the country, such as coffee or black tea with such intense aroma that could rival the best tea in the world. Among the other popular commodities were oranges, lemons, cigarettes, and Russian perfumes. The chic local women wore the perfume in abundance, which were, in fact, easily recognizable; short on delicate balance and refinement, they emitted such a strong and pervasive flowery smell that it was impossible to mistake their origin.

The two women sat in the dimly lit room and chatted amicably, sipping the freshly brewed coffee, while Alek sat at the kitchen table doing his homework. Mrs. Pavloska related her side of the whole story with such passion and attention to detail, as if she were talking about her own son.

Mrs. Brodski in turn shared the story of her visit to the police station, pausing from time to time, sighing, and taking deep breaths. Her facial expressions reflected that most unpleasant event as the story went on. On occasion, her eyes, stricken with painful sadness, swelled

DOMINIK POLESKI

with tears; and she reached for a white handkerchief in the left pocket of her handmade brown wool sweater.

Mrs. Pavloska listened attentively, seldom interrupting, and mostly with an affirmative "Aha, aha." Or, "Yes, yes, my dear." Or, "Those monsters!" Then she summed it all up: "The Almighty God has seen it all, and will not be so gracious when the time comes on judgment day, let me assure you of that."

As the time went on, Mrs. Brodski managed a few barely discernible smiles in the corners of her lips, especially when recalling the commandant's impassioned speech on the merits of the Party, its leadership or the friendship of the good Big Brother across the river, the Soviet Union.

Pavloska leaned over occasionally and touched the slim hands of Mrs. Brodski in a gesture of empathy, support, and unwavering unity. The women became quite fond of each other during the short time they spent together at the living room table, sipping coffee and talking. Pavloska seemed the most decent and pious woman Mrs. Brodski had met in a long time. Such manifestations of kindness seldom came her way, as far as she could recall and ever since she moved here with her husband, Jakub, in the early fifties.

Although in the beginning Mrs. Brodski seemed inconsolable, with time she regained much of her confidence and natural dignity. In the end, she eagerly shared some personal details of her early life, right after they crossed the border from the former Polish eastern territories, heading west with several groups of other migrants before the border was closed by the Soviet Union for good. Thousands of displaced families from the east managed to resettle within the present borders of the country in the first few years after the war, before the Soviets, relishing in its insatiable expansionist appetite, decided to keep what they conquered following their invasion of September 22, 1939.

Poland lost about a third of its land mass and a substantial part of its population. There was no turning the clock back—at least not for a foreseeable future. So it was, Mr. and Mrs. Brodski temporarily settled in this small, quiet town, hoping to move farther west shortly after, or out of the country, once contacts with any close or extended family members were established. Credible scraps of information were very hard to obtain, either from private sources or government agencies. Slowly they reconciled with a belief that most of them had likely perished in the concentration camps, or left the country by now and settled in Israel or the USA. Remnants of the once-large Jewish population of war-devastated Europe were making their way to Israel, especially following the country's establishment and recognition by the United Nations.

Jakub Brodski, however, fell victim to rather unfortunate circumstances, he had little control over. When making inquiries at the neighboring county town about the whereabouts of his family members, he came across a rather inquisitive party apparatchik. The bureaucrat, upon learning that Brodski was a former middle school history teacher and an accomplished musician from Lvov in the Ukraine (formerly a part of Poland), insisted that Jakub stay here, since there was a great need for all teachers in this part of the country. Jakub was literally assigned a post to one particular secondary school and given no choice. Soon his new personal identification document was made out to the address, which was to be only temporary but now became permanent, and that was the end of his traveling plans. Many other people were met with the same fate—not only teachers, but also some doctors, army officers, skilled tradesmen, and ordinary bureaucrats found themselves "assigned" in an ambitious and massive effort by the Party to maximize resources in an effort to rebuild the country from ruin and backwardness.

Mrs. Brodski continued with carefully selected pieces of her life's story, until it got quite late in the evening. She and Mrs. Pavloska both enjoyed each other's company immensely, and vowed to continue with a much closer relationship in the days and months to come. Actually, they'd known each other for a few years now, since the town was so small, sooner or later one was bound to see the same faces going about their business. Mrs. Brodski and Maria Pavloska ran into each other sporadically in the streets or in the shops, had they happened to be there at the same time, but it never went just past the basic cordial greetings and courtesy. Pavloska promised to make every effort to help resolve the issue with Alek, and what had now become a personal matter with Commandant Sokolowski, with possibly far-reaching and impossible-to-predict implications.

DOMINIK POLESKI

4

THROUGHOUT THE EVENING, Alek was restless, sitting mostly in the kitchen, pretending to study, but trying to listen in on the conversation in the living room. He heard some of it, but not all, and that made him uncomfortable. He didn't like being talked about. After all, many of the things he overheard, he's never heard before directly from his mother, and felt disappointed, almost betrayed. A few times, he got up and walked into the living room under the pretext of looking for something, then turned around and quickly disappeared again, when all he managed to elicit, were warm smiles from both ladies. Their conversation went on, and the tone varied with the subject discussed. At times, it was lively, then more somber and subdued, to be followed by short periods of complete silence, moments of reflection.

The two women made a commitment to keep in touch more often, as they bid farewell and parted at the door. Despite their age difference, the mutual affinity between them was unmistakable, and the beginning of rare friendship was forged.

Mrs. Brodski stayed up well into the night, immersed in her thoughts, pondering their future and regressing into the past, the time when her husband, Jakub, was still alive. Life was different then; they all felt safe, there was hope. With his untimely death, all that fell apart, their hopes and dreams of a better life like a house of cards. Mrs. Brodski sat impassively on the sofa in the dimly lit room, surrounded by profound, undisturbed, almost-divine silence. Instinctively, she caught a glimpse of Alek leaning against the kitchen's door frame.

He just stood there looking at his mother with all his usual intensity and those big black eyes, without saying a word. It seemed as if time stood still, and an overbearing feeling of sadness descended upon the room and permeated every corner. Since the death of his father, whom he only vaguely remembered now, he had learned to completely rely on his mom. She was his best friend, defendant, protector, and closest confidante; and he was absolutely sure he could always count on her.

Alek understood well by now the struggles she went through to put food on the table, to buy the clothes he wore or the basic school supplies. It all came at a great personal sacrifice, although she rarely talked about it—in fact, she always tried to maintain a positive attitude and, as if on purpose, keep the ever-present smile on her face whenever their eyes met. The meager monthly state pension allocated to her by the state after Jakub's death didn't go nearly enough to cover the basic necessities in most months, let alone any luxuries. She supplemented the pension as a part-time, seasonal employee at the local fruit and vegetable processing plant, and as an occasional housekeeper for families that were better off and could afford it. Nevertheless, it all added up to manageable subsistence, no better or worse than most folks in town; but under any normal circumstances, it would be called poverty.

The most vivid example that Alek could remember when things boiled over, his mom broke her silence, and in her rare departure from the norm, shared a most unpleasant event, which was, in a way, a turning point in the shopping routine in their household. Particularly one event that she confided to Alek must have had a great impact on her, since she talked about it with obvious pain in her voice. It happened at one of the stores, on her usual shopping errands before it officially became mainly Alek's responsibility. It actually happened at the old dairy store, when she was met with rude and spiteful remarks from the other shoppers and the clerks alike, as if in planned group collusion. As she stood in the overcrowded store, she had a feeling that there was a gentle sway of the throng turning into a push from the back, almost like a domino effect directed specifically at her. She quickly realized it was not an accident but a deliberate attempt directed at her, and no one else, as the overwhelmingly female crowd, suddenly roused from their typically expressionless demeanor and sullen faces, burst out laughing.

Mrs. Brodski didn't find it amusing at all; on the contrary, her immediate reaction was to leave that awful place at once. Some of the shoppers made little attempt to hide their hostile feelings. When "That Jewess!"—uttered with unmistakable contempt—reached her ears somewhere from behind, as she stood helpless, literally jammed between the mass of strange bodies, unable to retreat even if she wanted to. When she finally got close to the counter, after a long wait with no discernable queue, an order which only the locals seemed to understand, she was met with a provocative "What do you want?" from one of the two stout, red-cheeked, past-middle-age women behind the counter.

At that moment, Mrs. Brodski felt like saying the only thing she could think of saying: "Nothing. I don't want anything from you." And then just disappeared.

Stories like these increasingly had a profound and lasting effect on young Alek, and with time only added to his sense of aloofness and estrangement. He found life around town difficult to understand and adjust to, either among his peers or general population, since one could never know what to expect. He began to notice things he didn't see before, and hear things he had never heard before, which seemed to be the essence of life around here. Equally hard to understand were the customs at local social gatherings and celebrations, whether "men only" or conjugal. The frequently thrown-around saying "Women, wine and song" almost always found its way to the table, or to rapturous evening garden parties; but the "wine" part remained a mystery to him, when the drink of choice was always vodka, and extremely seldom anything else. The more vodka flowed, the more singing there was; and in time, little mattered whose woman it was, as the fun-loving men, with each passing minute, were more and more interested in the women sitting nearby, or directly across, but not necessarily their own, regardless of how disinterested or unattractive they were in comparison to their own wives.

That was the magic of vodka in appropriate amounts—it just seemed to work like a magic potion, never failed; it just blurred the vision enough to make *the grass look greener on the other side of the fence*, and always true to the old, popular saying, "Vodka warms you up, vodka cools you down, vodka will never do you harm."

The familiar and frequent ring of vodka-filled glasses bridged any social and ethnic divides, if only for the night, in an uninhibited display of rare happiness against what seemed like perpetual misery. Occasionally, someone brought out an accordion and tried his best to entertain the gathered crowd with his repertoire of the most soulful mix of Polish and Russian ballads, with the partygoers joining in with their vocal accompaniment. The parties were frequently punctuated with the customary cry each time they raised the toast, exclaimed by someone and followed by the rest: "One hundred years!" It was an enduring wish for longevity, or "Na zdrowie" (simply "To health"), and again usually initiated spontaneously by somebody from the gathered group, and then shouted in unison by the rest; and it went on and on through the night. By the end of the night, any common etiquette-inspired notions of civilized behavior were dropped in lieu of more unpretentious norms of the wide-open swaths of the eastern steppe. One might say a temporary uninhibited relapse into "the way things used to be." That too, of course, was an unequivocal testament to the proportional ethnic representation of the festive bunch.

There was no telling, though, when the jovial mood would just as easily take a somber turn, especially when vodka-induced patriotic sentiments surfaced, and the toasts exalted the undeniable greatness of the respective national heroes, dead or alive.

Finally, what would a good and friendly get-together be without reversion to the present and the customary litany of appropriate epithets hurled toward the benevolent, omnipotent, pervading, and ever-present ruling Party? It was all so foreign to Mrs. Brodski and Alek that she made up her mind long ago to have no part in the social scene of the town, and to never let her son anywhere near them, and thus increasing their isolation. It didn't go unnoticed, and itself became the subject of malicious speculations among the locals.

Alek was beginning to realize that he had reached a different point in his life, when with rapid physical changes came a sudden realization, although disheartening and unnerving, with which his mother could do little for him now. It dawned on him that he wasn't a little child anymore, and his problems were most likely beyond her capacity to solve. For years she was always there to intercede on his behalf when things got out of hand in his infrequent interactions with peers. But now...what was she to do? She would have to deal with the local thugs roaming the streets out of sheer idleness and boredom, like a pack wolves descending on unsuspecting prey; and it mattered little whether provoked or unprovoked—a reason could always be found, and their presence could always be felt. It was hardly a coincidence; rather, it was dictated by the law of mutual attraction that they stuck together through childhood, adolescence, and eventually adulthood. Most folks were well aware of the different groups at their various stages of maturity, and tried to live around them as best they could.

Alek looked at his mother with a strange curiosity, seemingly detached from the interaction and the usual emotional bonds that had bound them together for as long as he could remember. In a way, he was mesmerized by her silhouette as she was sitting silently there on the sofa, as if frozen in time. He admired her graceful tall and slim figure, her refined profile, and that sophisticated poise that reminded him of the biggest film stars of the day he had seen in magazines. Her shoulder-length wavy black hair, her big, dark eyes and long lashes, her nose with its slightly high bridge, and full lips that often smiled back at him—they all emanated an aura of a truly superior woman. Alek, for the first time, found himself looking at his mother differently—not so much as her child but, rather, as a man would look at a newly met woman, with a fascination he never experienced before. He was equally curious and embarrassed about it, and had a profound feeling that she somehow knew what he was thinking. *Dad was a lucky man*, he thought. *Too bad he hasn't lived long enough to see her now. He would have been happy. We all would have been happy.*

They both were deeply absorbed in their thoughts and reluctant to disturb the veil of magical and mutually understood silence. When already so much had been said, a space was needed; it was better to leave some things unsaid. The higher providence must do its divine work, if one is to believe what the clergy has been saying for generations, and to make any sense of it all.

In the following days and weeks, a period of relative quiet set in the neighborhood. Any given day resembled the next uneventful day, and all seemed to fall into its own usual patterns of repetition, like a circle, as if living through the same days and months over and over again. The weather was particularly uncooperative, the nights were cold, and the days had their generous dose of bone-chilling rain, often mixed with heavy, large flakes of wet snow. Gusts of bitter arctic air carried from the east, and as always, invited the customary comments among the townsfolks—"Nothing good has ever come to us from the east"—bearing in mind the Big Brother in the east, Soviet Union. The town's streets and sidewalks were quickly covered with a layer of slush, in places virtually impassible at the many surface indentations and potholes scattered about many sidewalks and streets. Occasionally, someone's foot would fall into one of them disguised in the slush, and then a litany of curses and profanities usually followed.

"When the only whore in town had a toothache, the nightlife died down," townsfolk used to say jokingly on days like these, as a cynical, but perhaps quite accurate, testimony to the town's size, isolation, and backwardness. Seven or eight thousand people, and no one seemed to know exactly, inhabited this godforsaken place year round, which swelled regularly every Thursday for the farmer's market day, yearly church fair day, or May 1, otherwise known as the May Day, or International Workers' Day. After the war, when the newly re-drawn borders were shut for good by 1947, the town's population was about equally split among Poles, Ukrainians, and Byelorussians, or Russians as they were generally viewed, since nobody quite knew what the difference between them was anyway.

They all seemed to live peacefully together in this small, decrepit border town, one might say, bound by the Slavic peoples' common threads: hard labor, women, music, and vodka—lots of vodka, probably the only staple in plentiful supply in these parts. The local ruling authorities thought, as long as those simpletons had plenty of cheap vodka, they'd be happy to keep quiet in a perpetual cycle of spirits-induced happiness one day, and a nasty hangover recovery the next day, with severely diminished mental cognitive faculties. Although the

DOMINIK POLESKI

drinking for the most part was a weekend tradition, many of the dwellers of the lowest class were seldom seen sober between the weekends, and left those who were mostly sober, or pretended to be mostly sober, scratching their heads:

"When do they work?"

"How do they work?"

"How can they work?"

Well, somehow they did it, trudging along at half capacity, so as not to exert themselves, carefully nursing their indispositions, with perpetually dulled senses, seemingly just like the rest and everything in this bloody country.

The tallest building in town was the church, a house of God, with its narrow, pointed tower crowned with a metal cross, and which housed a large brass bell that rang often, every day, few times a day; and no one knew why the hell it rang so often? Some folks would curse and spit whenever that big, hollow monster rang out, especially those who couldn't care less about the church, its teachings, and everything else it stood for. As for the baptisms, marriage vows, or the last rights, they thought they could do without them, and would do just fine, and, if anything, over the years would save themselves a significant amount of hard-earned money.

The congregation was mostly Polish, the faith Roman Catholic, and at the head of the St. John's parish was Father Antoni Pukalski, one of the town's best-known dwellers, and without a doubt its undisputed moral authority, at least among majority of the Poles. He was well known for his occasional fiery homilies on the sins of the flesh, which sparked passionate debates among some faithful, or equal amount of dismissive derision among the others, who were quick to point out his presumed hypocrisy.

Father Antoni was a man in his midfifties, although he appeared much younger, never having to do an honest day's work in his entire adult life, in the traditional sense. He was of medium height and build, with lively dark eyes that seemed to dance around, as if constantly on a prowl, and then suddenly stop and stare with piercing intensity at the object of his newfound interest, or desire. His most prominent facial feature was a rather big, crooked red nose that protruded from his pale cheeks like a sacristy's old, deformed door handle. That nose alone was a frequent object of mockery among the parishioners, who cared enough to even notice. Some folks swore on their ancestors' graves that they knew, or had seen "the red nose" gulping sacrificial wine in the back rooms of the compound's quarters. The sessions, although supposedly infrequent, lasted well into the night, sometimes in the company of his devoted Ms. Klementyna, an eager servant and maid, frolicking and mischievously playing hide-and-seek like a child with the horny priest. She actually lived on the premises, in one of the adjacent small, but tidy and cozy, rooms, dividing her time between the seemingly never-ending chores and prayer.

The story was that, Ms. Klementyna, now in her midforties, had succumbed to temptations of the flesh at the young age of just sixteen years. The culprit was apparently her distant, much older cousin. Those were the times when girls whose innocence was so suddenly and irrevocably pierced were disowned by their families, especially in profoundly devout, conservative circles, and thrown out of the house to restore the family's honor. From that time on, Ms. Klementyna decided to devote her life to God and vowed to modesty, chastity, and obedience. Although she had earnestly tried as a novice to a convent, she didn't actually last there more than a year for an unknown reason, and eventually ended up as a joyful, deeply religious and entirely devoted, servant to the parish priest, Father Antoni, and his younger assistant, Father Feliks. Yes, and a bundle of joy she was—cheerful, bubbly, although a little on a plump side, she was still quite attractive and desirable.

According to a great many, being close to the parish priest meant being as close to God as one could get, at least in this town. The other house of worship, which was a little less prominent and was in the eastern part of town, closer to the Soviet border, was the Eastern Orthodox Church. It catered to the Russian and Ukrainian faithful. The parish priest, or "the pope" as he was most commonly called, was a good friend of Father Antoni's from the Catholic diocese. He was a man of about fifty, or perhaps just a year or two older, and unquestionably the biggest inconspicuous womanizer this town had ever seen. In fact, his reputation was by then well established in the entire county. It was rumored that Pope Vladimir's clandestine holy services were in considerable demand among devout parishioners of the female gender. Many folks openly and sarcastically speculated that he was "dipping his aspergillum" in some "unholy waters" and wielding it indiscriminately.

Eastern Orthodox priests, unlike their Catholic counterparts, were allowed to marry, and some did so, preferring the stability of a family life, lest they be tempted by the devil and succumb to the weakness of the flesh. The majority of them didn't marry—and for all the right reasons, it must be said. They were those who truly devoted their lives to Christ and his teachings. Still, there were those among them who preferred to stay single, but it didn't mean celibate. The priesthood gave Vladimir and his Catholic counterpart a unique opportunity for a close, devotional contact with many young and middle-aged wives on the outskirts of town and surrounding villages, who craved the special attention bestowed upon them by the good shepherd. They were often terribly mistreated and neglected by their hard working husbands, who were gone for most of the day and who would rather tenderly caress their ploughing horses and completely forget about their wives' big, firm, and bouncy bosoms in desperate need of at least some attention. Besides, those big, hard, and insensitive hands, with an abundance of furrows and crevices, were not something to look forward to for any woman, in case the busy farmer eventually noticed his wife's existence. It must be said, however, that some female parishioners upon whom was bestowed the privilege of an intimate encounter, felt a pressing need to brag about being uniquely selected by either of the two men of God for a special blessing—a personal consecration, one might say. In this world, it was an honor, indeed, to be able to say at the end of their miserable, tumultuous lives with pride and nostalgia, when old, bent in half, and trembling: "I'm happy to say I was 'consecrated' by His Excellency Pope Vladimir, or Father Antoni, himself."

Pope Vladimir fell into the category of a married man with a family—whether by design or accident, it was impossible to tell. His own pious wife, Kalyna, was rather an unattractive, stout, and perfectly domesticated woman, whose dedication to her husband was unwavering, in spite of abundant unmistakable signs and echoes of his occasional transgressions. Kalyna, an all-around sickly woman, looked old and worn out for her age, with signs of constant worry and distress on her plain and pale face. One might even feel some understanding and sympathy for the poor preacher if sex was the last thing on his mind, paralyzed with fear, when she dropped her dentures in a glass and turned off the lights. The pride of the family, Kalyna's total devotion and preoccupation were lavished on their two pretty teenage daughters. Especially the older one, Tamara, who was a frequent object of attention of many mostly dim-witted local boys, some on the brink of mental retardation, showering her with whistles and stupid, lewd remarks.

Tamara wasn't the only one given this special attention—in fact, any girl that came upon this group of idle misfits, was certain to be met with the same fate, or worse. There always seemed to be a few small groups of them here and there, standing around, playing some kind of game with small coins or going somewhere, but certainly not in the direction of school. Few would be walking around with slingshots and mindlessly shooting at anything that moved—birds, cats, dogs, and sometimes even windowpanes, just to have a little fun. Other boys unassociated with these small gangs were equally susceptible to the bullying and harassment. Over the years, these teenage hooligans, as they grew in age and experience, would become the town's fearsome, well-seasoned criminals, and to be avoided. When some of them ended up in jail and disappeared from the scene for months or years, there were always the younger ones coming up the ranks to fill the void. And so it went on in a never-ending cycle for many generations.

Thursday was a farmer's market day in town, and it was always held at the same place for as long as anybody could remember—at the end of a short cobblestone side street, near the town's center, which at its very end flared into a sizable unpaved lot, resembling a large cul-de-sac, and adjacent to a small, perennially neglected city park. It was an ideal location for an open-air market of this kind.

Many peasants and farmers from the surrounding villages poured into town by train, by bus, by horse-drawn carriages, or, for the obviously well-to-do, by cars stuffed beyond capacity with goods and wares for sale or barter. Many locals also joined in these weekly affairs, peddling the fruits of their labor, their services, or a variety of manufactured products made locally in town, or brought from across the border, the Soviet Union. It was a rather feverish event, and always much anticipated, fulfilling the needs of people, since the state-run stores had chronic shortages of often-basic necessities.

The town came alive on those days, and inhospitable weather had little effect on attendance; they were all used to it, and well prepared. Nevertheless, they all knew what to expect, were well bundled up and ready to sustain themselves even in the worst of conditions, with a little help of a few shots of vodka, hidden in the thick layers of their heavy overcoats, or a quick dash to a nearby restaurant, well stocked with their own supply of bottles for the weekly occasion. For many participants, mostly locals, the market day was rather a day to socialize, meet friends or acquaintances, smoke cigarettes, drink and talk, while moving and stomping their feet and feverishly rubbing their hands to avert the advance of the penetrating, bone-chilling cold. There was the ever-present vapor mixed with cigarette smoke hovering around small groups of men standing around engrossed in animated conversations, which were occasionally punctuated with outbursts of profanities or loud laughter.

The market displayed a colorful array of vegetables, a good selection of dairy products, and always visibly restless chickens, turkeys, ducks, geese, rabbits, and piglets in wooden crates awaiting their fate. The market provided a great opportunity for local as well as visiting craftsmen and tradesmen from around the county to display their various products, such as stools, chairs, little tables, chests, cutting boards, rolling pins, tools, and ladders to be bought or sold. At this time of the year, always present were fur pelts and new or hardly worn full-length fur coats. The toymakers were also in full force on most Thursdays with their wooden blocks, simple trucks, wagons, and various figurines.

Also, there were usually one or two sellers of toys from the Soviet Union, which were actually very nice, of good quality and in great demand. They were quite different and had that distinctive, unmistakable

Russian appearance, and above all, they were not readily available at any state shops in Poland's eastern peripheries. The most popular among the boys were toy guns, and they seemed to have everything one could wish for—the detailed look, function, color, sound, and often accompanied by flushing red lights. There were the single-shot handguns or automatic multi-shot rifles, spitting plastic pellets or little darts at a touch of a trigger, while producing battery-induced, bullet-discharging sounds and rapid red flashes.

For the girls, Russian dolls were a must. Not only that they closely resembled real babies or downsized little girls in their appearance, but they also closed and opened their eyes; moved their lips, arms, and feet; and, best of all, were able to say a few basic words like "mama," or "papa," or a one-word greeting. The dolls' apparel was of the finest kind—exquisitely tailored colorful dresses, socks, and shoes. Every boy who had a sister who had one of those dolls was sure to know the more intimate parts of her wardrobe, as well as what was underneath the underwear, and thus the first venture into the world of the female anatomy; and what wasn't there was made up for by the imagination. The impressions were then eagerly shared with other boys in the neighborhood. Some of whom seemed to know it all, or got carried away by their imagination, or simply pretended to be more perceptive, had an aura of experience around them, and proclaimed to see a little more than the others, who could only utter with utmost certainty, "There was nothing there."

The market was a welcome alternative to depleted and scarcely stocked government stores, and still met the tacit, although somewhat reluctant, approval of the authorities. Any independent activity that in any way resembled a capitalist form of production or manufacturing on a larger scale was not tolerated and was promptly shut down. The open-air market, and with it small food-growing or manufacturing sectors was the limit of their tolerance and purported benevolence. The Party knew increasingly well they could not feed the populace under the collective farm system in the essential food production chain, or emulate the painfully obvious example of failure in the Soviet Union. Equally apparent was shortage of basic everyday services and unavailability of the most indispensable manufactured products. To avoid the most acute shortages, and in effect possibly a general discontent, the Party let the markets flourish in their limited scope for the time being.

It was universally understood, and in fact many, especially the government bureaucrats, were certain that the time would undoubtedly come, in the not-too-distant future, when the country would become the land of plenty under the expert guidance of the infallible Party. The abundance would flow like torrents of mighty rivers, flooding the countryside and the cities, to the envy of all the poor souls on the other side of the iron curtain and beyond. For once, the sacred communist credo "From each according to his abilities, to each according to his needs" would be fulfilled, and see the day of glory as prophesized. Those that doubted or opposed would find themselves on the wrong side of history, and forever condemned literally and swiftly, or, if lucky, in the eyes of future generations. Those that eagerly embraced the ideology would be vindicated and prosper in the new progressive world order on an epochal march toward new enlightenment, the liberation of the masses, and workers' paradise.

Although the paranoid authorities were concerned about even the slightest displays of public dissent, they had no reason to worry in this small town. People went about their lives, preoccupied with the hardships of everyday existence and had little desire to trouble themselves with strange concepts of the coming luminous future prophesized by that good old bearded man called Karl Marx. Very few people actually understood his elevated ideology, and even fewer took it seriously, although it's been a part of school curriculum for two decades now. The proletariat, the bourgeois, or class straggles rang hollow and was the last thing on people's minds. One thing they all seemed to understand, though, was the right to private property, which they considered a God-given right; and they were prepared to defend it, if required. Unlike their eastern neighbors across the border, who were stripped of all land in a massive collectivization and nationalization effort during Stalin's reign, the Polish farmers enjoyed a substantial degree of autonomy.

Here they were, every Thursday, selling fruits of their labor, and in return generate a modest income, or, some of them a rather significant income, which would allow them to buy much-needed goods or services the town had to offer. All the stores in the vicinity did a brisk business, as the crowds swelled, causing long lines. There was an undercurrent of subtle resentment directed toward the visitors from the farmlands, and occasionally, tempers flared.

The most common, spiteful, but mostly unsubstantiated perception was that the "peasants" had no manners, wore old or tattered coats, often-muddy boots, and smelled of manure. There were also other points of contention, which many found irritating, to say the least, like the fact that they seemed to have more money, or even the fact that many country folks flushed gold or silver fillings every time they opened their mouths or smiled.

Although the town was small, the locals nevertheless considered themselves a superior breed, city dwellers. Others found an issue with their horses, or rather, what they always left behind, usually along the stretch of the main street leading from the marketplace to a large, empty lot near the church, which doubled as a parking lot and a resting place for the farmers and their horses. The farmers, usually those with heavier loads, unloaded first at the market, and then led the carriages back to the parking lot, often leaving a trail of steaming horse manure behind them, which was, needless to say, frowned upon by townsfolk. The others with lighter loads, or relatively fewer goods to sell, parked first and then carried their merchandise on foot the short distance of about five hundred meters or so to the marketplace, which often required making two trips, while somebody else was watching over the merchandise when they were gone. Those with cars, trailers, or modified wagons of all sorts, usually parked nearby on one of the side streets, or right at the marketplace and occupied privileged spots with a preferable exposure, and that was just the way it had always been, and nobody ever questioned the natural order of things.

The market, besides its purpose as a commercial trading place, also served the locals and visitors alike as an invaluable source of information. One could often hear a lively conversation on a variety of topics, from

DOMINIK POLESKI

land cultivation, raising cattle, crops, availability of certain products, services or prices. Sometimes the subject of conversation was clearly on the lighter side, as participants swapped jokes, gossip, or family stories. There were also groups of people who ventured into what was generally considered a "forbidden zone"—that is, politics. Their understanding and interpretation of events or people in the news was seriously lacking and utterly naïve—in essence, harmless. Most often than not, by the time the story got to the market, it was most likely recycled several times since the original source, and Radio Free Europe was most likely the source. Eventually, it would be so distorted and devoid of credible information and substance, it could be dismissed as pure nonsense.

5

MS. KLEMENTYNA, THE priest's maid never missed the weekly market, and hurriedly scoured the stalls, knowing well what Father Antoni and his assistant Father Feliks particularly liked, and both of them were known for good appetite, especially father Antoni. It was a challenge sometimes to satisfy the two gluttons and their frequent visitors from out of town, clerics and nuns alike, and at the same time maintain—within reason, of course, specific days prescribed by the church of religious observations, fasting, and the Lent. Ms. Klementyna and the parish priest had a special understanding, and money was no object; there was plenty of it in the church's coffers. Ironically, quite often the same peasants dutifully coming to town for Sunday Mass and generously filling the collection basket were getting much of that money back from the purchases made by the church. Ms. Klementyna supplied only the most basic goods for current and immediate consumption, but the bulk of provisions were made by the farmers themselves, delivered directly to the church compound.

For the farmers, it wasn't just a convenient business arrangement, where the prices were usually fixed, with little room for negotiation, and Father Antoni more than willing to oblige. It was also a privilege to serve one of the town's highest authorities, its undisputed moral authority, and in the process do good deeds that would certainly not go unnoticed in heaven.

Mrs. Brodski, too, was out that day and mingled carefully among the folks at the unusually crowded market, despite the bad weather. As always, she was somewhat self-conscious and aware of the curious onlookers, either real or imagined. She thought that people stared at her for no apparent reason. At least the out-of-town folks couldn't have known her, she reasoned, so why had their eyes followed her as she passed by? *Am I just being paranoid?*, she asked herself. She wasn't sure about it, and of many other things lately. She knew she looked different from the women in town—at least all those she had seen.

On the other hand, there were many Jewish families living here before the war, and at least during its first three years of that horrible conflict. *Have they all forgotten them? Have they all erased the memory of their neighbors and friends by now?* Mrs. Brodski continued to question. She was tall for a woman, and at forty-two years of age very slim—even bony one could say, but very agile. She moved with dignified, carefully measured strides, occasionally looking down at the path in front of her and sideways, skillfully navigating through throngs of people moving around in different directions. She was wearing a long black overcoat, the same one she had worn for many years now, but it was still in a relatively good condition. On her head, she had on a thick gray wool shawl, and on her feet black half-length boots, which, although polished, betrayed considerable amount of time in faithful service.

The weather was most unpleasant, dark and gloomy with a mixture bone-chilling, intermittent drizzle and a light snow falling from the sky, with the temperature hovering around freezing.

Mrs. Brodski went about her business, stopping for few necessities carefully planned in advance and within her means, for there was no room for spontaneous expenditures, although it was almost always possible to negotiate the price with the sellers; nothing was written in stone. By this time, she already had everything she needed, but was still walking slowly and looking around for nothing in particular, just out of curiosity. This Thursday, she wasn't in a hurry to get back home yet; it was barely past noon, and she still had plenty of time before Alek would get back home from school.

Then unexpectedly, she ran into Maria Pavloska and was happy to see the old woman and her seemingly always-smiling and radiant face. Pavloska was equally happy to see Mrs. Brodski. They greeted and hugged each other warmly and planted kisses on both cheeks, as was the custom between old, close friends. They just stood there for a few minutes, briefly exchanging the latest news, and then vowed to meet again soon, in private, preferably in Mrs. Brodski's home.

Suddenly, Mrs. Brodski felt somebody's hand slip under her arm and forcefully grab her left wrist. Frightened, she abruptly turned around and instinctively jerked her arm back, trying to shake off the culprit. She met the steely blue eyes of commandant Sokolowski in full uniform, with a cigarette in his mouth; he wrapped his cold fingers around her thin wrist even tighter. His narrow lips twisted in a stupid, disparaging smirk as he cynically uttered, "Good morning. I hope I haven't frightened you, Mrs. Brodski. Don't be concerned. Let's go for a little walk, shall we?"

"Let go of my arm, please," she snapped back at him decisively.

Sokolowski, visibly content with himself, completely ignored what she has just said, and, in what would appear a gentlemanly yet forceful manner, steered her out of the market and onto the street.

"Sir, what do you want from me? Let me go, please let go of my arm," insisted Mrs. Brodski with increasing irritation.

"Please don't be afraid, madam. We must talk in private. There were just too many people at the market."

"I'm not interested anymore in anything you have to say, sir."

"Oh, please don't say that, madam. What I have to tell you is important, and concerns not only your son, Alek, but you as well."

"But please let go of my arm. It hurts," she said.

"I'm sorry, madam, I didn't mean to hurt you. Let's just go a little farther," said the commandant and released her arm. Mrs. Brodski sighed with relief, slowed down, switched hands carrying the canvas bag with the goods she bought at the market to the just-freed hand, and looked at Sokolowski with anticipation.

"Let's keep walking, madam. You should not be afraid. I just want to talk to you, and also tell you something you might be interested in. I'm not your enemy, and actually, you will be surprised if I tell you I'm on your side. I sympathize with you, Mrs. Brodski, a great deal, and I'd like to think I know what you're going through."

"You?"

"Yes, I am very sympathetic to your plight," Sokolowski assured her.

"What do you know about me? I'm afraid you have no idea what you're talking about," she said right back.

"I know a lot more than you think, Mrs. Let me explain…You see, I thought you'd come back to the station, you know, following your visit, but you never did. Frankly, I don't blame you either. It must be quite difficult for someone like you to deal with matters of this nature, and with the police in general."

They walked slowly in silence, arm in arm for several more meters, before the commandant, looking to the side at Mrs. Brodski, picked up the conversation again.

"First of all, in the matter concerning your son, Alek, I want to assure you, I treat this most unfortunate event, if I may call it so, very, very seriously. I've personally conducted a full and thorough investigation. I'd talked to my son at length, and so did my wife. I'd talked to his friends that could possibly hang out with Marek, and lastly, I'd talked to their parents. I'm sorry to tell you this, but they all say they had nothing to do with assaulting your son. They don't even know Alek. They don't have the slightest idea who he is, or where you both live. Believe me, Mrs. Brodski. I'm a father, and I care about my son, and the last thing I want is to raise a bandit under my roof. I'm so sorry about this, but I think I left no stone unturned."

Mrs. Brodski suddenly stopped, her arms stretched down still holding the shopping bag in one hand, her shoulders fell forward, and she bent her head slightly to one side as her sullen pale face, stricken with profound sadness, sank in resignation, and those big, dark eyes swelled with tears. Then she slowly turned sideways and looked ahead, toward some unknown, distant point where her anguished mind had just escaped.

Sokolowski sensed her absence and disappointment, touched her arm, and gently squeezed it, trying to regain her attention. "Mrs. Brodski, you must understand, I know my son well. He can stir up some trouble from time to time, believe me. I and my wife had our hands full more than once, let there be no mistake, but nothing really serious—you know teenagers…nothing of the kind you told us. No, never anything like that. Marek would never physically assault anybody, especially a younger boy, no, never. His friends are not the kind either. I know them, they are good kids. There must be a mistake..."

Mrs. Brodski resumed walking. Sokolowski followed her and quickly caught up in a few strides. Some passersby looked at them indifferently and continued on their way. They resumed walking side by side in silence for several more meters, engrossed in their own thoughts.

"I knew it, I just knew it," Mrs. Brodski said quietly, as if to herself.

"What did you say, madam?"

"No, nothing."

"I'm sorry, but you've just said something, I didn't quite catch that," inquired the commandant again.

"You know, Mr. Sokolowski, I had a feeling this would happen. I should have listened to Alek. He wanted to go with me to the station that day, but I didn't want him to go through all this testimony and questioning. He has suffered enough. He's still just a boy. Sir, let me ask you this, do you want a confrontation with my son in the presence of your son and those other boys?"

"No, no, that won't be necessary. And it will be counterproductive. I don't see how it could help matters in any way. In the absence of any witnesses, it would be your son's word against their word and, in the end, wouldn't solve anything. Frankly, I consider this case closed."

"Mr. Sokolowski, what makes you so sure there weren't any witnesses?"

"Mrs. Brodski, for our sake, let's just leave it at that, please. Trust me, it'll be better for all of us. Let's put it behind us and move on. I'm really sorry that such a terrible thing happened to Alek, and right here in our community."

The commandant made a gesture as if to say that he wanted to add something else, but paused to let Mrs. Brodski respond. She didn't say anything, just looked ahead while measuring out those equal slow paces on the uneven gray-tiled sidewalk. All around seemed gray to her—the sky, the street, the buildings, the trees, and even the people hurriedly moving in both directions, as if in some preconceived, obscure pattern. It all weighed heavily on Mrs. Brodski's already-somber mood, as she tried to digest the cruel reality of what Sokolowski had just said, and to compose herself and not show him any weakness.

The commandant of the People's Militia looked at her momentarily, as if trying to assess her state of mind, and with a noticeably subdued and much gentler, almost-concerned tone, began again: "The other thing I wanted to tell you is of a rather delicate nature, and I'm only going to tell you this—or rather, make a friendly suggestion, because in spite of what you may think about me, I actually sincerely do care about people. Frankly, I don't even know how to tell you this. I'm afraid you might take it the wrong way. Nevertheless, please don't be offended. I'm really concerned about you and your son, of course."

"I have no idea what you're trying to tell me, sir, but do not worry. I won't be offended, I promise," said Mrs. Brodski.

"Well then, I think I know how you've been struggling on your own over the years as a single mother in this town, where opportunities are few, and let's face it, life is not easy around here. Have you ever given a thought about having a man in your life, like a companion, you know... meeting someone?"

"No, I haven't, and I don't think I will. That is the last thing on my mind. Why the hell would I want a man? You've said it yourself, life is tough around here. Why would I want to complicate it even more than it already is? I appreciate your concerns, and I trust you're sincere in what you're saying, but in spite of what you're thinking, I'm doing just fine."

"Please, madam, don't be defensive. It's just a suggestion. You seem to be implying that a man in a woman's life is nothing but a burden. How is that?" asked Sokolowski, surprised by her answer.

"Sir, I haven't seen another man since Jakub's death about six years ago, and I don't intend to now. Yes, I'll be honest, I've struggled at times, financially and in many other respects. I know perfectly well that my son needs a father, a role model, especially now in his adolescence. But I just cannot imagine a Gentile man within intimate proximity—it's out of the question."

"Mrs. Brodski, this is not how I see things. On the contrary, this is exactly what you need. I know what you're saying about your son in need of a male role model in his life. I and my wife have it all, and we're a good, close family, but I'd be lying if I'd say it's all nice and easy with our two boys. We have our challenges, like this alleged incident with your son, just to name one, but I'm absolutely convinced it is much better to share support and responsibilities between the two of us. I don't know what it is with you people about someone being a Gentile? How does it change anything? What does it matter?"

"Maybe to you, sir, it doesn't, but to me, it makes a world of difference. The prospect of a Jewish widow being seen with a local Slavic man is just unthinkable. What would people think? What would they say? Have you thought about that?"

"I think you're exaggerating and needlessly concerned about that. There are few eligible man around here who are interesting, and would be interested, I'm sure. Why not open up to the possibilities and give it chance?" continued Sokolowski.

"There might be possibilities, but there is only one certainty in my opinion. None of those men you're talking about is any good, as far as I'm concerned," retorted Mrs. Brodski.

"I'd respectfully disagree with you there. I know there are a few respectable widowers, and there are few old bachelors who, for whatever reason, never married. They are good, hardworking men. Some of them are professional, decent men, with good positions and salaries."

"Well, I haven't heard of or seen any of the men that you've just described. Besides, as I said, I'm not interested, and that's the end of it."

"You haven't seen any good men, and you won't meet any if you stay at home constantly. There are different social functions around the town from time to time, you know. It's not only the church that people go to. As a matter of fact, I don't go to church myself—and not only because of my position, but that's a different story."

They walked in silence for two or three minutes, passing some old, decrepit gray buildings, the church, and a small group of people that looked at them with interest and politely bowed their heads with respect at the sight of Sokolowski. The commandant seemed to relish the attention given him, however brief it was; and it only added to his aura of importance, which was only too visible on his radiant face and

DOMINIK POLESKI

in his manner. He then picked up where he left off in his monologue: "I just want to add, Mrs. Brodski, so there are no misunderstandings. All I've said to you today stays between us, so please don't share it with anybody, not even your own son, Alek. It is a very delicate matter, as I said before, and we don't want any trouble. We're practically neighbors, it's such a small town…I wish you well, Mrs. I hope you'll take my advice—at least give it a serious thought, if you know what I mean. As for your son, I'm sorry once again, but there is nothing I can do. I've done all I could, to be fair. If there is anything else I can do for you, or help you with, I'll be happy to. You know where to find me."

"Mr. Sokolowski, I must tell you, I'm greatly disappointed. I don't think justice has been served, or ever will be. I've realized more than ever, we cannot count on anyone, not even the police, to protect us from harassment. Obviously, I was mistaken. I can only blame myself for it, and in retrospect, I should have never gone to the police station in the first place," Mrs. Brodski summed up.

"There is nothing I can add to that, but I assure you, Mrs., I have great empathy for what you're going through as a woman and as a single mother, and I'm sure you wish things would be easier, but don't we all? Please take into serious consideration all that I've said to you today. Good day, Mrs. Brodski."

Commandant Sokolowski then turned around abruptly, and hastily walked away in the direction they came from. Mrs. Brodski, stunned by the sudden end to their conversation, made a half turn and looked at the quickly receding tall figure, and quietly said, "Good day…" She stood there for a few seconds motionless, as if frozen, unable to move and to make any sense of what had just happened. Then just as quickly, she composed herself, and she too walked away. She hurried back home, where Alek was most likely back from school and, as always, anxiously waiting in anticipation.

Over time, it became a routine: both were worried if either one of them wasn't home at the expected time, and hostilities toward them intensified, whether real or imagined; but nevertheless, over the course of just the past year, mother and son experienced their share of indignities at the hands of neighbors and strangers alike, as if just the daily grind of life itself wasn't enough. The weather was quickly turning into full-blown winter, with increasingly bitterly cold air and the accompanying penetrating, easterly wind with a daily dose of light snowfall, which within just a few days covered the town with a white blanket and quickly transformed their life into survival mode. It was already almost a tradition among the folks here and every year at about this time, when people expressed their surprise at the early onslaught of winter, its particular intensity, and as always summed it up with the same line: "Nothing good ever came to us from the east." All around the town and the surrounding villages, the preparations for Christmas were in full swing.

Miraculously, the stores appeared to be better stocked than usual; the assortment of goods was noticeably wider than at any time before, as if by well-planned and premeditated government policy to project an unshakable image of the Party's benevolence, infallible economic guidance in achieving a successful consecutive five-year plan, and cultivate the image of resultant growing prosperity in every corner of the new socialist country. Despite the increasingly colder weather, the town became noticeably livelier. It seemed there were significantly more people on the sidewalks, more horse-drawn carriages, cars, and supply trucks on the streets; and of course, the farmers' market was also busier than ever. As always freshly cut Christmas pine trees were in great demand, of which two kinds were sold—spruce and fir. The trees emitted such a strong, unmistakable aroma of the pine forest that it instantly brought back familiar memories of the past Christmas celebrations in the buyers, onlookers, or idlers alike. Just the smell of the trees alone could elicit sighs and smiles on peoples' faces.

As always, at this time of the year, there were also a few enterprising vendors and manufacturers, in a country that officially banned capitalist-style private businesses big or small, which produced and sold products that were not readily available, or were scarce, in the government-run stores. Chronic shortages had become rampant and acute over the years, to the point where it all became the norm, a fact of life, rather than an exception. The eastern outskirts of the country were particularly affected—in fact, neglected, as most people felt, not even taken into

DOMINIK POLESKI

account in any centralized economic plans of the ruling Party. People quickly learned to fend for themselves, ingenuity spread like wildfire, and a vast private enterprise network flourished, right under the radar of the Party bureaucrats and its extension—the guardians of law and order, the People's Militia. The weekly market was the best example of that unofficial transformation, from dogmatic socialism as the basis of economic development, under the banner of collective control of the means of production and self-sufficiency, to vibrant widespread sector of small private entrepreneurship. Especially on the last two Thursdays before Christmas, the market was overflowing with farmers' goods, products, and variety of small livestock dead or alive, poultry, fish, fruits, vegetables, fur coats, pelts, hats, mittens, toys, and, of course, a wide variety of colorful Christmas ornaments or gifts. Shopping at the market during those days was more than just a necessity—it was an unforgettable experience, an extended holiday season leading to and culminating in an ancient Slavic Catholic tradition of Christmas Eve on December 24. Very little had changed in these parts over the years; the whole town had its very own special flavor, a taste and smell unlike anywhere else in the world, for this god forsaken place for the inhabitants was their world, from birth till death.

6

THE MIDDLE OF December 1967, just like the year before, was a unique and much-anticipated occasion to buy and sell, to browse, socialize, to see and to be seen, to present oneself to the community, and to meet people otherwise rarely seen, if that was what one wished for, or unintentionally could not avoid, and later was glad nevertheless. Even the sizable population of Orthodox Christians of Ukrainian and Russian descent were out in full force, taking advantage of the opportunity for their upcoming Christmas celebrations shortly after the New Year, on January 7. People were buying, bartering, and haggling over prices, standing around in pairs or small groups and either talking loudly, whispering, or bursting with laughter while flushing their gold teeth, as was the trend of the day; and quite often, clouds of cigarette smoke hung above their heads. The atmosphere and the smell of the entire market and much of the town in those days was most uncommon, unique, and so irresistible that it was an integral part of the people's life and culture; and for many, it added to their very sense of existence, and every moment of it to be enjoyed and savored like a precious relic, and then remembered and talked about for many months after.

In the evenings, the lights on Christmas trees started to appear in the windows of many homes, adding charm and mystery to the aura of this festive holiday season, especially when the town was quiet by then, people were back in their homes after a day full of activities, and a light snow was falling from the sky, sparkling in the dim yellow street lights perched high above on tall wooden lampposts lined up on one side of the few major streets.

Alek liked this time of the year, not because he celebrated Christmas in any particular and meaningful way, being a Jew, but because it was impossible not to be affected by all that was happening around town. Other than his eighth-grade classmates at school, he didn't have anyone he could call a true friend. His school relationships didn't spill into his private life after school—not for lack of trying, but mainly because he had so little in common with them. He didn't attend any regular religion classes, as they were known, which most of the boys and girls dutifully attended as an extracurricular subject; he didn't go to either one of the two churches in town; and he didn't celebrate any of the Christian holidays, particularly Christmas and Easter, but also anything in between.

The school was out usually a week before Christmas, but there was always a rather well-celebrated yearly event for children of grades 5 to 8 at the elementary school he attended, and grade 8 being the last year before graduating and moving on to middle or trade school. This social event was usually referred to as the Winter Ball, and not officially called a Christmas Dance due to secular system of education in the country; but in effect, that's what it was. Every year it was held at about the same time, give or take a few days, on the first Sunday following class dismissal for the winter break. For many boys and growing teenagers, it was a much-anticipated event, which gave them a first look at girls long secretly admired in classrooms but now dressed in pretty new dresses and looking their absolute best. It was a chance to make first awkward advances and stake out their claims, since more than one teenage boy was always interested in the same great-looking girls.

The girls certainly relished the attention, but also had their own favorites as well, secretly whispering among themselves and exchanging furtive glances. Those that were hauled to these celebrations by one or both of their parents were visibly embarrassed by the fact, and once they found themselves in the main room, which was the school gymnasium, they grouped with other boys and girls, trying to avoid their parents throughout the evening. Quite often, it was not an easy task, since some parents were equally determined to see their pride and joy dance with a girl or a boy, and if possible, to take a precious photograph; and that was the last thing the children wanted, especially the boys. Traditionally, a live band composed of local talent, that played the current most popular pop tunes while the children ate snacks, drank soda, and danced the best they could, sometimes encouraged by their snooping and meddling parents, or teachers. For many children, it was their first attempt at dancing with the opposite sex, and at that particular, fleeting moment, the most important event in their short lives, to be remembered for many years to come.

To touch a girl other than one's sister, and to feel the warmth of her hands and her breath, and the closeness of her young, rousing body, to smell her hair was nothing short of a miracle, dreams fulfilled, the ultimate experience unrivaled by anything else. Many, who before had only seen their parents in similar circumstances, regarded the ball, as the first steps into adulthood, a source of pride or embarrassment, depending on one's performance dancing or talking to and making a connection with the opposite sex.

Alek never attended these celebrations marking the beginning of school winter break, and could not quite remember how it all started. He was well aware that he didn't quite fit in, and asked his mother not to force him either. Mrs. Brodski understood well her son's apprehension, and did exactly that—at least for the last two years. However, Alek usually went out for an evening walk alone, along the better-lit streets, rarely venturing beyond the areas he walked many times before. It was one of his favorite pastimes, a way of connection with the town; whenever he felt confident, safe, and curiosity was impossible to resist, he just walked. Alek had a habit of looking in the windows of people's homes, mostly from a safe distance and at nighttime, when the lights inside were on and the curtains were wide open, or there were none at all. He could see everything that was going on inside; it was an inconspicuous peek into their lives, without them even knowing it. Occasionally, he approached the windows closer whenever a real family drama was unfolding inside, right in front of his eyes. He looked with fear, and just as quickly hid, crouching just below the windowsill for fear of his presence being detected, and the consequences could be disastrous.

DOMINIK POLESKI

Most men in town and the surrounding villages seemed rather short, as if they had their growth stunted in childhood, and then could never catch up. To make matters worse, their physical development, in some mysterious way, was often paired up with their mental progress as well. One would be mistaken, though, to think: *Harmless little fools they are.* Undoubtedly, fools they were, yet anything but harmless and cowards. They were cocky little bastards, they were scrappers, and they were ready to take on a man of almost twice their size, if such a man should unknowingly stray into town. A liberal dose of vodka gave that extra edge in courage, while subduing any remnants of rational thought, and even any woman who had the misfortune to be married to such an abominable earthly creature could attest to that. All those blue bruises, black half-shut eyes, swollen and bloodied lips spoke for themselves. Alek had seen his share of domestic violence on his night excursions. He had seen and heard loud sobbing, the wailing and outright screams of women being reprimanded by their drunken, out-of-control men for what was commonly referred to as "insubordination," and which usually happened at regular, never-failing intervals.

The women desperately pleaded, "Please, for God's sake, stop it. Please don't...I beg you. Oh please, for the children...please stop. I'm sorry, I'm sorry...Do you hear?"

Those pleadings, those desperate cries only riled up the all-powerful beast even more, and a barrage of fists followed in rapid succession.

"Shut up! I said shut the fuck up, or I'll kill you, you stupid bitch," shouted the man as he pounded his helpless prey with his dirty fists. Such generous methods of dispensing marital love and affection were not unusual in these parts; instead, it was almost a requirement, a bold and unequivocal statement of who was the boss and who was in charge around the house, lest it be forgotten.

On the day of the school Winter Ball, Alek decided to actually come near school. He just couldn't resist the temptation of seeing it for himself, what he's been missing for the past few years. It was a rather mild night for this time of the year, with a steady, light snowfall; but he was bundled up well for the weather and not worried in the least.

He stopped from time to time to listen for any sounds, to see if he was being followed; but he couldn't hear a thing, and moved on.

The snow crunched and squeaked beneath his heavy winter boots, and he left behind a trail of footprints in the fresh white powder. Once near the vicinity of the school building, he walked slowly; he didn't want to be seen, ready to hide in case the door swung open and someone left the school unexpectedly. Alek came close to the gymnasium and circled around, listening to the music and the muffled voices coming from inside, and he felt sad. He looked high up and inside through the small barred windows; but they were too high above the ground, and the only thing he could see was a kaleidoscope of reflected shadows, dancing around the ceiling. He moved away from the gymnasium and slowly walked along the main wing of the building, which housed most of the classrooms. Most of them were dark, but Alek was particularly drawn to those that had lights on, casting yellow beams onto the snow-covered ground just outside.

He looked inside one room; the light was on, but there was nobody inside—just the rows of student desks and chairs, the teacher's desk up front, and two blackboards just behind it, on the main front wall, with something written on them with white chalk. It felt surreal, eerie; so Alek moved on, passing a few dark classrooms, then almost at the end, another classroom with the lights on. There were two figures inside, a man and a woman. She was sitting on the teacher's desk with her legs crossed, and he was standing near her, with an accordion in his hands and quietly playing a soulful ballad.

Alek was startled by what he had seen, and on impulse, he ducked just below the window. He recovered quickly and slowly lifted himself up, just enough to see inside without being seen himself. He recognized the faces: The woman was none other than Ms. Lubinska, the young and well-liked math teacher, consistently judged by male students as the most beautiful female teacher of the school, and quite possibly, one of the most beautiful women in town. The man was Mr. Buzynski—a rather handsome old bachelor and a music teacher. Alek was standing on his toes, with both hands on the thick but disfigured sheet-metal windowsill, which was rolled into a small tube at the end, and covered with snow and ice.

Ms. Lubinska was well dressed in a fashionable and daring red dress, with a long cut along her right leg, almost right up to mid-thigh and gleaming black high heels. Mr. Buzynski wore a black suit and tie and a white dress shirt. They both must have taken a break from all the activities and commotion in the gymnasium, and hid away, oblivious to the outside world. He played the accordion with utmost devotion, occasionally swaying gently from side to side, looking straight into Ms. Lubinska's eyes with a simple but sincere smile on his lips, such that it left no doubt that it came right from his heart. She was visibly moved, almost aroused, looking straight back at him. She was blushing.

Alek looked at them for a moment mesmerized, then moved to the side, away from the window, with his back against the building wall, breathing heavily and observing the steam coming out of his open mouth, as his eyes swelled with tears of sadnesss, he couldn't move for a minute or two, and just stayed there in the shadow, listening to the quiet sound of the accordion; but he did not dare to look in there again. He looked around, and there was absolutely not a soul around to be seen, just a few yellow lights glistening in the windows of residential houses lining the nearest street about a block away, and the snow falling gently and quietly adding to the strange feeling of loneliness. There was a pungent smell of burnt wood in the air, most likely coming through the chimneys of the row of dark houses, with barely distinguishable outlines, which, interestingly, didn't show any signs of life. It was time to move on and head back home, where his mom was certainly concerned and waiting in anticipation as usual whenever he went out and was absent longer than usual.

Along the way, Alek passed by two groups of Christmas carol singers, who went from home to home, spreading the holiday cheer by singing their hearts out below the windows or near the front doors, waiting for a gesture of goodwill from the occupants in the form of a small donation. It was a long-held tradition, and always expected at this time of the year, as if it were an integral part of Christmas celebrations. The church too had its tradition of visiting homes, with one priest going around town with his devout altar boy, and the other priest servicing the surrounding villages. The visit was usually short, taking just few minutes, unless prior special arrangements were made with Father Antoni for a longer stay. The priest mumbled a few barely comprehensible lines of prayer, blessed the home and its inhabitants with a sign of the cross, and then, with a gentle smile to the children, gave out small colored pictures of Jesus, Virgin Mary, the current pope in the Vatican, or some unknown bearded saint. It was an unwritten law, a common understanding for as long as this tradition went on, and anyone could remember that the visiting, uninvited priest was to be rewarded with money. The visiting cleric by his gesture was to intercede with God on behalf of the family; and the outcome, at least at that moment, was never in doubt.

The amount given varied and was perceived to be voluntary, but depended on the material well-being and financial possibilities of the inhabitants, whose family name the priest knew in advance; and if not, just one look around the house was enough for him to know what to expect. Usually, the amount was an equivalent of one bottle of vodka, and if for whatever reason they wanted the priest to stay a little longer, the amount went up from there. It went on smoothly, as a well-rehearsed procedure, with mutually understood glances, bows, nodding and gestures, culminating with the priest finally taking the money, and almost like a skilled magician, drawing aside his long black overcoat, underneath which he wore a black cassock, and slip the money below it, into a specially made deep sack, hanging alongside and fastened around his waist. Then followed the final wishes of "Merry Christmas, Happy New Year, and good night." It was not unusual for an argument to ensue following the priest's visit, when mostly the husband usurped the right to the name of a rational thinker in the family and lashed out at his well-meaning and unsuspecting wife: "Hanka, you stupid, why the hell did you give that scoundrel so much? Do you realize how tight the money is around here?"

The priest never visited the Brodski household, for he knew well they were poor Jews, and as such, lived in their own world, which had very little in common with prevailing beliefs. This only contributed to Alek's feeling of alienation in the life of the community, where so much closely revolved around the observances of the Catholic Church's calendar of events throughout the year.

Christmas was a time when most of the residents went to church at least once, almost always on December 24, Christmas Eve, and usually the next day on Christmas Day, and those who didn't would not admit to it. Alek and his mom never went to church, and there was no synagogue in the entire county. Although, over the years some well-wishers suggested to Mrs. Brodski more than once that it couldn't hurt, after all, "We all believe in the same God," and "It would look good," went the arguments, they stayed away. Similarly, they did not participate in any social gatherings, since they were only a family of two and didn't have any close friends, and the people they knew were acquaintances and neighbors, except perhaps the recent addition of Mrs. Pavloska.

The social scene at the time of Christmas was dominated mostly by family and friends' visits, especially on Christmas Day, and then December 26, known as the second day of Christmas, when sumptuous, traditional meal consisting of several dishes were served and lively conversation carried over an endless flow of vodka. Christmas Eve was usually celebrated within the closest family, and sometimes with invited-only closest friends, and very little alcohol, if any was consumed then, since midnight Mass was still awaiting them. The focal point of this gathering was the breaking and sharing of a thin white rectangular wafer signifying the body of Christ, and the exchange of wishes for the future.

Mrs. Brodski and Alek spent those days at home, although on few occasions in the past, they were invited to some of the neighbors' homes, and either declined or went there just for a brief visit, sampled some of the foods, exchanged good wishes, and then went right back home. Perhaps three or four times since they came here, they were also pleasantly surprised by a neighbor's knock on the door, who brought over some traditional Christmas food to share. Christmas leading up to New Year was a time of intensified activity in the two government-run liquor stores, as well as the clandestine booze-distributing pit stop of Ivan Alkashov, also known locally as Ivan the Terrible.

This older, small-time bootlegger and hermit was a bundle of unkempt hair; lips twisted in a wild, menacing snare of a primitive, carnivorous primate with bloodshot, fogged-up eyes; and just a few teeth left. Despite his unsavory appearance, in reality, he was a good man, a gentle soul leading an ascetic life, minding his own business, and doing quite well while serving the community in his own way. He used to say with pride, "For domestic consumption only"; but that's how it all started, and to his surprise, the word got around, the business picked up, and he had to diversify and sell the overproduction of his handcrafted, throat and gut-burning moonshines, with significantly higher alcohol content, than the government sold vodka. Over time Ivan perfected his formula and his equipment, and added few flavors to the otherwise pure, twice-distilled potions. Christmas was a time of the greatest demand, especially for the flavored spirits like lemon, raspberry, cherry, and honey.

Ivan didn't drink much himself, and mostly on special occasions, or when he had unexpected visitors, or a regular customer who came just at the right moment when he was in especially celebratory mood for no apparent reason and the customer had an urgent need to share something "very important" with the bootlegger. Those were indeed rare moments when Ivan opened up about his past, although he never revealed much, besides a few general details about a great deal of suffering he went through in the past at the hands of NKVD, the Russian secret police. He seldom smiled, and almost never laughed—at least nobody could actually recall him doing so.

Perhaps apart from the moonshine, he was best known locally for the occasional woodcarving of somber figurines of visibly distraught, suffering people, mostly peasants, beggars, and martyred saints with what seemed like pained expressions on their contorted faces. Ivan's favorite saying was the often-repeated "The world changes in front of my eyes, time seems to pick up pace with every day, and I don't have much time left to live in the past."

The other well-known small-time local entrepreneur of a different kind was a long-haired mystic, naturopathic doctor and healer, a longtime resident from the east, Afanasy Palushkin. It was said that his grandfather married a Polish woman of noble descent, and was exiled by the late and the last Tsar Nicholas II to the furthest depths of Siberia for revolutionary, subversive activities against the state. Afanasy somehow managed to find his way to the eastern outskirts of Poland in the aftermath of World War II confusion, where just across the river to the east, there was nothing but the Soviet Union for thousands of kilometers, spanning two continents and nine time zones.

The inherently adventurous Palushkin apparently had enough of the happiness in the land of his grandfather, and decided to try his luck in the land of his grandmother. His supposedly God-given healing powers were first applied quite successfully on farm animals, but he soon discovered there was a big demand for his services among the people, especially women. Naturally, then, he moved into a more rewarding practice, laying his miraculous hands on their aching and ailing bodies; and they flocked to him like flies.

In time, the healer became part of the local small but tightly knit society consisting mainly of town administrators, bureaucrats and their spouses, some teachers, two medical doctors, and a few shrewd business people who engaged in officially banned for-profit commodity trading—mostly gold, gold coins, precious stones, and furs, but also more common and affordable jewelry, watches, cigarettes, tea, coffee, and toys from Russia to Poland, and on to other socialist countries, where supplies were scarce and the demand great. His home was modest, but large for a single man living in an old communal housing, on the western side of town, in a somewhat secluded area. Over the years, Afanasy had managed to assemble an admirable collection of antique Russian icons, Orthodox crosses, Bibles, and variety of other religious artifacts, which were a reflection of this profoundly pious man's true character and lifelong interests.

December 27, a day after Christmas, coincided with the twenty-fifth day of the Hebrew month of Kislev, the beginning of Hanukkah, the Feast of Lights. Preparations were under way at Alex's home actually at sunset the day before, Tuesday December 26. His mother had done some final cleaning and cooking. The table was covered with clean white cloth; and the ritual nine-branched candelabrum, the menorah, was in place, along with big white plates with the wide soup bowls on top of them, and cutlery. It was set for three people.

"Who is the third one for, Mom?" asked Alek.

"Mrs. Pavloska will be coming tonight," she answered.

She had barely finished her sentence when there was a knock on the front door; and sure enough, Mrs. Maria Pavloska was standing there in the dark, all bundled up. Mrs. Brodski quickly turned on the outside light just above the door, and there she was, smiling warmly and stretching out her arms in a friendly gesture of greeting, as if between old friends. Mrs. Brodski threw her arms around the old woman, planted a kiss on both of her cheeks, and then pulled her right in.

Once inside, Pavloska removed her overcoat, fur hat, and shawl; and then with a purse on her arm, proceeded farther inside, enthusiastically encouraged by the happy host. Alek got up from the sofa and, without a hesitation, approached Mrs. Pavloska, greeting her courteously and respectfully, like a well-mannered, young man should. She pulled out a small box out of her purse, handed it to Alex, and said, "This is for you, young man."

"Thank you, thank you so much, Mrs.," replied Alek, taking the little box hesitatingly in his right hand, with an obviously surprised look on his face. Then he looked at his mother for a sign of approval, but she just smiled without saying a word, which he understood as a consent. Mrs. Brodski invited Pawloska to sit down on the sofa while she still had some work to do in the kitchen, informing them both that the dinner would be served shortly.

"Do you need any help with it, Zofia?", asked the guest.

"Thank you, but I'll manage. I've got almost everything ready. I don't have anything extraordinary prepared, just the usual, but I hope you'll like it."

"Don't worry about me, do what you have to," said Pavloska. She took her place at one end of the sofa and then furtively looked around the room with interest. Mrs. Brodski was in and out of the kitchen while pacing quickly, and still exchanging few words with Maria, and then taking some dishes out of the living room cabinet and adding things onto the table. The intense, pleasant aroma of a cooked food filled the entire living quarters, supplementing the already cozy and joyful atmosphere of the home. Alek also made a few trips to the kitchen, checking impatiently on the state of the dinner to be served, or perhaps to avoid being left alone with Mrs. Pavloska, and be engaged in an uncomfortable conversation, or be subjected to questioning, as was usually the case with adults pretending to be interested in all the details of their lives. Most teenagers found this so irritating, avoiding it awkwardly at all costs, under any pretext, however feeble, and at the same time trying to maintain an impression of politeness, and reciprocate with equally pretended interest.

Soon a large bowl of chicken soup arrived, and Mrs. Brodski invited them both to take a chair at the table. But indicated that she would like to recite a quick prayer before they began the feast, and it would be perfectly acceptable to remain seated in this informal setting. She then bowed her head and proceeded with the following words: "Blessed are You, ruler of the universe, who has sanctified us with His commandments, and commanded us to kindle the Hanukkah light. Blessed are You, Lord our God, ruler of the universe, who performed miracles for our forefathers in those days, at this time. Blessed are You, Lord our God, ruler of the universe, who has granted us life, sustained us, and enabled us to reach this occasion."

Before they proceeded to eat, she asked Alek to light up the first candle on the menorah. He eagerly pulled out a box of matches from the top drawer of the cabinet the candelabrum was sitting on and struck the first match, but was unable to light it up. He then repeatedly struck it few more times, until it broke. He, was visibly embarrassed and unhappy with himself, pulled out another matchstick, and struck it against the small box twice; and to his relief, it lit up. He had difficulty lighting up the candle, only succeeding almost at the last second, when already the match between his fingers was at its end, like a twisted, burnt little stick with the flickering, dying flame. The all looked at the candle for several seconds, for it seemed at first that its small flame was about to die, but after the initial doubts, it slowly regained its strength and burst into full unhindered glow.

They immediately began to eat the chicken soup with delight, expressing much appreciation for the culinary prowess of the host, and listening to Mrs. Pavloska's brief summary of Christmas celebrations in the previous few days. Mrs. Brodski and Alek listened to it with genuine and sincere interest. Following the soup, Mrs. Brodski served the traditional potato pancakes, called *latkas*, which she had already fried before and kept them warmed up and ready on the stove. At one point, and as he would every year, Alek asked his mother for the story behind Hanukkah celebration, since he could never remember all the historical details, and which seemed to him so distant and incredible, almost like a fairy tale, a good bedtime story. She reluctantly agreed but didn't want to impose on Mrs. Pavloska, unsure how she would react to the story, she probably had little interest in it, she thought.

Nevertheless, Mrs. Brodski actually wanted to relate everything and however little she knew, well aware how lacking her knowledge of the history of her nation was. Over the years, she learned to rely on her husband, Jakub, when he was still alive; but since his untimely death, she and Alek were on their own in this often-hostile environment. She picked up the mostly empty dishes from the table, took them back to the kitchen, and came back with a pot of tea and a plate of biscuits. Then she returned for the tea cups and small desert plates, poured the fresh tea into each cup, and then sat down and began.

"I'm not really good at this, but what I know is that, it was during a period in our history during Greek domination and influence in virtually every aspect of life of Judea. In 175 BC, Antiochus, an Athens-born warrior ascended the throne, established dominion over Judea, and Jerusalem was converted into a Greek city.

A proclamation was issued that forced all citizens to follow Greek religion, including pagan religious rituals. Soon, even the temple was used to slaughter pigs on its altar. In 168 BC, in the marketplace of a small town called Modein, northwest of Jerusalem, Syrian soldiers erected an altar. The soldiers' captain ordered Mattathias from the men assembled, a Jewish priest and elder, to sacrifice a pig to Jupiter in honor of Antiochus. He didn't move, but another man came forward, offering to perform the sacrifice. The intention of the soldiers was to execute those who would refuse to eat the meat of the pig. Mattathias snatched the sword from the captain, killed the traitor who offered to perform the sacrifice, then killed the captain. Mattathias's sons surrounded him and, together with their followers, fled to the hills.

"It was the beginning of the so-called Maccabee uprising, during which a decision was made to temporarily suspend the ordinance against fighting on Sabbath, giving them a military advantage over the unsuspecting enemies. For years, the Maccabees' victories brought them back to Jerusalem, where their immediate task was to re-consecrate the Temple, by removing the stones that had been used for pagan sacrifices, and they built a new altar.

"On the twenty-fifth day of Kislev, 165 BC, they lit the sacred lamp, but realized that they had enough oil for only one day, so horsemen were dispatched in every direction to find more lamp oil. After eight days, someone had finally returned, but remarkably, the lamp had continued to burn with what was initially thought to be only one day's supply. The Hanukkah, therefore, commemorates the re-consecration of the Temple, and the miracle of the lasting oil."

Mrs. Brodski abruptly stopped her narrative and looked at Alek and Mrs. Pavloska, as a sign that it was the end of the story, after which there was silence. She invited them to have some more tea and biscuits. To break the silence, she asked Alek to open the gift he received from Mrs. Pavloska. He got up eagerly and walked over to the small stand beside the sofa and picked up the small package. Then he returned to the table and began unpacking it at once. Alek's eyes lit up, and a big smile appeared on his face; it was a fashionable man's wristwatch with a black leather strap. He thanked Pavloska for the gift with visible delight and emotion in his voice.

She explained that it was her husband Stanislav's merit, and that he still works for the National Railways and regularly rides the freight trains to the Soviet Union and back. He quite often brings back with him goods and products in short supply on this side of the border, and which command premium prices, but on the other side, they're readily available and inexpensive. Just like the first time they talked at length,

Pavloska offered Mrs. Brodski an array of goods, if she were ever in need of such things, at substantially discounted prices, of course.

Mrs. Brodski thanked her for the offer and expressed her gratitude for Alek's present and for her unwavering support. In the meantime, Alek excused himself from the table and moved back to the sofa, where he began looking over his new watch, now his most prized possession, and tried to set the dials to the current time, while the two women continued on with their amicable conversation. At one point, and quite unexpectedly, Pavloska asked hesitatingly and in a subdued voice, "Zofia, have you ever given a thought to possibly having Alek baptized?"

"Baptized?" repeated Mrs. Brodski, taken totally aback. "What in the world are you saying? You cannot be serious, my friend."

"Oh yes, I am. I have to admit, I was a bit afraid to bring this up, I wasn't sure how you'd react, but please think about it. It would solve many problems, I think. You know as well as I do, people around here are not very understanding, and baptizing Alek here, in our church, would certainly help the matters. It would make your lives easier. We're all children of the same God—and after all, our faith derives from your faith, and most importantly, the Son of God was one of your people. I'm sure our priest, Father Antoni, would welcome you both with open arms, and the people would come around too, just a matter of time. You think about it, dear. I'm sorry if I hurt your feelings in any way, but I'm suggesting this thing to help you. You know, I care about you both."

"Yes, yes, I know. Don't worry, I'm not offended at all. I'll think about it," replied Mrs. Brodski, giving the impression she would rather change the subject. Never in her whole life, not even for a split second, had she ever thought about abandoning what was dearest to her heart, her faith, and her Jewish traditions, just to gain wider acceptance in the community or "make lives easier," as Pavloska said. The idea of a Christian, especially Catholic, baptism seemed absolutely inconceivable to her. She wondered about the old woman's motives, or whether it was entirely her own idea, or there was someone else behind it, and she was just a messenger? Soon, she was left only with her thoughts and impressions of Pavloska's visit, since it wasn't long before the old woman got up and bid both of them farewell. They stood there at the door for a few seconds and looked at the quickly departing silhouette, and only went back inside and closed the door when Pavloska had disappeared around the corner of the adjacent building.

Early in the new year, on January 6, 1968, the government ran daily newspapers, in a short front-page article announced unexpected and sudden change the previous day, in the leadership of the Czechoslovak Communist Party, without giving any specific reasons, but described them as welcome and necessary for the country's future economic and social development within the socialist framework of reforms, and unshakable fidelity to Marxism-Leninism. Antonin Novotny was voted out, and Alexander Dubcek, a Slovak with a liberal reputation, replaced him as the first secretary of the Communist Party. Many considered the shake-up inevitable, and yet highly suspicious. Czechoslovakia, a friendly country on Poland's southern border in the brotherhood of Eastern Europe's Warsaw Pact nations, was generally viewed here as an orthodox, tightly controlled communist state.

People craving more information than the official media could provide were once again glued to their short-wave radios, listening to every word of Radio Free Europe reports, and then exchanged the information among themselves, with much speculation of what was really happening in the highest echelons of power, and what it all meant for the rest of the Soviet Bloc countries. Although most of the reports beamed incessantly by Radio Free Europe were considered as trustworthy, yet there were those who refused to believe them and dismissed them as a subversive western propaganda.

The Vietnam War was the major topic of numerous television reports, radio broadcast, and newspaper articles, and particularly intensified shortly after the New Year with an attack on a US Army base by the Vietnam People's Army and the Viet Cong on January 1, 1968. In officially censored statements, the government expressed its jubilation at the early successes of the Vietnamese, as well as its unwavering support for the country's brave people, fighting the overwhelming, and merciless, American imperialist forces. The government took this opportunity to announce new, vigorous efforts to help the Vietnamese with supplies of food and medicine, and appealed to the people for financial donations through a network of collection centers in all cities and towns across the country—at post offices, banks, schools, places of employment, libraries, and a number of stores.

Alek, as well as all other students were compelled to donate to Vietman relief effort a relatively insignificant amount of 2 zl, for which they received a small pocket, single-page 1968 calendar. His mother however was asked to contribute a few times at institutions she happened to be in on business at the time, and dutifully donated a nominal amount each time, to avoid controversy and suspicion with her reluctance, although every coin counted in their household. The almost-incessant informational campaign in the mass media on the course and specific details of the Vietnam War began to worry the people, in whose minds the World War II was still fresh.

Following the unprecedented Vietnamese offensive in the first two weeks of the new year, the shelling of district and provincial capitals in South Vietnam was reported as an imminent victory, not only militarily but ideologically as well, over the decadent imperialism of the USA. The communist North Vietnam's assault at the end of the month, known as the Tet Offensive, was particularly widely reported and analyzed by the government's tightly controlled media. It was the final, triumphant nearing end to the American aggression and undisputed victory, and a source of pride of the forces of communism over the imperialist capitalism. A great many folks in town turned to the Radio Free Europe for alternative sources of information and, armed with their own perception of unfolding events, sparked heated, impassioned debates, in their limited capacities, on who is right and who is wrong, and what it all means for the country, Europe, and the world. There were those who viewed the Vietnamese advances as an undisputed example of the strength of the unstoppable forces of communism on the right side of history, on its march toward liberating their country from an imperialist aggressor, and imminent ultimate global triumph of "liberty, equality, fraternity."

They argued—after centuries spent under the boot of monarchs, aristocracy, and ruling bourgeois classes—over what can be more appealing than the most just cause for the new world order, "*from each according to his abilities, to each according to his needs."* The prevailing opinion however, and the equally strong conviction, was that the red plague or the red menace had to be stopped once and for all, and if it was in the Far East, then they were all that much better off. At the end of January, Poland's communist authorities announced the removal from the National Theatre in Warsaw of the popular play *Forefathers' Eve* by the country's nineteenth-century national poet Adam Mickiewicz, and the last appearance was set for January 30, 1968. Initially, the play began in November of 1967 and was meant to commemorate the fiftieth anniversary of the Russian Revolution of 1917. The play was deemed subversive, with decidedly anti-Soviet accents prompting some in the audience to loud verbal outbursts of hostile sentiments toward the Soviet Union. Immediately, following the last show, most of the audience in a seemingly spontaneous show of defiance, some with unfurled banners with decidedly anti-government and anti-Soviet slogans, then marched toward the monument of A. Mickiewicz to picket and demonstrate against the play's suspension, demanding its reinstatement and "freedom of artistic expression."

In the days following two of the demonstration organizers, University of Warsaw students Milnik and Szeifer were relegated and arrested. In their defense, fellow university students organized a petition with a few thousand signatures, submitted to the parliament, demanding their reinstatement. Simultaneously, an unprecedented campaign of fliers was orchestrated at the university, further voicing demands for the liberalization of the educational system, the politics of the central government, respect for freedom and democracy, repeated calls for reinstatement of relegated students, and direct talks with the minister of education and rector of the university. The circulated campaign of words intensified with time, and unknown opposition fractions joined in with their own agenda, directly challenging the legitimacy of the ruling Party and calling for its overthrow.

It all culminated on March 8, at the university's central square, where a few thousand students gathered in a mass display of defiance, listening to student speakers reading out resolutions explicitly calling for democracy and liberalization of public life and politics, freedom of expression, and demands for reinstatement of other relegated student leaders involved in the flier campaign and petition, namely Kantor and Modelski. When busloads of plainclothes and uniformed policemen, along with dozens of secret agents, pulled up and surrounded the protesting students, it was just a matter of time before tempers flared. The overtly aggressive behavior of the police was met with passive opposition from the students, who were beginning to disperse once guaranteed by the university staff of the next peaceful rally, without outside interference. Unexpectedly, the police began their brutal, coordinated assault and mass arrests. Scores of students were injured, some severely, and the main leaders and instigators were dragged away to the awaiting police vans, as onlookers chanted, "Gestapo! Gestapo! Gestapo!" In the following days, more arrests followed as the student rallies spread to other universities all over the country in solidarity with the students at the University of Warsaw.

The news of the protest spread like wildfire, and soon reached almost every corner of the country, including its eastern outskirts. The press at first reported only a sketchy course of events, minimizing their significance and scope; but it soon became apparent that the news could no longer be contained or stifled. The protests were just too widespread to ignore; even in the tightly controlled media, it was no longer an option. On March 11, the ruling Party's daily, the *People's Tribune*, published the official government version of events under a heading, "Around the events at University of Warsaw." The article placed the blame for the demonstrations squarely on a privileged class of students, branded Banana Youth, which suddenly came out of the woods, and with such a highly visible presence.

In the Brodski household, the Jewish holiday of Purim, which fell on Sunday, March 14, was a welcome break from the increasingly politicized life in the neighborhood and on the streets. The student protests became the favorite topic of quiet discussions and fervent speculations among family, friends, and neighbors. The ever-watchful and well-informed Radio Free Europe did not disappoint with their around-the-clock broadcasts, while the authorities were doing their best to jam them, but with mixed results at best.

Mrs. Brodski and Alek didn't share the excitement of the general population, and didn't quite understand the significance of it all, which almost everybody else seemed to attribute to these events. After a few days following the initial wave, they became rather indifferent to all the attention given to some student protests in the capital; they had other things to worry about. In the morning, Mrs. Brodski asked Alek to read the story of Esther from their Christian Old Testament, the only Bible they had. She didn't want to wait for the evening, had other things planned for the day, and wanted to keep Alek occupied. She was disappointed with Alek's lack of enthusiasm, but not entirely surprised. Over the years, he had displayed ever-increasing resistance to observance, much less celebrations of any Jewish holidays in an environment where the vast majority of his peers were devout Christians, or so it seemed, and there was no room for anything else.

Alek read the Bible aloud and reluctantly, as it related a story of a Hebrew orphan girl in Persia, known as Esther, and who became a queen of Persia on the throne of King Ahasuerus, and through an unexpected turn of events, prevented the genocide of her people at the hands of the king's scheming viceroy, Haman.

In the meantime, Mrs. Brodski listened periodically to her son's reading, while busy making the traditional *hamantashen*, small, triangular pastry filled with fruit preserves, which she always made in small quantities each summer. She was planning to surprise Maria Pavloska and her husband, Stanislav, with these tasty treats later in the day. For his efforts, Alek was rewarded with several coins, despite his lackluster reading, which at times was becoming torturous; but his mom, being in a particularly good mood, just rolled her eyes and smiled.

7

O N MARCH 19, 1968, the unthinkable happened: the conference of the Warsaw branch of the Party, chaired by the first secretary of the Polish United Workers' Party, V. Gomulka, and was transmitted nationally by the state radio and television. In his lengthy speech, Gomulka outlined the genesis and course of the student protests, alluding to active revisionist opposition, and described the instigators in the following words: "In the recent events that took place, actively participated university students of all backgrounds and descent. Parents of these young people occupy responsible and high positions in our country."

Gomulka emphasized that although there was certainly a presence of dubious nationalists in those circles, whose interests did not necessarily coincide with those of the country's, they did not, however, constitute any threat or danger to the socialist system and the country as a whole. In the following weeks and months, an unprecedented shakeup took place in the government and in the Central Committee of the Polish United Workers' Party. Numerous ministers and members of the Party resigned under pressure, or were replaced amid mutual accusations of incompetence, disloyalty, ideological corruption, or outright subversion.

The two distinct Party factions, competing and vying for a greater share of power, were set for a showdown. One of Polish ethnicity, grouped around the general secretary V. Gomulka and known as the Boors, were under attack from a highly influential group of ardent Stalinists trying to undermine them and wrestle control of the leadership. Ultimately, the Polish communists prevailed in the much-publicized and openly contested struggle for power and ideological supremacy within the ruling party. Normally tightly controlled state media were unusually transparent in their reporting—at least it went significantly beyond the usual minimum on the inner workings of the Party apparatus, and perhaps purposefully created an atmosphere for open debate and much speculation within all walks of society in the entire country, at least for the foreseeable future. Those who still didn't trust the media were glued again to Radio Free Europe—the favorite and widely considered as the most reliable source of information; it was broadcasting around the clock from its German headquarters in Munich.

It soon became apparent, the personnel changes encompassed not only the ruling political elites but also many university rectors perceived as too liberal, or those who deviated from the official communist academic curriculum and therefore created fertile breeding ground for revisionist student activities were promptly replaced with people sure to follow the official Party line. The purges swept through the justice system; and numerous judges, prosecutors, and internal Security Bureau officers, mainly remnants of the old Stalinist guard from the 1950s show trials, were replaced with members of younger generation with relatively clean slates. Also, the state radio, television, most daily newspapers and magazines of any significance lost a number of journalists, chief editors, and managers.

Almost simultaneously, the media devoted much of its coverage to continued political and social reforms, dubbed the Prague Spring, taking place just south in neighboring Czechoslovakia, initiated by the new communist party leader, Alexander Dubcek. There was much excitement in the air, as the news of a radical political program called "socialism with a human face" was related by the media, passed on, and debated by all who paid any attention to politics on this side of the border.

The new Action Program, launched in April, announced the far-reaching liberalization of the most important aspects of people's lives, including freedom of press; freedom of speech and movement, with economic emphasis on consumer goods; and the possibility of multiparty system. The program would also limit the power of secret police, and covered foreign policy, including both the maintenance of good relations with Western countries and cooperation with the Soviet

Union and other communist nations. The people's hopes were instantly revived, although cautiously, and met with great deal of skepticism. The political turmoil in the highest echelons of power seemed so remote and so far removed from their lives that it all seemed surreal, almost as if it had nothing to do with the country itself. An isolated group of people, risen over the years to the ranks of mythical gods in the minds of the citizens, were not expected to relinquish their status, power, or institute any changes to the status quo; and true to its common saying, "Nothing ever changes around here" became a self-fulfilling prophecy. People resigned themselves to poverty, hardship, misery, and hopelessness as a fact of life, and learned to live with it, and around it.

In the wake of increased tension, and occasional hostility in the community as a result of continuous political upheavals in the country and abroad, ceaselessly broadcast by the media, the Brodskis withdrew even farther into their own small world within the confines of the walls of their old communal housing apartment, not much even around this town, but it was a little haven of their own. They had no television, but they had a good, cabinet-style short-wave radio, which in its day was probably the best in its class, manufactured in the country, and could easily pick up most of the stations across Europe. The other option was Radio Moscow, equally accessible and with its own agenda, closely aligned with the official government view on rapidly developing stories.

For the first time, Alek and his mom, sitting in a comfortable sanctuary of their home, heard of supposedly officially unreported, but passed on by few who escaped, surviving village eyewitnesses to Radio Moscow, who escaped the carnage of My Lai village massacre by the American troops of over five hundred Vietnamese civilians. They were horrified by the news, although they viewed it with suspicion. It just couldn't be the America they thought they knew from all the sources. Then, to their surprise, they heard on the radio parts of a translated Lyndon Johnson Address to the Nation, in which he announced steps to limit the war in Vietnam and declared his decision not to seek reelection for the presidency. It was broadcast on all the national news outlets.

The Passover holiday of Saturday, April 13, wasn't high on Mrs. Brodski's list, amid general apathy she and Alek increasingly felt, as their problems with limited resources mounted, and the daily grind of a hard life, as well as a profound feeling of isolation and loneliness, was creeping in. She had absolutely no intention of celebrating for seven days in a town where they were the only Jewish family, at least as far as they knew; and there were the usual obligations of school and work in an environment where probably nobody knew what Passover was, or even cared. It took Mrs. Brodski a considerable effort to prepare the traditional dinner the night before, or something that would at least remotely resemble what she remembered from her childhood. With difficulty, she made three pieces of unleavened bread, the matzo and, separately, the matzo ball soup with parsley, supplemented with a few boiled eggs, and a sweet salad of shredded apples with walnuts and cinnamon.

Alek helped to set the table on a white tablecloth already in place, and brought in plates, cutlery, and cups for the tea, while his mom brought in the food from the kitchen. It was about thirty minutes before sundown when she lit a single candle and they finally sat down to eat the meal, but not before they both bowed their heads and she said a short blessing: "Blessed art thou, Lord our God, Master of the universe, who sanctifies us with Your commandments, and commanded us to kindle the light of Shabbat and of the Pesach holiday. Blessed art thou, Lord our God, Master of the universe, who has kept us alive and sustained us and has brought us to this special time."

Although it was a modest meal, they both enjoyed it and took their time to savor all that was there on the table, while talking and reminiscing on the years gone by in this small town, where it would seem not much ever happened and every day was just like the day before, yet there was so much tell. Just the adjustment to the new environment of mostly Christian population of this small community, where it was virtually impossible to be anonymous, yet they'd felt isolated here and lonely, despite the fact most people here seemed to know each other, or at least they had met or seen somewhere more than once. For Alek, his school posed the biggest challenge: he just didn't fit in, and not for the lack of trying. Sooner or later he found himself at the receiving end of cruel and crude jokes or horseplay.

8

THE PREPARATIONS FOR the annual May Day celebrations were in full swing around the county and around the town, although there was much uncertainty and apprehension among the people in the aftermath of the political turmoil in the capital, with ramifications across the country. The national holiday on May 1, 1968, as always, was preceded by major cleanup and decorating operations by supposedly voluntary crews made up of anyone from elementary school children, middle school youth, to employees of different government institutions. Within a week, red became the dominant color, the color of the proletariat, the symbol of the blood spilled by the heroic previous generations in their struggle to defeat the "bourgeoisie" and free the masses from oppression.

The Polish flags, made up of equally proportioned white and red longitudinal stripes, fluttered in the wind alongside red Soviet flags, adorned with the characteristic trademark hammer and sickle. They were placed on virtually every lamppost, prominent buildings, schools, and state businesses, and along all the major streets. Red canvas banners extolling the virtues of socialism and the leading role of the Party spanned the distance between the tallest trees and aligned lampposts on both sides of the main street. The Town Hall and the bulletin board in the town's center exhibited black-and-white portraits of the movement's forefathers—Karl Marx, Fredrick Engels, and Vladimir Lenin. Joseph Stalin was out of favor by now and resting in eternal obscurity. Even the poorly stocked main bookstore proudly displayed thick volumes of the "Works of Lenin" in its front windows. It did generate some curiosity, but little genuine interest.

The main event was the parade, which moved through the main street and culminated at the old sports stadium, where the gathered crowd would be greeted by local dignitaries and minor Party officials from the district office, who descended here for the occasion. At the head of the parade, a goose-stepping battalion of the local army unit, followed by a rather large contingent of uniformed railway workers with a band up front, mutilating their trumpets, horns, flutes, and drums in a strenuous attempt at what seemed like the national anthem, followed by an even more muddled version of "The Internationale." Next in line was a small group of a voluntary fire department unit, on an old red fire truck that gave out frequent muffled, sputtering sounds, as if in its last throes. Yet, somehow it moved along slowly, defying the odds and inviting some laughs from the onlookers along the way.

There were other trades represented, but the most populous groups were the teachers, with their pupils and students of various ages, from the town's two elementary schools and the middle school. There was Mr. Buzynski, the popular music teacher in the crowd of teachers, and nearby, but not together with him, was the young and pretty Ms. Lubinska, as always radiant with a lovely smile and a clearly visible sense of contentment on her face. Particularly, the teenagers showed little enthusiasm for this big event, and many seemed rather embarrassed to be there at all; but it was a common knowledge that participation in the May Day festivities was mandatory.

Alek was among the group of grade 8 students—the last year of his elementary school before going on to secondary school—right here in town. Either because of his height or by assignment, he was marching in the back of his class, and on the outside of a loosely organized column. There was a rather serious expression on his face, while the other boys and girls seemed to be enjoying themselves without restraint, talking and interacting. For many boys it was a perfect and long-awaited opportunity to strike up an awkward conversation with a long-admired girl, or pull off some hastily arranged prank.

Alek looked as if he'd rather be anywhere else but there. As usual, he was dressed in his customary black trousers, matching jacket, white dress shirt, and black shoes. It all seemed to be at least a size or two too big, and hung on his tall, skeletal figure as though on a coatrack. Alek could have been easily mistaken for one of the teachers, but his face betrayed that he was still in his early teens. He looked sideways at the spectators, only down occasionally, making sure not to accidentally kick, trip, or run into the boy in front of him when the marching column slowed down its pace for no apparent reason. The citizens who didn't participate in the parade, as well as many visitors from surrounding villages, lined both sides of the main street and looked curiously at the passing procession, and a great many of them were trying hard to spot somebody they knew.

Mrs. Brodski stood anxiously on a sidewalk, close to the curb, for what seemed like hours, waiting to catch a glimpse of her son passing by with the rest of the festive crowd, just like many other parents, grandparents, and siblings waiting for their turn. Finally, Alek appeared in sight, and as the group came closer, his mom leaned over toward the street, to make herself even more visible, and started waving and smiling lovingly, as only a proud mother could. He was completely absorbed in his own thoughts within the marching column, without even as much as a brief glance sideways, and would have passed her by had she not shouted his name when he was just a few meters away.

Alek immediately looked in the direction of the coming familiar voice, as if awakened from sleepwalking, and smiled back timidly, and at the same time slightly lifted his right hand and made a few waving gestures back to his mom. He kept looking her straight in the eyes for a few more seconds as he was walking by, and in just a few strides, left her still standing there and smiling.

Soon the long-marching throng spilled through the wide-open gate of the stadium, as the loudspeakers played instrumental versions of well-known revolutionary and patriotic songs. The parade participants all took their designated places as predetermined by the event organizers and directed by a few volunteer crowd controllers right from the gate. Alek stood quietly among his classmates on the edge of his column, slightly aloof, almost as if he didn't belong there. Nobody seemed to pay attention to him anyway, neither the boys nor the girls. He was perceived as a loner, engrossed in his thoughts, someone who didn't bother them and didn't want to be bothered; he just kept to himself. That trait alone, however, got him into trouble sometimes, when the school bullies badly wanted to know what Alek was up to. What was he thinking about? That aloofness seemed to project the wrong impression, an aura of superiority or provocation, which didn't sit well with the local young thugs.

Alek just patiently stood there, looking ahead at the center stage, paying little attention to the commotion all around. He was thinking about his mother, wondering if she was still here somewhere among the spectators, or if she went back home shortly after the parade passed through the center of town. He looked sideways, and even turned around quickly to see if she was standing somewhere nearby. With her height and distinct features, she would be rather easy to spot; but she was nowhere to be seen. For a moment, though, he had a feeling someone to his right, about ten paces away, was actually staring at him. Alek didn't like being looked at like that; it made him nervous, but nevertheless, he turned his head slowly again in that direction and looked. He recognized the face: it was the same boy he had seen that fateful day back in September, standing there at the entrance to the alley, just looking at the whole scene unfold, but with obvious fear and genuine concern in his eyes. He looked rather short then, but he seemed about fourteen years old now, and much taller, standing with his classmates but seemingly detached and, just like Alek, standing in the outer row of his group.

Their eyes met for a few seconds, but the boy lowered his gaze. This time Alek sensed a strange curiosity in his rather sad eyes, and puzzled by the encounter, he then quickly turned his face back toward the center stage. He couldn't concentrate on what was happening in front of him; but he waited a few more minutes looking straight ahead, pretending indifference or lack of interest, but again instinctively turned his head back to the right. The boy wasn't there anymore; he just disappeared, nowhere to be seen. Alek looked around for several more seconds, but the boy was gone, as mysteriously as he appeared among the group of students nearby, staring at him just a few minutes ago.

The dignitaries and important local officials, including Commandant Sokolowski, alongside visiting minor Party apparatchiks, stood on a specially constructed and freshly painted wooden platform—or a rather large stage, ready for the biggest spectacle this town had ever seen. It was adorned with several Polish flags with equally proportioned white-and-red horizontal stripes, alongside an equal number or Russian flags, with the well-recognizable emblem of the hammer and sickle, conceived during the Russian Revolution of 1917. Over the years, it had become the most recognizable symbol of the communist movement, the alliance of industrial workers and their peasant counterparts, under one banner of dictatorship by the proletariat. The dignitaries stood on the stage without any particular order, mostly middle-aged and older men dressed in dark suits, few with nondescript female companions, most likely proud wives by their sides, occasionally waving their hands in friendly greeting, their red, well-fed faces glistening in the hazy early-afternoon sun.

The townsfolk looked with great curiosity at the assembled visiting and the few local communist leaders, since they'd never seen such numbers here before—certainly never on this scale. For some, it was yet another reason to speculate on the reasons for this unusual presence; and for others who took it literally for what it was, it gave them a feeling of importance, of the growing status of their town. The grand finale had begun at last.

The highest local Party official, the town's mayor himself, Comrade Kutasiuk, stepped up to the microphone, tapped on it few times with his index finger, cleared his throat, and started to speak, first welcoming the visiting distinguished guests from out of town and the local officials, the pillars of society gathered on the stage, all dressed in dark suits and ties. Then the mayor turned his smiling face to the gathered civilian crowd and the parade throng, now all settled in relatively orderly groups of spectators on the large grassy field opposite the platform. He sincerely welcome all the gathered, especially emphasizing the young people, the students as the guardians, the torchbearers, and the county's best hope for the future. Each time Kutasiuk mentioned a specific group of people, a somewhat timid applause followed from the crowd, and visibly more spontaneous from the dignitaries.

The mayor looked to his right, then to his left, bowed his head, and with a slight hand gesture, introduced a few of his closest comrades by name. He then repeated one of the names, looking to his right at a stocky, middle height, past-middle-aged balding man with a reddish face, and let it be known that it was his rare honor, indeed a privilege, to welcome Comrade Baranski, the regional Party secretary. The mayor then enthusiastically announced that the distinguished guest would like to take this opportunity to speak to the citizens of this fine, historic town. And then he slightly bowed his head again, looked at Baranski, smiled invitingly, and pointed to the stand with a microphone as he stepped aside.

Comrade Baranski, elegantly dressed in a new dark suit, white shirt, and a distinctly dark-red tie, slowly crossed the distance to the microphone in just a few short steps, thanked the mayor for the introduction, and pulled out a sheet of prepared notes from the left pocket of his jacket. He then scoured the crowd with his eyes, as if looking for familiar faces; and once satisfied, he began to speak.

"Dear comrades, distinguished guests, ladies and gentlemen, and fellow countrymen! On this day, we're gathered here to celebrate a very special occasion. Since the inception of the People's Republic of Poland at the end of World War II, May 1 came to symbolize the indelible spirit of our beloved country. It is a spirit which endured foreign invasions and occupations by our enemies, who thought it could be extinguished, and the country permanently erased from the map of Europe.

"Over twenty years later, we can unequivocally state that neither the spirit has been extinguished, nor the country or national identity erased. We have risen stronger than ever on the ashes of Nazi Germany and our own bourgeois aristocracy, which brought this country to the brink of existence in 1939. The brave army of the Soviet Union, with the Polish People's Army by its side, had liberated our motherland from the greatest evil humanity has ever known. Upon the unprecedented destruction, a new, free, democratic, and socialist homeland was established. We are forever grateful and indebted to our Soviet brothers and sisters for the unimaginable sacrifice they made to liberate our country and to build our socialist Poland. All along, the Polish United Workers' Party had been instrumental, and its leadership unquestionable in our efforts to rebuild the country from the massive destruction inflicted upon us by Germany.

"The Party has been our guiding light in freeing ourselves from the chains of the old, decadent bourgeois order, and uniting all segments of society in our march toward justice and prosperity for all, under one socialist banner. Workers, peasants, and working intelligentsia stand arm in arm as equals, united by a common purpose, and today we celebrate their day. This day was written in the blood of the early socialist martyrs in the fight for a better future for all, so we can celebrate this day as a crowning victory of the working men and women across this country, Europe, and around the world.

"It's been 120 years since *The Communist Manifesto* was first published, but its resounding truth and credo that the proletarians have nothing to lose but their chains has finally been fulfilled, as demonstrated by the tangible achievements of our socialist country and the lives of all of you standing here today. The victory over fascism and bourgeois capitalism has been achieved; and the rotten world order of social injustice, inequality, and exploitation of men by men has been buried in the dust heap of history. The capitalist system, which for centuries enslaved the societies of Europe by division and exploitation of the many by the few has been replaced by a new socialist doctrine and the immortal words of Karl Marx: 'From each according to his abilities, to each according to his needs.'

"Dear fellow countrymen, I should mention, and as you all know, this year, November 11, marks the fiftieth anniversary of our country's independence from 150 years of partition and foreign domination by three European empires of the old world order. The new socialist order of Marxism-Leninism—built on the ashes of those empires in a spirit of cooperation, respect, and brotherhood of nations—withstood the test of time, and has become the envy of those still oppressed in every corner of the globe, and a beacon of hope, the new standard for all future generations. When the prophetic words of *The Communist Manifesto*

'Workers of the world unite!' were first published in 1948, few knew that one day they would became a universal reality, and the most potent force in the world today—for united we stand, divided we fall."

Secretary Baranski went on and on for several more minutes, extolling the virtues of socialism and dramatizing the battles and subsequent victories of the labor movement. His face turned red as a beet, his eyes inflamed with passion as the lofty words were pouring out of his mouth. Finally, it was impossible to tell whether he was intoxicated by the achievements and triumphs of socialism, or the vodka he drank shortly before the celebrations had started to kick in and taken over with clearly visible effects. He wiped his perspiring low forehead with a white handkerchief he pulled out of the left pocket of his trousers. On a few occasions, the speech was punctuated by a shrill, contemptuous whistle from one of the local bums hiding in the rear of the crowd. Then a determined uniformed policeman made his way through in the direction of the source of the whistles, while the people weren't making it any easier, refusing to budge and move to the side. Clearly frustrated, the cop uttered some incomprehensible threats, slowly squeezing through the throng. Meanwhile, Baranski's speech took on a more somber tone, and the crowd became impatient and visibly restless as he continued.

"Comrades, my fellow countrymen, our work is not finished yet. There is still much to be done on our path to where we want to be. Sadly, there are still those in our society who would want to turn the clock back, to where things used to be. To those people, we say, there is no turning back, so either join us, or step aside, because we'll have you moved. To those imperialist and bourgeois sympathizers we had extended a conciliatory hand, but with much regret, I confess that our gesture was rejected. Therefore, we were given no choice but to fight with unwavering determination the traitors and agents of the decadent, imperialist West, the saboteurs, agitators, and liberal scoundrels wherever they are. The enemy doesn't sleep, but is lurking in the shadows, trying to subvert our motherland and instill chaos and confusion in the minds of citizens.

"We must be vigilant, and any attempts at subversion must be ruthlessly eradicated, and the perpetrators brought to justice. The role of ordinary people under the infallible guidance of the Party is instrumental in protecting this country from domestic opposition elements, class enemies, spies, and traitors. We must trust the Party and its policies as a crucial and indispensable force in our common struggle for a free, democratic, just, and prosperous socialist Poland. Working men and women from all walks of life, from east to west, and from south to north, unite! Thank you."

The dignitaries and the Party officials started clapping vigorously as soon as comrade secretary finished his speech, but the crowd stood unmoved and silent for a few seconds, which seemed like minutes, and stirred the elites on the platform into a visible state of consternation and the citizens were gasping in disbelief; they had never heard a speech in their town like this before, given with such passion and conviction that it rivaled or exceeded the best speeches on television given by the secretary general or the prime minister himself.

Finally, a few sporadic, single claps started it all, and then more and more adults and children in the crowd joined in, to what became a rather lukewarm and scattered applause. The crowd's reaction wasn't received well by the comrades. Many were obviously bewildered, some visibly dismayed and agitated, looking around at themselves and then back at the less-than-receptive crowd with anger and contempt. The people stared at the stage, probably equally surprised by their reaction. Many made some derogatory comments and freely exchanged opinions of utter indignation among themselves, with anybody who happened to stand nearby. It quickly turned into a collective murmur of discontent and muffled sporadic chattering, followed by few outbursts of hostile shouts. The spectators were undaunted and expressed their resentment as if certain of impunity and assured anonymity in this large crowd, which otherwise would have been unthinkable for fear of serious consequences. Again, the hecklers in the back started to jeer and whistle; the so-called local "criminal element," was in full force and doing their best to show what they thought of Baranski's speech and the dignitaries on the stage.

Sokolowski's team moved in again, with the main law and order enforcer, Kovaluk, right in front, wielding batons ready to strike. Kovaluk was well known around town for his reliability and diligence in what he thought was fulfilling his duty. He was a frequent object of ridicule, as a perfect specimen for the job: medium height, a bit on the heavy side, yet strong and stupid. Some derisively dubbed him "the man of the cross," in reference to his apparent lack of education, some said illiteracy, and swore they had seen him sign his name with a cross on a dotted line.

Likewise, the Party did not tolerate discontent, independent thought, or divergent opinions among its ranks; in fact, any opinion was viewed with suspicion. Even those in line with the official Party position were suspected as not genuine, or possibly sarcastic. They all had to be vigilant; there was always someone behind, watching. The preferred course was to leave the thinking and formulating of opinions to the leaders of Party. This ever-present, omnipotent entity portrayed itself as the infallible source of wisdom, of profound ideas which only they understood. Only the Party held the secret, an exclusive monopoly on the ultimate truth; and the masses were there to listen, comply, and obediently fulfill the Party's directives and all those five-year plans in virtually every sector of the country's economy, the educational system, cultural and social life.

The mayor, Comrade Kutasiuk, again stepped up to the microphone and asked for attention; in fact, he had to repeat it a few times: "Attention please...attention, attention please!"

Many residents and visitors from the surrounding villages did pay heed to the mayor's plea and turned their eyes to the stage. He announced the beginning of the entertainment part of the May Day celebrations, mainly by the children and the youth of both the elementary and secondary schools, interspersed by a few words of introduction and praise from their teachers and principals. Proud parents were overjoyed by the performance of their pupils in the choirs trying their best at the well-known patriotic songs, solo performances, and poetry reciting. Many people in the audience reacted with sincere appreciation; even those who had the most basic knowledge of Polish literature were familiar with the heartfelt, timeless verses of the great poets like W. Broniewski, K. Galczynski, or A. Slonimski. Of course, any event of this kind had to include some well-known Russian literary giants such as Alexander Pushkin and Vladimir Mayakovsky.

For almost two hours, the entertainment session continued uninterrupted in a well-organized and obviously previously rehearsed sequence, except for brief announcements from selected teachers or the principal. Slowly it was all coming to an end, and the people and children in the audience were all becoming tired and restless. Many people began to move around the large grassy field, to stop and talk to someone they knew, or someone newly acquainted, and then there were those slowly moving toward the exit gate and leaving the stadium inconspicuously.

Alek didn't even notice when his mother approached from the back and stood behind him, slightly to his right side, making an effort not to disturb him, but rather secretly observing him with that seemingly ever-present gentle smile on her lips. After several minutes, Alek must have sensed somebody watching him, turned around, and their eyes met; and he was quite surprised but relieved to see the familiar face and smiled back. She squeezed his right arm gently and, with a little push forward, gave a signal it was time to leave the stadium. He had no objections; in fact, it was on his mind since shortly after coming here. He had no patience for any public gatherings; they made him tired and uncomfortable. He just couldn't concentrate during official ceremonies, whether public or those frequent school assemblies he so dreaded. Alek always had this uneasy feeling that he was observed, that people stared at him for no apparent reason. He was well aware of the difference between him and all the other teenagers, and possibly all the other people in town. They all had distinctly Slavic features, and he had visibly Jewish facial characteristics.

At times he felt like an unwelcome outsider, a foreigner with no place to call his home. Over the years, however, some things didn't make much sense to him, as he witnessed numerous instances of animosities and hostility among the Slavs themselves. It seemed to him that there was no love lost among the Poles, the Ukrainians, and the Russians either. Although on a surface the town seemed to rest in almost-sleepy peace and tranquility, from time to time true feelings would come to the surface, and then back to normal, and then the people went about their business as the best of friends.

One thing Alek had also noticed was that it was the older generations, the parents and grandparents, that fed the fires of ethnic resentments among them. The reasons for it were as foreign to him, as often his own presence here in this community. He overheard on a few occasions from some arguing men about historical wrongs unleashed by each of these countries on another, about prolonged occupations and resultant border disputes. However, what was probably most disturbing was the fact that many kids, like little vultures, were running around and spreading the same venom. Constant vigilance became Alek's daily reality at public events, school playground, or the town's streets. He was also concerned about his mother; she was the only person he was close to, and she was more than just his mother—she was his loyal friend.

They moved swiftly, navigating through the crowd, trying to reach the gate of the stadium as fast as they could, hopefully without bringing too much attention upon themselves for leaving early, well before the vast majority of the gathered crowd. Just behind the main entrance gate, Alek immediately noticed the same teenage boy standing just outside the stadium gates and waiting, and looking—looking at him and his mom leaving, as if in a well-planned, premeditated move to actually be seen.

"Mom, look, there he is again," said Alek.

"Who is there?"

"The boy I told you about last fall. He was the witness to the whole scene, standing there and looking, just like now," said Alek, slowing down and pulling his mother by the sleeve.

"Are you talking about that young man standing by himself over there to the right of the gate?

"Yes, that's the one."

Mrs. Brodski stopped and looked back at the boy with renewed interest, at someone who was a total stranger and yet somehow an integral part of their lives, and by some inexplicable coincidence a silent witness to its turning point. She looked intensely into the boy's eyes for a few crucial seconds, and he looked back at her with that same penetrating but a sad, almost-anguished gaze of someone who was deeply troubled, or perhaps just lonely and engrossed in his own little world, and yet detached from it all, just an observer. She smiled, and he smiled back for a few seconds, with that same faint smile she still remembered from all those years ago. He then turned his eyes away with a placid demeanor, looked briefly sideways at something, and then walked away.

Right at that moment, Zofia Brodski unmistakably realized she had seen those eyes before. She had seen the boy before, without any doubt, several years ago, perhaps six or seven years before; and she was absolutely certain of it.

"I think I know him. I've seen him before, I'm sure. I can never forget it," she said to Alek as they walked away.

"What are you saying, Mom? How do you know him? You never told me that."

"It was something that at the time was nothing to be concerned about, a trivial thing, and had nothing to do with you. Actually, I had almost forgotten it, buried it deep in my memory until today."

Once outside and well on the main street sidewalk, they slowed down again, and walked at a leisurely pace back home, sharing few personal impressions of the whole scene they just left behind; but mostly, they walked in silence for several more minutes. Then Alek began to have a strange feeling of most uncomfortable remorse. He realized he had seen the boy over the years a few times before, as he was growing up and in the most unexpected circumstances, when least expected. Whether by chance or he was intentionally following him, he couldn't tell.

As they walked, enjoying the fair spring weather, they held their heads up high, not as was their usual habit of mostly looking down, trying to avoid eye contact with most strangers. The weather improved as the day went on, with frequent bursts of weak sunshine between some scattered clouds, and the temperature was still quite low, at only around 14 degrees Celsius; but still, it was a perfect day for an afternoon stroll. With all the visitors from the surrounding villages, there was more traffic on the sidewalks and the streets than usual on any given day, but not particularly because of the significance of the May Day but, rather, because of people taking advantage of the statutory holiday, and as such, was a much-appreciated day off work and an equally cherished day off school. Alek and his mom were happy for a day, at times almost elated, walking slowly, not in a hurry to go back home, savoring the moment, or perhaps even to be seen or to meet someone they already knew. They looked at the buildings decorated solemnly with flags and banners, at the streets cleaner than usual, at the freshly manicured lawns and flower beds, and at people passing by, dressed in their finest, absorbed in their own world or in intimate conversations with their companions, paying no attention to the mother and son.

On this particular day, Alek wanted to be noticed, and wished that someone would stop and greet them like an old, loyal friend, someone who even from a distance would smile, recognizing them at once, and be so truly happy to see them, and then shower his mother with compliments she's never had for many years now. They passed some familiar old houses with front gardens already coming alive, and the owners bent over, cleaning up the previous year's withered plants and planting new ones. There was quite audible music coming through the open windows from one of the old wooden houses along the way, a new tune on the radio, the unmistakable guitar sound of the Rolling Stones, invoking strange nostalgia, distant imaginary images, and mystique of the free West, somewhere well beyond their reach.

"Mom, tell me about him, I want to know. What happened several years ago?" asked Alek, breaking the silence.

"Son, this is so insignificant—a child's play, I'd say. I have almost forgotten it completely until today, and it just came back to me. I don't think it is worth talking about."

"No, Mom, you've got to tell me. I want to know. I want to understand, why does he keep showing up? What is this all about? We don't even know who he is."

"Alek, don't take it so seriously. Don't let it become your obsession. It's a small town, people bump into each other all the time. Living in a place like this, one way or the other, we all have an effect on each other's lives, whether we like it or not, and sometimes we don't even realize this. Look, we all live under the same sky, breathe the same air, and sooner or later, our lives, in a mysterious way, are interrelated, at least to some extent."

"Mom, please don't…What happened several years ago? Tell me."

"Alek, in all honesty, I never thought I'd ever be talking about this. It's just so irrelevant. Do you really want to know about something I only suspect is related to the young man we've just seen?"

"Mom, but few minutes ago you said you were sure, and now what?"

"You know, I wish you'd drop this, but obviously, it won't happen. You just won't let go of it."

"Mom, please don't make it any harder than it has to be. This is all quite bizarre, wouldn't you say?"

"Perhaps…"

"So, what's the story?"

"It's not much of a story, but subconsciously, I guess, in a sense, it probably had an effect on my thinking somewhat over the years. It was a summer vacation, a nice and sunny day five or six years ago. Some children gathered behind the big, wooden fence dividing our courtyard from the neighbors' adjacent courtyard. You know, those few families of different ethnic backgrounds on the other side and, as always, with several kids of various ages playing? Few of them approached the fence and were talking among themselves. I was in and out of the house, and I overheard what they were saying. One of the boys was visiting, because I had never seen him around before, and the other kids were showing him around the courtyard. One of the boys said to the other two, just on the other side, and I could clearly hear them: 'Look, behind this fence that old Jew Brodski used to live," said one of them, whose voice I had heard several times before."

***

"Where is he now?" asked the new boy.

"Oh, he died a few years ago in that big fight we had over here," answered one of the local boys. He pointed to a few sharp pieces of fire equipment displayed on hooks attached to the old wooden shack several meters away and added, "All that was used in the war."

"My dad fought in that war too. It was our yard against them on the other side. It was a real war, I tell you," the other boy said proudly.

"So, who lives there now?" asked the visiting boy.

"In that first apartment across, just behind the fence, only his wife and son, Alek, live there now," came a reply.

"Do they come out of the house sometimes?" asked the new boy again.

"Oh yeah, for sure, but not very often. If you'll look through that hole in the fence, if you're lucky, you might see the devils."

"Why did you call them that?" continued the visiting boy.

"Because that's what they are, my dad said," one of the other boys answered quickly, with confidence and authority in his voice.

***

"The new boy slowly approached the fence and looked through the hole in it for several seconds, looking around our yard. I was bent down, pouring water out of the washbasin, just a few meters from our door. I caught a glimpse of the boy with those characteristic frightened and sad eyes, looking at me, obviously expecting to see the devil. I smiled to him, and a few seconds later, he smiled back. But just as quickly, he moved away, clearly embarrassed. Instinctively, I stood there waiting, curious what would happen next, and again he stuck his face in the hole and looked at me again—just to make sure, I think. I smiled, and he smiled back for a second or two, and then jumped back again, away from the fence, and I went back inside. That's the whole story, Alek. I don't know why it stayed with me for all those years. I wasn't really thinking about it, not at all. I thought it was just child's play. Nevertheless, it was one of those rare encounters, which, for whatever reason, remained with me."

"I really like the story, especially that it is so strange, but true. Is that what the people on the other side think of us, Mom?"

"No, not at all. There are many good families crammed together in those old buildings, and as everywhere, most people are good. But there must be a rotten apple among them too."

"Do you know any of them personally?"

"Yes, of course. I know the tailor Kaminski and his wife—very decent folks, friendly, always helpful, always smiling. They'd never say a bad word about anybody. Whenever they see me on the street, they stop and chat a little. I've been to their home a couple of times, and Mrs. Kaminski has been here at our place too. You just don't remember, or weren't home at the time."

"Do they have any children?"

"No, they don't. They're childless."

"Anybody else that you know?"

"I know Mrs. Terpilowski and her husband, Franek, who is a semi-retired electrician. They're older, but also very good people. They have three children, two daughters and a son, who is the youngest of the three. One of the daughters is married and lives in another city. The other daughter is studying at the university in Warsaw, and the son, I think, is in the third year of the local middle school. All well-raised, respectful children."

"Thanks, Mom, for telling me all this. I would have never known."

9

AROUND MAY 7, the national media, the Soviet Union, and Radio Free Europe reported that the so-called May Offensive was launched in the early morning hours of May 4, in which the Vietnamese began the Phase II of the Tet Offensive by striking 119 targets throughout South Vietnam, including Saigon. By this time, the prevailing mood on the street was that America lost the war, and there was no doubt the communist Vietnam won, and with it the entire block of communist countries in Eastern Europe, under the banner of the military alliance of Warsaw Pact.

Within two weeks, and unexpectedly, a letter arrived from the Citizens' Militia station, which was handed to Alek by a mailman, when he just happened to be briefly outside. Alek looked it over and went right back inside and handed it right to his mother. She looked at it, surprised, and flipped it in her hands before tearing the envelope open between her fingers and removing a single white sheet. It was an awkwardly typed two-sentence text, most likely by the undersigned, dated just three days prior, addressed to Mrs. Zofia Brodski and signed by the commandant, Captain Sokolowski, himself.

Alek stood beside his mother, who was sitting on a chair at the kitchen table, sensing the importance of what she was holding in her hands. She looked at him for a split second and then began to read.

> *You are hereby requested to appear in person at eight o'clock in the morning of Monday, May 20, 1968, at the office of the Citizens' Militia of the Polish People's Republic, at 195 Warynski Street. Failure to appear may result in appropriate legal action taken by the state against you.*

She finished reading, sighed, and looked at Alek defiantly, as if trying to assure him with her demeanor that there was nothing to worry about. He was curious beyond that, and asked, "What does it all mean, Mom?"

"I'm not sure what it's all about, but obviously, they want me to appear at the station next week, on Monday. There is nothing you should be concerned about. Maybe Sokolowski changed his mind about your case. I'll go."

"No, Mom, we'll go this time."

"I don't think it's a good idea to have you involved in all this. Besides, I've dealt with Sokolowski before, and I know what to expect. Actually, he seemed like a reasonable man. Maybe somewhat narrow minded, but reasonable.

I wouldn't go as far as calling him a good man, but for a cop who is just following orders from the county headquarters, he has shown his human side—maybe even deviated from the protocol, and possibly sometimes goes out of his way to at least look tough officially, but be fair and reasonable."

"Mom, I'm going with you this time," said Alek again.

"Oh, son, what about the school? Are you going to take time off school again? You've been missing many times this year. I'm really concerned."

"Don't be, Mom. I'll make up for those few hours, no problem."

"I don't want to sit here and argue with you endlessly, Alek, but we'll see."

***

On Sunday, May 19, Alek already couldn't concentrate on anything else, but was mostly silent, thinking about what the next day would bring. His mother was probably equally apprehensive, didn't talk much, unless absolutely necessary, and just went about her chores, quietly engrossed in her own thoughts. A summons to the police station was never any good, and it was always better, if possible, to live quietly beyond their reach, not to give them a reason to learn your name.

When the next day arrived, May 20, Alek and his mom were up quite early, long before they needed to get ready, eat breakfast, and walk about ten minutes to the station. Again, they didn't talk much, but knew well what each other was thinking. Both were calm and composed, without any visible signs of fear or apprehension. They both dressed in their best clothes—Alek his usual black trousers, white shirt, and dark, almost-black jacket with a tinge of gray in it, and the same pair of well-worn black dress shoes he had had for over two years, which used to be too big but now fit his feet perfectly.

Mrs. Brodski put on her long-sleeved beige blouse, simple black skirt, dark-gray cardigan with front buttons, a light-gray trench coat, black shoes, and an old black leather purse. Just before they left home, she looked herself in the mirror, then at Alek from head to toe, and once satisfied, she smiled approvingly, and they left. They walked at an even pace, mostly in silence, passing several kids on the way to school and a few adults on the way to work or the stores.

Two old delivery trucks whirred noisily by, leaving behind a trail of white smoke. They quickly covered the distance and soon found themselves in front of the gray two-story concrete building near the town's center. The same heavy, double wooden entrance doors led to the building's vestibule, and the same three flights of steep concrete stairs with rusting railings all the way up. Although there were no visible streaks of urine, or all the filth as previously, left late at night by the drunkards spilling out onto the streets from the nearby restaurant at closing time, looking for a perfect place to relieve themselves, and with a dose of newly found courage proportional to the amount of consumed vodka, to make a bold statement of what they thought of those communist guardians of law and order.

This time the walls were reasonably clean, but the characteristic foul, nauseating smell still persisted inside the building, especially on the ground floor, as if its indispensable feature, one could not be without the other. They ascended the stairs slowly, carefully scaling each worn-out concrete step, Mrs. Brodski first, with Alek right behind. When they reached the second floor, they stood for a few seconds looking at the door to the office of Citizens' Militia. There was not a sound coming from anywhere on the floor, just that eerie, unnerving silence.

Mrs. Brodski slowly pressed the door handle down and then pulled it and stepped inside, with Alek close behind, holding the door ajar. At first they didn't notice anyone inside, but then at the same time, the officer must have heard the creaking of the door and lifted his head from behind the desk in the rear of the large room, leaned back in his chair and looked straight ahead, as if to let them know that he was already waiting for them. It was Commandant Sokolowski himself, in full uniform and alone in the office, puffing a cigarette. He quickly got up from his chair, greeted them from afar rather cordially, and then without hesitation approached the front counter where mother and son were standing. He walked around it to his right, opened the small wooden swing door, and invited them inside, with what seemed like a sincere smile.

"Please come in inside. I've been expecting you. We have a lot to talk about, so let's sit down. At the moment, there is nobody else here but you and I, of course, so we have this big room to ourselves, and we can talk freely, all we want. There is nothing to be concerned about."

Mrs. Brodski hesitated for a second, looked at Alek, but then stepped right through and followed Sokolowski inside. The room had its own distinct strong mixture of stifling, putrid smells dominated by old wooden furniture, tobacco, sweat, and cheap Russian cologne in various proportions. The commandant again took a seat behind his clattered large desk and asked them to sit down on the two wooden chairs already pulled up on the other side. He looked at them intently for a few seconds, as if trying to get a feeling for what they were thinking, and then quickly looked around the room.

Sokolowski seemed tired and deeply absorbed in his own thoughts, almost disinterested in the meeting, as if he would rather be somewhere else. He rubbed his unshaven chin a few times with his left hand in an obvious struggle to regain mental concentration, looking for just the right words to begin. He then lowered his gaze on some documents on his desk, took one more deep puff of his cigarette, and proceeded slowly to extinguish the butt smoldering between his fingers in a large glass and overflowing ashtray. Once satisfied with newly found focus, he looked at his guests with renewed confidence and began to speak with a quiet, almost-subdued tone.

"I'm glad to see you both here today, thank you for coming. I realize the letter must have given you a cause for concern, but I'd like to assure you, there is nothing to be concerned about, or to be afraid of. There is a certain protocol we must follow here, and that's all. My coworkers are on duties in town today, and won't be in for a few hours, so we can have some privacy."

"Yes, I must admit, we both were a bit concerned. I've never been summoned to the police station in my life before. It's all a new experience to me," said Mrs. Brodski, visibly unsure of herself despite Sokolowski's assurances.

"Well, as I said, there is nothing to worry about, and it has nothing to do with that incident with your son, Alek, last autumn, I'm sorry to say this. What I want to talk to you about is an entirely different matter. You must have heard about the student protests in early spring—first in Warsaw, then around the country. It is not a secret, it's been reported extensively by our media, and of course, by Radio Free Europe. I don't suspect you listen to that propaganda bombarding our airwaves around the clock, but there are some that do, and I know it. There is opposition to what we're trying to do in this country. The enemies of the state are trying to derail everything we've achieved since the end of World War II. We all know that there are some changes taking place at the highest levels of the government and at universities around the country."

"Yes, I've heard something about that, although I don't pay particular attention to politics. But people talk about it around the town," Mrs. Brodski interrupted.

"Let me just make my point here," Sokolowski began again. "It's not only our country that is going through this transformational period, but other countries too. There were protests in places like France and Germany. The protests in France were particularly violent and on a large scale, joined by trade unions, and the strikes swelled to some 8 million people on indefinite wildcat strike. Soon the demonstrations spread to provincial cities and almost brought down the government of Charles de

Gaulle. I'm sure you know all this—our media covered everything quite extensively. What happened here in Poland was completely different. We don't have those problems, and I'm sure you're aware of it. In Western Europe, they have some fundamental structural problems, which is only to be expected sooner or later under their capitalist system, which enriches few at the expense of the vast majority.

"Nevertheless, it's not what I wanted to talk to you about. There have been some changes in our country too as a result of political reforms following the student unrests. Our borders have opened up for some people. They can now, for the first time, legally obtain passports, and without any problems, as was sometimes the case before, and they can go. They can just leave the country if they don't like it here, or are struggling in any way, or whatever the case may be."

"I don't understand, sir. Who can go?" asked Mrs. Brodski.

"The Jews, of course."

"The Jews?"

"Yes, the Jews can go, if they want to. Or Poles and others who think life is better somewhere else. They're free to go."

"Why?" asked Mrs. Brodski with genuine incredulity.

"Let's just say, there is suspicion—actually, I should say a reliable information—that many high-ranking politicians and influential people are behind all those protests, all that mess and subversion."

"They are? What's that have to do with us?" asked Mrs. Brodski, quite astonished after what she had just heard.

"Actually not much, probably only a handful of leaders in politics, the justice system, academia, and those in mass media, like the leading newspapers and magazines. Please don't take it personally, Mrs. Brodski; as far as I'm concerned you're one of us, good people. On the other hand, it might be your only chance. There is a unique window of opportunity as never before, and it would be in your best interest to take advantage of the situation."

"Are you telling me we should leave our country because of some apparent or imaginary transgressions of certain individuals in public individuals in public life, and of whom I've never heard?" Mrs. Brodski asked with determination.

"No, I didn't say that. All I'm saying is you're on your own, just the two of you, with hardly any friends, and no extended family. There is a big chance for you two, while all those undesirables are leaving with a one-way ticket," Sokolowski continued.

Alek was completely lost and couldn't quite understand the conversation unfolding in his presence, but for whatever reason or no reason at all, was equally at ease and just listened to the commandant's monologues and his mother's occasional interjections. He had full trust in his mom's judgment, who had proven over the years that she could hold her ground in any circumstances. He has seen his peers on many occasions being embarrassed even to be seen with their parents in public, and to have them intercede on their behalf was unthinkable, an ultimate humiliation. Alek was proud of his mother; he had seen her come out on top successfully in many verbal confrontations. She would make fools of those who tried. Quietly, deep down, he greatly admired her; she was above all those petty posturing, jostling for attention, recognition, and social status, even in this obscure town, on the outermost eastern outskirts of the country.

"Sir, why are you telling me all this? I still can't understand what some Party bureaucrats in politics and all those other positions you've just mentioned have to do with us. You're implying something that I personally don't identify with, just because I'm Jewish."

"Yes, yes, that's true, but it is a completely different matter. You don't seem to understand what I'm trying to tell you. I'm only telling you this out of the goodness of my heart. There is nothing in it for me, please believe me. This might be your best chance at a better life, somewhere else, abroad…What's keeping you here?" Sokolowski persisted.

"Sir, please tell me, where in the world can we go, and why would we want to go anywhere out of the country?"

"What do you mean where? Where you belong, in Israel, of course…"

"What are you saying, sir? I was born in Poland—actually, in the east, what's now part of the Soviet Union, and so was my father, and so was my grandfather, and God knows how many generations before them."

THE JEW

"You do as you please, but let me tell you, the time of reckoning has come," Sokolowski said emphatically.

"I don't understand you, sir. I have no idea what you're talking about. This must be a misunderstanding. Why did you summon us here?"

"Mrs. Brodski, let me be frank with you. My own father, who was in the AK, the Home Army, during the war as a young man, was persecuted after the war and imprisoned in 1953 on false, totally fabricated charges of subversion as an oppositionist to the new system, along with many others like him who fought for liberty. He was locked up on Rakowiecka Street in Warsaw; tortured by the UB, the Security Bureau; tried; and sentenced to death in 1954. Almost a year later, the sentence was commuted to twenty-five years by the secretary general, Comrade Boleslav Bierut himself. Then my father was released virtually on his deathbed several months after Bierut's death in March of 1956, and he died shortly after. He was a true Polish patriot, but not according to some overzealous party bureaucrats. Do you know who the interrogator was, or the prosecutor, or the judge at his trial? Do you?" asked Sokolowski.

"No, I don't," Mrs. Brodski answered without hesitation.

"Let me tell you, then. They were bloodthirsty scoundrels."

"I'm really sorry to hear that, sir. I really sympathize with you, I really do. If what you're saying is true, then I have nothing but words of sympathy for you and your family. I believe the perpetrators must be held accountable, even now, if they're still alive."

"Wishful thinking, that's all it is. Those bastards are untouchable. For your information, my father was a well-known commander in the underground, with many successful actions against the Germans to his credit. He was best known by his pseudonym, Falcon. Yes, he probably was against the new communist government the Soviets installed in the country after the war, with the help of Polish communists, but so were most people at the time, I'm sure, but that's not a reason to kill a good, courageous and honorable man.

"Yes, yes, I'm so sorry to hear this, sir. Such an awful tragedy, it's incomprehensible. Please accept my deepest sympathy for you and your family, sir," said Mrs. Brodski.

"I deviated from the subject, perhaps, into personal matters which don't concern you in the least. We all carry things around that weigh heavily on our souls, and I guess it doesn't take much for them to surface. I know you and your family have suffered terribly during the war, but my family has suffered not only during the war, but many years after, as I've just told you. We all have our demons to contend with. Nevertheless, I sympathize greatly with you, and if you'll ever need a good reference, if you'll decide on applying for passports, of course, or anything else for that matter, you can count on me. Please do not hesitate. I'll be here to help."

"Thank you, sir. I'll take your word for it, although I'm not sure what we'll do. We both know these are uncertain times, and things could change from day to day. Just a few months ago, who would have thought we would be talking about it."

Commandant Sokolowski suddenly became restless, looked hastily around the room, as if trying to make sure they were still alone. The he pulled out a cigarette from a package on his desk and lit it up. He then looked at the clock on the wall, leaned back in his chair, away from his desk, and turned to his guests with a penetrating gaze. Then without a word, he took a few deep puffs, and blew the smoke above his head. The distant sound of steps, still at the bottom of the concrete staircase outside, could be heard, and the sound of which was getting closer and closer with each step. The commandant hastened to explain, "One of my men will be here soon, so we must be careful. But there is nothing to be concerned about."

Unexpectedly, Alek moved impatiently in his creaky wooden chair, turning to his mother and, visibly worried despite Sokolowski's assurances, said, "Mom, can we go now, please?"

"We'll be going soon, son. Don't worry, just wait few more minutes," replied his mother.

"Please wait, I haven't finished yet," added Sokolowski. Lowering his tone, he looked intently at Mrs. Brodski, then at Alek, and then back at Mrs. Brodski and began again with unmistakable concern and sincerity, "What I said to you today stays between us. Please do not share it with anyone. You know, during the May Day ceremonies, as you had probably seen, we had rare visitors from the regional Party office and the interior ministry district offices, some very important and influential people. I talked to them about the situation in the country, the changes that have been taking place in the highest places in the capital, and the challenges we're facing here, locally. It confirmed what I've known already myself—some individuals are allowed to leave the country, the doors are open. You might consider taking a trip to the district passport office in Biala and apply for passports. I'm telling you this out of my genuine concern, and you would be well advised to take this opportunity. It might not come again soon."

The front door swung open, and another uniformed middle-aged policeman appeared, with a rather cheerful look on his face. He greeted them all cordially from a distance, not a bit surprised at the company the commandant entertained, as if it were a normal and frequent occurrence. He proceeded to get behind the counter and then walked over to the nearest desk and sat down, as if with a well-rehearsed routine.

Alek and his mother seemed confused by the sudden addition to the room. Both turned around and looked at him curiously for a few seconds, unsure what to make of it, or if they should continue with the conversation. Sokolowski's demeanor had suddenly changed—from being somewhat nervous and restless, to being relaxed and fully at ease.

Mrs. Brodski took it as a sign, as the commandant had previously assured her—there was nothing to be concerned about—and she said, "Sir, I'm sure you were sincere in what you've said to us today, and we do appreciate it. We'll certainly consider the options. It is a very interesting suggestion, although I must admit, I'm quite surprised by it. Never a thought has crossed my mind to leave my country, and the country of my ancestors."

"I understand your apprehension, but it might not be as bad as it seems at the moment, Mrs. Here, the possibilities, as you're well aware, are limited, but somewhere else, they might be endless," added Sokolowski.

DOMINIK POLESKI

"Perhaps, but this town is our home. There is no doubt, life here is tough sometimes, and as you know, we have faced some hostilities, but we also have a few friends here, and we've managed to survive thus far. Is there anything else you'd like to tell us, sir?"

"No, this is all I had to say. Please think about it. I thank you for coming in. I'm glad we had this conversation. I still feel somewhat guilty about that incident with Alek back in September of last year. I hope nothing like that has happened to you again."

"No, sir, it has not, although I'm quite careful to stay out of harm's way," Alek replied confidently.

"Good for you, son. These things happen to many other kids too. I don't think you were specifically singled out because of who you are."

"I don't know, sir," said Alek. He turned to his mom again and added, "Should we go now, please?"

"On a different note, Mrs. Brodski, I've spent a considerable amount of time on matters that concern you and your son, and it might raise suspicions. We're quite busy here at the station with our own work, which requires immediate attention, and we're understaffed. You must have heard what happened recently—the whole town is talking about it. It's actually quite funny," said Sokolowski.

"No, I haven't heard anything in particular, especially not about something funny, but I'm not around town much, and I don't know many people."

"I'm not even sure if I should go into this, but to end our meeting on a positive note, let me tell you, because as I said, the whole town is talking about it. Last week there was a break-in at the rectory of our Catholic church, and the thieves discovered that our good shepherd, Father Antoni Pukalski, was actually a very frugal man. The box-frame of his couch was half full of money, literally filled with stacks and wads of money, I'm told. Apparently, it wasn't some loose change either, but banknotes, paper money, lots of it. How the thieves managed to uncover that, I don't know. We're conducting our investigation. They cleaned out most of it, but probably left some of it because they came unprepared for such a big haul. Nevertheless, they also ate most of the torte Father Antoni had in the fridge. And to top it off, they drank two bottles of red wine he stored in his cabinet. It seems the thieves had quite a party there", and the commandant let out a hearty laugh.

"Yes, that's very unusual for this town, and it is actually quite comical, I must say. Do you have an idea who was behind it?" asked Mrs. Brodski, smiling, quite amused by the story.

"No, we have no idea. But I imagine Pukalski wants us to pursue this matter at all costs, no matter what, until the culprits are found. No, he doesn't want to cover it up, although this whole thing is quite embarrassing for the church."

"Why would it be embarrassing? I'm not sure I understand."

"Why? You know, I don't go to church, but everybody knows how he's always soliciting more and more money from the pulpit, how poor the church is, how there is always a shortage of money to cover even the most basic expenses, et cetera. Now we all know, but is he shamefaced about it? No, not at all."

"Well, I'm not familiar with those things. I've never been to the church, or discussed matters of the Catholic faith with anyone, so it would be inappropriate for me to even comment about it," Mrs. Brodski said diplomatically.

Mrs. Brodski got up from her chair almost at the same time as Captain Sokolowski, and with it giving a signal the meeting had come to an end. Alek was caught off guard, listening to the incredible tale and smiling, but he soon sprang to his feet. The commandant extended his hand to Mrs. Brodski, then to Alek, and thanked them again for coming, smiling broadly. He led them slowly back to the front counter and to the small gate on the side, swung it open, and held it to let them through. He then bowed courteously and said, "Good-bye!" Mother and son both turned to him just before the exit door and equally politely nodded, smiled with great relief, and said, "Good-bye."

Once outside, they hurried down the three flights of stairs, as if afraid of being called back to the police station, their feet stomping hard on the cold concrete steps, making loud echoes. They didn't slow down past the front door, but continued in a hurry for several more meters, before realizing they were actually outside and had left the police station well behind. They walked in silence, still strongly under the impression

DOMINIK POLESKI

of the meeting they'd just had, oblivious to the traffic on the sidewalk and the vehicles passing them in both directions on the street, and they were sad.

It was a fair and warm day, with a few gray and white clouds scattered against the otherwise mostly blue sky. Home was the only place they wanted to be. Small and crammed as it was, it had always been a place of refuge, away from the small, often-inhospitable world outside. Soon they reached the familiar courtyard surrounded by the old, gray, mostly single or two-story houses. Every one of those buildings, depending on its size, was divided into a few separate dwellings, each one with its own entrance, either from a common corridor, or a direct entrance from outside.

Alek and his mom lived in a small, two–room corner apartment with a tiny two-piece washroom—and all of it with a separate entrance from the inside courtyard, secluded at the back of the building. Their building and the courtyard were separated from the adjacent courtyard with two similar buildings by a tall, wooden fence running barely two meters away, parallel to their kitchen window and the front entrance. Over the years, the old, worn-out fence had become recognized as a natural divider between two different worlds often inhabited by distrustful and competing families, and their attitudes were often passed on to their children, who carried on the same traditions in the courtyards. Each courtyard had a life of its own, which revolved around the protected and unwritten neighborhood-specific rules, which were more or less never questioned and universally understood. Children and adults alike, although inconspicuously, liked to peek through the gaps between the wooden planks or holes left in place of missing knots. It was more a force of habit, a curiosity, than any particular reason to see what was going on, on the other side of the fence, especially for the older folks who didn't work outside of their homes; and gossip was an indispensable part of their everyday lives.

Outside the neighborhoods, it was all back to normal, as between the best of friends: smiles, friendly gestures, courteous greetings, handshakes, and, often, customary kisses planted on both cheeks. Alek and his mother spent better parts of the next few days pondering the future, trying to make sense of what Commandant Sokolowski told them about emigration with such certainty, and what they had no way of confirming to be true. He either knew something others did not, or he was just repeating and spreading some unsubstantiated rumors.

10

OVER TIME, THE rumors became a reality, confirmed repeatedly in conversations, occasionally by the major government-run media outlets, and the always-reliable Radio Free Europe. Alek's restless imagination carried him away to some faraway places, and perceptions of which accumulated in his mind over the years from stories he read or heard, and which now came to life again and seemed closer than ever. The numerous discussions they'd had on the subject of potentially leaving, failed to produce a consensus, much less any concrete plan of action. The subject of a final destination was left open to further contemplation, although Alek had full trust in his mother's judgment. Time and time again, the experience had thought him she was right, even when posturing and defiantly arguing with her over little things, or at times in his world, matters of great importance. Admitting it to her sometimes didn't come easy, since everything she said sounded so true and convincing.

Occasionally, Alek tested his mother's patience and resistance level by venturing a little farther in his arguments in an attempt to stake out his own sphere of influence. To his surprise, he found his mother to be a rather passive and reluctant participant, and thus withdrawing from conversation with clearly visible sadness, before any serious argument erupted.

June 5, 1968, became another extraordinary day in the mass media, when the only subject of the news, analysis, and around-the-clock speculation was the assassination of Robert Francis "Bobby" Kennedy, a United States senator. The somber-faced television announcers anxiously read a prepared short statement and repeated countless times on the radio waves: "Today, at twelve fifteen in the morning, American senator Robert Francis Kennedy was shot three times and wounded in Los Angeles, California, at the Ambassador Hotel by a twenty-four-year-old assassin, Palestinian-Jordanian immigrant Sirhan Sirhan. The senator was immediately transferred in a grave state to Central Receiving Hospital, and later to the Good Samaritan Hospital for surgery."

The tragic event became a continuous story, with photographs of the senator splashed across television screens, until a day later, the same announcers read another brief statement: "American senator Robert Francis Kennedy died at 1:44 this morning at the age of forty-two, of the gunshot wounds sustained a day earlier. By his side were his wife, Ethel; his sisters Jean Smith and Patricia Lawford; his brother-in-law Stephen Smith; and his sister-in-law Jacqueline Kennedy."

The senator's death gave the authorities and the state media a unique opportunity to exploit the tragedy for their own purpose of emphasizing political violence and the instability of the American capitalist system, and the Western decadence in general, and once again an unmistakable proof that it had run its course and was undoubtedly in its last throes.

The beginning of June also marked a momentous day in the Brodski household. The decision had been made, although with much often intense deliberation: they would emigrate. It was agreed on a general concept of leaving the country for good, but the final destination was still left up in the air, and a subject of further numerous discussions in the following weeks, which still failed to produce a consensus, although America and Israel figured prominently in their deliberations.

Ultimately, however, they were at the mercy of some yet-unknown bureaucrat in the district passport office, who would undoubtedly expect at least some attempt at securing a visa to a country he would deem acceptable, and which in his mind would not compromise in any way the good name and security of the country. It had always been common knowledge that most passport applications were denied without any explanation, although with an appeal process in place, which was long and arduous, leading to the same result: passport denied with a brief note attached—that the applicant had a right to appeal the decision further to the ministry of the interior.

DOMINIK POLESKI

Although it was not recommended to pursue it, so as not to bring unwanted attention to oneself, those who did appeal to the ministry were expected to receive a customary letter stating the obvious, that this office "upholds the decision of the lower administrative instance," and dutifully inform the applicant of one final possibility, the appeal of the last resort—the general secretary of the Party himself. Those desperate and persistent enough to take that route, in the best case, had never received a reply, or they had their place of residence exchanged for a period of "rehabilitation" in a political prison, with a generous doze of indoctrination, or even in some rare cases, those particularly unruly, never to be heard from again.

Alek's mother harbored increasingly nagging thoughts of emigrating to Israel, to live happily and work among their own people. Although Israel was a foreign country, somehow at times it seemed closer than the country they were born in, and so were many generations of their predecessors. She knew well that since the end of World War II, remnants of the Jewish populace from across Europe, so horribly decimated by the Nazis, were settling in, in the newly established state of Israel in 1948. The Jews finally had a state of their own, a place where they could live in peace and not be afraid as to where the next threat to their very existence was coming from, at least that was the prevailing hope and dream.

Nevertheless, leaving Poland was an arduous and lengthy process shrouded in uncertainty. Obtaining the passports was dependent on producing a valid visa from the embassy of the country of the final destination in the capital. Visa application had to be supplemented by rigorous medical examination in a designated medical clinic. The trip to Warsaw itself was a serious undertaking, requiring careful preparations, time, and money. What followed was a flurry of activities in the Brodski household, during which time it was decided that to ensure any chance of obtaining the passports, Israel was the only reasonable option.

Then followed two tiring trips to Warsaw to obtain the visas, and which were successful, resulting in emigration permits and promissory notes, but still without the passports. The trip by train covered about two hundred kilometers but took about four hours each way, with frequent stops along the way. It gave Alek a rare, and perhaps the only opportunity to see the country beyond his small town. He was glued to the window for most of the time as the new, fascinating world passed before his eyes. The train stations along the way were old historical buildings, usually freshly painted white or beige, with some decorative elements in gray or black, like the year it was built at the top of the building, and below it, a big sign in bold, black lettering with the name of the city or town. An indispensable feature at every station was, somewhere on top of a secondary, adjacent smaller building or specially constructed billboard, was a familiar slogan in red lettering on white background, extolling the virtues of the ruling party or the achievements of the socialist country.

Every time the train slowly pulled out of the station, picked up speed, and left the city or town behind, a whole new world opened up before Alek's eyes, unlike anything he'd ever seen before—the countryside. Far at a distance, solitary or small clusters of predominantly gray and white houses with a few old farm buildings dotted the horizon, surrounded by vast wheat or potato fields with some still new, some barely sprouting vegetation. The scenery changed seemingly every few kilometers from farmlands and forests to rolling green meadows with a few scattered ponds or patches of shallow wetlands, with the familiar presence of white storks, always migrating here every spring from Africa and calling these areas home, for a few months every year.

Two weeks later, they took another day trip by train to the district passport office in the nearest biggest town, population of about forty thousand, and which was just over thirty-five kilometers away but still took well over one hour each way to cover. The train stopped at every small, impoverished village along the way, just long enough to let a few new travelers on board, and sometimes it stopped in between any settlements in the near vicinity for no apparent reason at all. The travelers impatiently paced the corridors, exchanged their best opinions on the unwelcome interruption, looked out the windows; a few men disembarked for a few minutes and looked ahead of the locomotive, trying to see for themselves the reason for the sudden stoppage. Those occurrences were always a perfect occasion for widespread grumbling on the failures of everything in this supposedly socialist paradise, where not even one thing worked faultlessly.

It gave Alek the unique opportunity to relax and immerse himself in thoughts and dreams of what was to come, oblivious to all the commotion around him. Quietly, he thought of eventually ending up in America, somewhere in one on those big metropolitan centers on the East Coast. The American films he had seen over the years and the stories he's read all implied life was good there, certainly better than anything this godforsaken town had to offer, and until quite recently, with no way out. Suddenly, with all the political turmoil, the meaning and implications of which he could barely comprehend, there was a glimmer of hope, a narrow opening to escape the confines of this isolated, decrepit eastern town right on the border with the Soviet Republic of Belorussia.

For Alek, the sudden prospect of a long journey abroad and a new beginning became a source of rare, yet still concealed, daily joy, should it all turn out to be just wishful thinking, an elusive dream with not even the slightest chance of realization. In the following days and weeks, it became an increasingly frequent, almost-routine escape into the unknown, magical world, which gave him comfort, a sense of contentment, and ever-growing hope while dealing with the vast government bureaucracy at every level in the district passport office. It also became apparent that the whole endeavor was so difficult, demeaning and time consuming, that soon they began to doubt the sense in the whole undertaking.

First, there were the lengthy applications to be filled, a few original documents to be submitted, such as confirmation of their residence from the town hall; record of employment for Mrs. Brodski, and for Alek, an enrollment confirmation from his school; birth certificates for both of them; and, finally, processing fee, which in itself was a significant amount of money, at least in their household. The passport office was conveniently located, with various local municipal government offices in the most prominent building in the town's square and, most importantly, the district Party headquarters. It was a common perception that entering that building was something one would do as a last resort, when all other options had failed, or when there were no other options.

Clients, ordinary citizens, were mistreated right from the front counter by rude, conceited, and incompetent staff, usually young women, with average looks, questionable education, and an embarrassing lack of knowledge on a whole range issues within the scope of their respective departments. Most of the women seemed to be in a permanent state of agitation and were exceedingly impatient; and any prolonged or persistent questioning from a reluctant client would set them off, and with assured impunity. The secretaries, clerks, and most department managers were especially abrasive, often outright abusive toward country and small-town folks, whom they generally considered lesser beings for their dress code, language skills, manners, and overall personal hygiene. The prejudice was prevalent in most government offices; in fact, it was an inherent part of the system, and generally accepted as a fact of life. Openly challenging any of the employees, from the lowest in rank to the management, was not recommended, and could only guarantee an absolute failure, not to mention a humiliating lecture right there on the spot, laced with an array of derogatory epithets.

At the best of times, to get anything done usually meant two or three trips to the institution. Briberies, one of the greatest achievements of the socialist experiment, were the most common assurances of business done quickly and efficiently, usually on the first trip, unless some bureaucrat higher up the ladder thought it was not enough. The same rules applied to the small district passport office serving the city, surrounding small towns and villages within about a fifty-kilometer radius.

Comrade Rakowski, the Party member in good standing, was the head of the department, with a staff of just a few employees consisting of his deputy and four female clerks. Rakowski was a tall and rather thin middle-aged man with a small moustache, as was usually the norm for a civil servant or a policeman. His services were in great demand, and his powers vast. He knew it well and used them to his best advantage, like a god in matters of life and death. For many folks, obtaining a passport to go anywhere beyond the country's western border for reasons previously meticulously planned for years, and was quite often kept secret till the very end, was a dream come true, an opportunity of a lifetime.

Comrade Rakowski was well known for his spiteful, malicious streak, and devotion to the socialist cause (whether genuine or pretended was impossible to tell). Undoubtedly, he must have served his masters well, since he was at it for over six years now, and as comfortable in his position as anybody who knew how to play the game well. Over the years, the bloody, cancerous system became a perfect breeding ground for venomous, conscience-depleted pricks like him.

His deputy, Stasiuk, was also quickly making a name for himself, closely following in his boss's footsteps, the familiar, proven path to guaranteed success in his career, Party rank, and financial security. Almost all the employees in the passport department—or any government office for that matter, right from the first female clerk behind the counter—had an aura of superiority about them. The way they walked, the way they talked, even the way they looked at the clients, was enough to scare off even the most determined or the most desperate souls. It was not that uncommon to hear profanities directed at them from the waiting clientele, or the ever-so-popular saying among the males in these parts, thrown for their indolence: "She's like an old whore, not so sensitive anymore."

Since there were no other options for those who decided to travel abroad, they all had to endure the indignities and abase themselves in highly deferential postures, preferably with unmistakable signs of profound veneration toward those superior beings on the other side of the counter, or in any of the small private offices, behind closed doors. Here too, as in all government offices, hung the familiar and ever-present three portraits on the main feature wall, across from the double entrance door. One was the ever-present black-and-white likeness of the first secretary of the Party, Vladyslav Gomulka, then in the middle the white eagle on red background; and to the right hung the black-and-white picture of Prime Minister Jozef Cyrankiewicz sternly peering down from above.

11

A FTER REGISTERING AT the front counter, the Brodskis were asked to sit in the waiting room, which was actually a long corridor with several wooden chairs along the nondescript beige wall on both sides and few randomly spaced "No Smoking" signs. Most of the chairs were already taken up by other vividly disillusioned people, silently waiting hours for their turn to be served. They all waited, Alek and his mom and all those other strangers from the surrounding towns and villages, sharing furtive glances, seldom more than a few words, bound by common understanding, fate, and fear of the unknown. They already had the applications ready, which consisted of two double-sided pages of flimsy, low-quality paper folded in the middle; the fee, along with two photographs each; and all the supporting documents looked over by one of the clerks.

The sluggish clerk rather indifferently flipped the pages, and with what seemed like an approving nod and a few scant, barely comprehensible words, signed and stamped the applications at the top and directed them to the waiting room. From time to time, one of the irritated and callous female clerks would come out from behind the counter and call out somebody's family name once, twice, or even three times, if there was no immediate reaction, and the person called out didn't immediately jump to his feet. Many people, for no apparent reason, were waiting there for hours, until growing increasingly restless and from time to time walking up in frustration to the front counter, demanding to know what they were waiting for, or the status of their applications.

There was also among the clients a tall and bearded middle-aged man attracting much attention, pacing nervously back and forth with his head down, absorbed in his thoughts, and letting out a curse from time to time. He didn't elicit much sympathy, if that was his intention; on the contrary, the folks looked at him with disdain and apprehension, afraid he would unexpectedly turn his anger toward one of them. The common understanding was that every newly submitted application would be followed by an interview, or those who had submitted their passport applications weeks before were there on their second or third visit to finally pick up their new, long-expected document. The whole process was rigged and wrapped in a veil of uncertainty, from initial submittal of the application to finally receiving the ready passport or official notification in the mail that the application was denied without any further explanation, but always with an added note: the decision could be appealed.

In cases where the applicant was required to appeal and appear at least once more, it usually meant there were other expectations, which were an indispensable part of the whole process. A subtle, unwritten message was being conveyed, and financial considerations were now at play; the great wheel of government bureaucracy had to be greased. Those who knew the game well, and came with an envelope stuffed with some cash, were usually the lucky ones who would eventually leave the passport office with a smile on their faces and a passport in their pockets. Those who knew how to play the game but refused to play it, convinced they had the law on their side and approached the process with a dose of visible hostility, were doomed to fail, or in rare cases, even worse.

There were stories passed around of such rebellious individuals charged with subversion, or for contacts with foreign agents and plotting against the state. There were also people who were never exposed to any dealings with government offices or agencies, and simply just didn't know or were too naïve thinking all was well and in great order in the socialist motherland with the ever-caring, benevolent government of the people, for the people, and by the people. They would soon find out that naiveté or outright ignorance were not mitigating factors, wouldn't get them anywhere, and the only option was to learn the game fast and play by the unwritten rules.

Mrs. Brodski and Alek were both very nervous about the affair, since they'd never had to deal with any government authorities at this level, so serious and unforgiving, where everything seemed strangely foreign and overwhelming, permeated with fear and elevated to almost life-and-death significance. To make the matter worse, they didn't know how to play the game; in fact, they didn't even know such option existed in the first place. The relative comfort of waiting in the corridor for what seemed now like at least two or three hours was suddenly interrupted by a loud female voice: "Brodski!"

People looked in the direction where it came from, but nobody moved. Alek and his mom were completely absorbed by their own quiet conversation, oblivious to the surroundings beyond their two chairs, as if forgetting the life beyond. The young female clerk who came out from the main office around the corner stood at the head of the narrow waiting room and looked impatiently over the two rows of people sitting along the walls on both sides of the corridor. Visibly unhappy about the lack of immediate response, she bellowed again, "Brodski! Is Brodski here?"

Alek caught the sound of their name and sprang to his feet, still somewhat confused by the sudden, least-expected interruption, followed by his mom, who also heard her name this time loud and clear. Mrs. Brodski surged forward first, with Alek right behind her toward the front and the first office on the left side. By this time, the clerk retreated promptly back to the main office as soon as she saw two people respond to her call and up on their feet.

They burst through the door and remorsefully approached the long front counter. The clerk was already standing there, impassively looking down at some papers. Instinctively, she lifted her head, as if expecting the clients to arrive there on the other side, at that precise moment. Mrs. Brodski began apologetically in a subdued voice, "I'm sorry about it, Mrs., but we didn't hear you call out our name. You know, we were so distracted by the noise, all those people..."

"No need to explain, Mrs. Brodski. I understand."

"Thank you, that's very nice of you. You must be so busy here..."

DOMINIK POLESKI

"Yes, we're very busy. The summer season is near, so naturally, people travel everywhere, and many more travel abroad than ever before, as people prosper and can afford it, or have relatives in other countries. Of course, nowadays, we have many more clients like you, who would simply like to emigrate. It is written Israel in your applications. Any particular reason why Israel? You don't like it here, Mrs. Brodski?"

"Oh no, no, it's not that we don't like it here, not at all. We love this country. This is our home, the only country we've ever known. You see, there are just the two of us. My husband died several years ago, and it's been a struggle at times, you know. All my close relatives didn't survive the war, and the few distant cousins that I know of and which are still alive, just stayed there on the other side, in the Soviet Union."

"Are you Jewish, Mrs. Brodski?"

"Yes, we are."

"I'm sorry for being so intrusive, and it's actually none of my business, but I'd like to ask you, just out of curiosity, is the reason for your emigration to Israel to be among your own people? Do you feel alienated here?"

"You see, before the war, my family lived in the eastern parts of Poland, but since the border was redrawn and it was annexed by the Soviet Union, we moved out west and settled on this side of the border."

"Well, it's a matter of opinion whether it was annexed, but I'd rather not talk about it. When are you planning to travel, Mrs. Brodski?"

"We're not sure. It all depends if we'll be granted the passports, which I hope won't take long."

"Since we're dealing with emigration, not just a short trip abroad, as most people waiting here are planning to do, you'll have to see Comrade Rakowski or Stasiuk. This is certainly a more serious matter, and in cases such as this, decisions are not taken hastily. I'm afraid you'll have to come back here another time, Mrs. Brodski."

"I'm sorry to hear that. I thought it would just be a simple procedure and all could be done in one day. We were waiting here for hours. I took a day off work, and Alek, of course, a day off school, and now we're told we'll have come back another day? It's seems so unfair."

"I know. Life is unfair, don't we all know that? It's not every day we have someone here who, for whatever reason, wants to emigrate. These things are not taken lightly here. We like to know why. Why would anyone want to leave this beautiful country and go somewhere else?"

"I've explained it to you already, but of course, it's not that simple. There are many other little things which we've taken into account."

"I'm sorry for the inconvenience, Mrs. Brodski, but you just might have to explain all those reasons to Mr. Rakowski. I have nothing to do with it. These are the procedures. You'll be notified in the mail when to appear next time."

"How soon will we receive the notice to appear?"

"You should be getting it within two or three weeks."

"So, is this all for today, nothing else that can be done?"

"Yes, Mrs. Brodski, this will be all for today. I'm sorry once again for the inconvenience, but we must follow some strict regulations here, especially if it's about more than just a passport for a short trip abroad."

"Yes, I understand."

"Good day to you both!"

"Good day, madam!"

Alek and his mom turned away from the front counter and just stood there in silence for a few seconds, looking at each other, not quite sure what to do. There was visible concern on their faces, a feeling of helplessness. Slowly, without a word, they began to move toward the door. Once outside the office, they both looked one last time at the people sitting on both sides of the corridor waiting for their names to be called. Alek pushed the double, heavy wooden door open, and they left the corridor and then descended the few old, worn-out concrete steps down and onto the sidewalk. Once outside, they stopped again in front of the building, appearing lost, and looked around within the immediate vicinity, then at each other, quite unsure of their next move, and they were sad. Passersby walked around them, trying to avoid collision and hurried indifferently ahead, preoccupied with their own business.

Alek stood about three feet away from his mom, looking straight into her dark, tear-swelled eyes and waiting for her to decide the next move. She reached into her purse with one hand and ran her fingers through the contents, and once satisfied, she looked around the city square. She noticed a sign—"Dairy Bar"—above the door of one of the government-run businesses that filled the square on all four sides, and regained her composure somewhat. With renewed determination, she said, "Alek, let us go and eat something. It'll do us good. What do you say?"

"Sure, Mom. Where to?"

"How about that Dairy Bar on the other side?" She pointed to the row of dilapidated stores and small businesses on the left side of the street.

"Sounds good. I'm hungry."

Without any further hesitation, they started walking in the direction of the bar, silently and in unison, looking at the enticing sign from a distance, above large dark-green wooden door. Soon they found themselves at the entrance, separating two large misted-over windows, one on each side with sagging old beige curtains, marking the approximate size of the bar. Alek reached for the door handle first, pulled it open, and held it for his mom.

Once inside, they were hit by the strong, pleasing smell of cooked food. The bar was almost full; only a few scattered seats remained empty. The furnishings and décor were basic, but functional and designed for the massive daily turnover of indiscriminate working-class clientele. Several wooden tables with metal legs and tabletop glass covers were scattered around the sizable room, each with four matching plain wooden chairs. Each table and every other piece of furniture had a rather old, overused, and well-worn appearance. The entire floor area was covered with gray porcelain tiles with numerous cracks and chips, and over the years filled with multiple layers of grime. Here too hung the three portraits on one of the walls—one of the white eagle, First Secretary Gomulka and Prime Minister Cyrankiewicz watching over the diners from above.

Alek and his mom approached the service counter, behind which two corpulent and busty, past–middle-age women with rosy cheeks stood, with a third younger and relatively slim but pale woman moving around behind their backs. The Brodskis looked up at the back wall, a big part of which was covered with the establishment's menu on a large plastic panel with black lettering. The menu didn't entirely or accurately reflect its name, *Dairy Bar*, but none of the items served were meat based. The bar served two types of cereal with milk, potato-and-flour pancakes, cheese-and-potato–filled pierogis, cottage cheese crepes, eggs, a variety of baked goods, yogurt, coffee, and tea.

They both ordered potato pancakes, the latkes, and the always-popular grain coffee, which became a cheap, universally available substitute for the much more expensive real coffee, usually available at better restaurants and cafés. Without much difficulty, they were able to locate two vacant chairs at one of the corner tables, sat down, and ate in silence, avoiding curious, meaningless glances and sarcastic attempts at conversation from a young couple sharing the table with them. Alek devoured his portion rather quickly, and with time to spare, looked at his mom, who was taking her time, visibly engrossed in thoughts on what he could only guess were matters related to the passport bureau.

Alek looked around the premises with great interest, since it was one of only a few times in his life they were eating outside of their own home. He recognized that a majority of customers were most likely out-of-town farmers from surrounding villages on a business trip to the district capital or out for a shopping excursion, intermingled with possibly a few locals.

The peasants were quite easily recognizable by the clothes they were wearing, and even by the way they were moving around and behaving, as opposed to the local residents, who were certainly better dressed and showed more ease of movement, refinement, and confidence. The peasants were mostly dressed in outdated dark, oversized, and well-worn clothing, reminiscent of the 1950s style. The women had colorful scarves over their heads, some tied under their chins, and still others had them just loosely wrapped around. Most men wore old-style dark suits, usually with stripes and long, wide lapels. The matching baggy turn-up trousers they were wearing all seemed too long, with excess folding onto their black dress shoes. Many men were sporting a beret on their heads, which was almost an indispensable part of any farmer's attire, so easily

DOMINIK POLESKI

recognizable by city dwellers, and what over the years became a frequent subject of jokes or of the popular saying, "In the summer or in fall, by his beret you can always tell a peasant from them all."

Alek couldn't help but smile just thinking about it, while looking at the people all around. His mom noticed it, but didn't say a word; instead, she also just smiled warmly.

"We have to go now, son. We must hurry back to the train station to catch the three o'clock train home," said Mrs. Brodski.

"Sure, Mom, I'm ready."

They both took a few quicker sips of their grain coffee, got up, thanked the young couple, and left without looking back. Once outside, Mrs. Brodski led the way out of the large city square and into some side streets and straight to the train station, which was on its southern outskirts. Despite a considerable distance to cross, they walked briskly, and the march was most enjoyable. New imposing, concrete apartment buildings and mature, leafy trees lined up both sides of the street, and green belts with "Keep off the grass" signs separated the sidewalks from asphalt driveway.

Somewhere halfway to the station, they crossed a small bridge over a narrow river that ran through the south side of the city, with a strip of green meadow on both banks with a multitude of colorful, wildflowers, children playing, running around, and flying kites. Soon they boarded their train at the second platform from the old, historic station building, already packed with mostly commuting workers from the villages, and probably some travellers, on a day trip to government offices or shopping excursions. It was difficult to find two vacant seats next to each other, although there were a few scattered single seats here and there, and Mrs. Brodski soon took up one of them.

Alek preferred standing in the corridor to sitting squeezed in a packed compartment with eight strangers gasping for fresh air, and the people who would try to engage him in a meaningless conversation, and ask questions as soon as the train pulled away. Besides, he had this well-entrenched, preconceived idea: sitting in a compartment meant being exposed to all those foreign, foul smells emanating from a group of exhausted people, and their often-tattered clothing, and who, like many times before, were on their way back to the suburbs and nearby villages. The contents of their belongings spread out on the shelves above their heads or in full bags at their feet, and that ever-present stifling air, once the sliding door of compartment was closed behind, was of equal concern to Alek. He was particularly sensitive to all those inconveniences, growing up quietly in relative seclusion, rarely interacting with people beyond the circle of his peers and out of necessity in school, or with a few neighbors who were evidently indifferent, or the two or three he considered quite positively disposed toward him, with no visible signs of prejudice.

There were several passengers in the corridors of the train carriage, mostly men, some with their arms resting on the lowered windows, taking in the scenery passing them by, and some with their backs leaning heavily against the walls of compartments, many of them smoking. The few partially open windows created a wind draft with the fast-moving train, with a surge of fresh air from the outside clearing up the interior from the clouds of cigarette smoke. The familiar whistle of the steam locomotive could be heard occasionally coming from the front of the train, ahead of every railway crossing along the way. Steam engines were still a prevailing sight in these parts, where distances were short and the train covered this stretch of eastern track few times a day.

Alek, overcome by curiosity and nostalgia, stood by one of the windows, looking at the scattered dilapidated buildings along the way, near the railway track and the houses farther out in the distance, nestled between kaleidoscopes of cultivated farm field patches in a serene, fabulous setting. The warm early-evening wind blowing in his face was, in its strange way, a welcome relief, gently soothing and alleviating the accumulated pain over his tormented mind, as tears swelled in his eyes. The end of the school year was near, and as every year at this time, a period of particularly intensive studying, final assignments to be handed in, and final exams to be passed. The end of eighth grade for Alek also meant temporary freedom at last, but most importantly, awaiting application to a secondary or trade school, and where the final marks from elementary school were vital for acceptance.

DOMINIK POLESKI

The two-year trade school was usually reserved for somewhat dimwitted students, or "late bloomers" with limited or no ambitions, and as a last resort or transitional period, when all other attempts had failed. Entrance exams testing proficiency in Polish language and literature, and of course, mathematics was standard and compulsory at the only local middle school, although probably with a reduced level of expectations than it would have been at most secondary schools in larger metropolitan areas. Some students opted out for better boarding schools in the district or provincial capitals, which meant living away from families and only occasional home visits on major statutory holidays, but worst of all, living with a group of teenagers one would have otherwise never met, or care to meet.

Alek's academic performance was mediocre at best, although he didn't find it exceedingly difficult; but, rather, the number of mandatory subjects and the volume of repetitive homework was more than he was able to process and attend to at any given time, especially when it so often interfered with his daydreaming. The only logical choice for Alek was the local secondary school, although he was reluctant to pursue his education further in an inhospitable environment he was already too familiar with. The official end-of-school-year celebration came and went, marking it the last day when attendance was closely monitored and expected.

As always, certificates were handed out with a transcript of final marks, which for many students and their parents was a cause for celebration; but for just as many, it was a day of complete disappointment, almost a disaster. It wasn't uncommon to see parents and their offspring huddling together and sobbing, or outright confronting their children and shouting in despair, or the pupils with their heads down, sitting somewhere in a secluded school corridor, while inconsolable, utterly devastated parents were nervously pacing around, asking, "What now?"

It was commonly understood that good education almost always meant success, position, relative prosperity, and a ticket out of this small, forgotten town to a new dream world of the country's large urban centers, where opportunities were knocking at the door, and drastically increased for those who joined the ranks of the Polish United Workers' Party.

For Alek, it wasn't about career anymore; but in the worst case, survival for at least four years at the secondary school, enduring all the special attention from his peers, as can only be generously bestowed on the town's only Jew. The Jew was always within easy reach for all those who made it their life's purpose to relive their frustrations on a helpless target, or unabashedly show their contempt and hostility for no apparent reason other than just plain ignorance, if only to make them feel good about themselves for a few minutes at a time, or otherwise they had nothing else to show.

In the best case, the application for admission to secondary school was just a temporary measure, while patiently waiting for the passports from the district office. But just in case it would take longer than they thought, the final, positive result was never in doubt. Their anxiety was dispelled in the beginning of July, when a summons to appear at the passport office within two weeks came in the mail, typed on the same flimsy government office standard sheet of paper, by the same obviously long-outdated typewriter with clearly visible indentations around each letter, without any additional explanation or a hint of whether the passports were granted or declined. If it weren't for the stress associated with the whole process, another trip by train to the district capital would have been a welcome break from the depressing too-familiar poverty-stricken and perpetually hopeless surroundings of their own decrepit little town, if only for a day.

12

ALEK AND HIS mom were back again in the same two-story
building housing the City Hall and a few essential federal
government offices, serving the city and surrounding areas. They were
on time, as directed at ten o'clock in the morning, but again at the front
desk, they were asked to wait in the same long corridor with chairs lined
up on both sides, serving as the waiting room. They spent the time
looking at the people coming and going and all those waiting, until
well over one hour later, a female clerk came from around the corner
and called out anxiously, "Brodski!"

Alek and his mom quickly got up and headed in the direction of the
female clerk, standing there just outside the door to the passport office.
Mrs. Brodski smiled and walked right behind her, with Alek lagging a
few steps back.

"Please follow me. Comrade Rakowski will see you now."

They walked past the front desk, then through two L-shaped
corridors to the very back, which housed a few separate offices, each
behind a closed, heavy wooden door. The clerk stopped in front of the
last door on the left-hand side and knocked. The man inside responded
after a few seconds: "Come in, please." The clerk opened the door and
let the Brodskis in, and then closed the door behind them.

Comrade Rakowski, who was sitting behind a large old, oak desk,
immediately lifted his head, looked over the visitors, and respectfully
got up, and, with a barely visible smile on his lips, said, "Please, sit
down." He pointed with his outstretched right hand to two wooden
chairs on the other side of his desk, and then sat down again. Alek and
his mom pulled the chairs and hesitatingly sat down too, looking at
Rakowski's next move. He looked down silently at some documents

scattered around, for what seemed like a minute or two, while Alek quickly looked over his rather large office. There was one large, slightly open window with long, almost-down-to-the-hardwood-floor lace curtain gently waving in the light breeze coming through the window. Distant, muffled street noise could be heard from the outside. The air in the office reeked heavily of tobacco with a mixture of cologne and the characteristic smell of the interior of old buildings and furniture. There were several documents spread out across his desk and a few piles of stacked papers on both sides, some pens and pencils, and, of course, a crystal glass ashtray with a few cigarette butts already in it.

Directly behind Rakowski up on the wall were the ever-present three portraits. There was a rather high brown wooden bookcase with several volumes of neatly stacked books, mostly in dark-red or brown hard covers, two matching filing cabinets, an old, plain couch up against the wall with the window, and a small coffee table beside it.

Rakowski was wearing a white dress shirt with sleeves rolled up halfway to his elbows, with a slightly loosened navy blue tie around his neck, and without a jacket. The jacket was hanging on an ornate old coat hanger in the left corner of the office behind them. Rakowski lifted his head up and began in a slow, measured tone, "I've looked at your passport applications carefully. It says here that you're a widow, Mrs. Brodski, and that there are just the two of you in your family. You have also indicated that you're planning to emigrate to Israel. Why Israel?"

"We are Jewish, sir."

"I know that, but why do you want to go to Israel?"

"We want to settle down there. I think it will be good for both of us."

Rakowski looked at them with his piercing, steely bloodshot blue eyes and with a little smirk in the corners of his lips, and continued. "Are you not happy here in Poland, is that the reason?"

"Sir, it is not the main reason. I'm a single mother with a son fast growing up, with limited resources—a job at a fruit and vegetable processing plant with hours cut in half every winter and spring—no family that I know of, very few friends, and no possibilities for any improvement in the future, as far as I can see. As a mother, I have to think about the future of my son."

"You think that Israel is the solution to your problems, Mrs. Brodski?"

"I think living among our own people would certainly open up some opportunities for both of us. I've heard that the government is letting people out, all those who want to emigrate."

"Actually, it's not that simple, Mrs. Brodski. I don't know where you've heard this or who told you, but that's not exactly the whole truth."

"Mr. Rakowski, there must be something to it, because even our media were alluding to this, and people are talking."

"People are talking? And what are they saying?"

"That people can go, whoever wants to is free to go"

"Let me tell you, Mrs. Brodski, and I'll be frank with you. Of course some of our citizens of Jewish descent, Poles and others can leave the country, if they wish to—and in fact, many have already left, but those were different people."

"What do you mean, sir? I don't understand."

"What I mean is, those are people who occupy high positions, mostly in the government, academia, judiciary, and mass media—in a sense, privileged members of our society who were still dissatisfied with what the country has given them. Those are most ungrateful, subversive scoundrels who now spit at the motherland, and who were secretly trying to undermine the socialist order of our society and, it must be said, in their typical fashion, gain even more power and control, as if they haven't had enough already.

"Sir, we are not interested in politics, or in what happened in the highest circles of the government. That's something I've never really understood. For us, it is the everyday life which is the motivating factor, nothing else."

"Mrs. Brodski, you sound very naïve. Are you trying to tell me you've never heard about the student protests.

"I've heard about the protests, of course. It's not a secret anymore, it's a common knowledge, which was covered quite extensively by the media at the time, but I don't know much about the background of those unrests, and I'm actually not that interested in it either. As I said, we both have our own concerns, far removed from what's happening in the capital."

"I see your point, but as I said, those are the people who are mostly leaving the country now. If they don't like it so much here, and their goal was to subvert all that we've worked so hard to build on the ashes of World War II, then let them go. We'll be better off without them."

"Mr. Rakowski, I really don't know much about politics, nor do I want to. For me, the most important thing is the future of my only son, Alek, and my own."

"Please don't make it sound like it's been such a tragedy for you here in our democratic, prosperous, and socialist country. There are opportunities here for everyone, if we only try."

"Sir, believe me, we've tried everything."

"Maybe you haven't tried hard enough. How do you get by, then, if you're saying your hours at work are limited during winter and spring?"

"I do some housekeeping."

"I don't mean to pry into your private life, but what happened to your husband, if I may ask?"

"Jakub died of leukemia about seven years ago."

"I'm sorry to hear that. Have you ever considered remarrying, Mrs. Brodski? You're still young, and an attractive woman."

"I've been asked this before, but to answer your question, no I have not. I'm quite happy the way I am."

"I respect that. It's your choice, but things would have been easier."

"Perhaps, but my options are limited in that small town; There are no Jewish men there that I know of, and as I said, I'm not interested anyway."

"How about you, young man, why would you want to go abroad— and to Israel of all places?" Rakowski turned suddenly to Alek, when he least expected it.

"I don't know. As Mom said…," answered Alek with uncertainty. He was clearly caught by surprise. In the presence of his mother, he always relied on her to take care of family business, and knew she would never disappoint. Faced with direct confrontation, he was lost for words, especially in matters he knew very little about, although they discussed these topics previously at length.

"What do you mean you don't know? You must have thought about it. You have no family there, no friends. You've never been there before. Why the hell would anybody want to go there? That country is practically in a permanent state of war, especially after the Six-Day War just over a year ago."

"I have no friends here either," Alek answered quietly.

"Oh, I don't believe that, young man. Everyone has friends at your age. Maybe not always the kind of friends you'd like, but friends nevertheless."

"I don't. I used to get picked on sometimes at school, and I'm glad that is over. I get harassed on the streets too, so I try to avoid some areas as much as I can. I think I'd like to see other countries too."

"Yes, we all do. We live in uncertain times now, and this country, while not perfect yet, is certainly an example of peace, economic stability, relative prosperity, equality, and social progress; and the so-called West can only dream about that. You must know what's happening around the world, even in America?"

"Not really. I don't know those things, but from what I've read, seen in magazines, and heard on the radio, it all looks good," added Alek.

"Mrs. Brodski"—Rakowski turned again to Alek's Mom—"I don't know what nonsense you've been feeding your son, but I think you both should think long and hard about this emigration business. There is no better place for both of you than our country. There have been enormous opportunities for women here, as never before in history, thanks to our superior system as opposed to the Western social and moral decadence, which is still stuck in the nineteenth-century mentality, it seems to me. Let me tell you one of my favorite quotes from Marx: 'Social progress can be measured exactly by the position of the fair sex in society, the ugly ones included.'"

After saying this, Rakowski began to laugh briefly, visibly proud of himself, and reached out for a package of cigarettes on the right side of his desk, near the ashtray. He pulled one out and lit it, inhaling deeply and then releasing a big cloud of white smoke above his head.

Mrs. Brodski paused for several seconds and retorted, "I don't know about that, but I haven't experienced all that many opportunities, or seen any progress in the last few years—at least not personally, certainly not in these parts. My position is not something to be envied."

"Well, maybe you've haven't been looking in the right places, or hard enough? Have you thought about upgrading your skills or learning something new?" Comrade Rakowski was clearly in control of the conversation, visibly enjoying his position, which gave him unfettered power over average mortals, and he didn't miss an opportunity to use it; in fact, he seemed to enjoy every minute of it. After a few seconds' pause, like a well-indoctrinated, professional propagandist, he added, "Again, Karl Marx quite accurately also said, 'From each according to his abilities, to each according to his needs.'"

Mrs. Brodski and Alek didn't say anything to that, just sat there impassively, looking at Rakowski with further anticipation. Momentary silence enveloped the room, except for the gentle rustle of paper between Rakowki's fingers as he began to slowly flip the pages of their passport applications. He lifted his head up, took another puff of cigarette, and looked at Alek and his mom with a visibly changed expression on his face. A few drops of perspiration appeared on his forehead, and suddenly he seemed tired and disinterested, almost impatient. In unmistakable sign, the appointment over which he was presiding and was in total control of over the average mortals across the desk was coming to an end. He looked at the window for a second or two, and then said, "Mrs. Brodski, and you, Alek, thank you for coming here today. I sympathize with your plight—however, I'm not the sole decision maker. I make recommendations, send them to Warsaw to my superiors, and they either approve the applications or they don't. It's a chain of responsibilities to ensure the system is fair and serves what's best for the country."

"When can we expect to hear from you?" asked Mrs. Brodski.

"You'll hear from us. I'd say within a month, you can expect something in the mail. But one way or the other, we'll let you know," said Rakowski.

Although his answer was vague, it didn't sound promising; but they had no option but to wait patiently as he said "something in the mail."

Rakowski got up behind his desk, which was a clear sign the meeting was over. Alek jumped to his feet, his mom followed, and the three of them walked slowly to the door. Rakowski grabbed the handle, opened the door, and asked them to follow him to the front office through the narrow corridors they came from. Once they reached the familiar large room, he turned around and in a very cordial, but official manner bowed his head politely, shook their hands, and assured them they'd be getting a response from his office in the mail within a few weeks, without giving the slightest hint of what it might be.

Mother and son then proceeded toward the exit door, passing few workstations, the front counter, the long corridor, then few steps down and out through the main entrance door and onto the sidewalk. As the first time around, once outside, they seemed somewhat disoriented and stopped for a few seconds to look around for an exit street out of city square. They soon found themselves well on their way to the train station, and this time well before the rush hour and ahead of the throngs of passengers filling in every possible seat, with scarcely any standing room in the corridors, as was the case before on their first trip.

Nevertheless, there were many passengers, just like them, coming back from a necessary trip to the city, usually on a business trip to government office or a shopping excursion, as was evident by the baggage they carried with them. Although Alek was naturally uncomfortable in all crowds, or even in smaller groups of unfamiliar people, he was greatly intrigued by the working-class men and women and the peasants who in such large numbers traveled regularly to the city, and then back home. He found them irresistible to look at, at their behavior, manners, and attire; it all had a special allure to him, as if at a distinct species of human beings. Years of hard, exhausting labor had left its indelible mark on them, on their bruised and scarred hands with vividly protruding veins, and those tired, sad faces with often-deep but premature furrows burnt by the sun.

It was commonly perceived by the city dwellers that there was a characteristic smell emanating from the peasants, a mixture of the outdoors, the wind, the soil, and a tinge of stable manure, as they claimed, which only added to the widespread but hidden resentment of the visitors on a day trip from the villages. Yet there was an unmistakable look of dignity, determination, and resilience in the eyes of the farmers, and strangely, easily discernable politeness, one might say, almost apologetic expressions in their behavior, as if humble gratitude for just being there. There was never any noticeable sign of anger or the slightest irritation in those folks; on the contrary, for the most part, they seemed good-natured, almost serene, perhaps resigned to their fate of hard but rewarding temporal life in anticipation of life everlasting one day, when the good Lord decides it's time to go. After all, everything was in the hands of God—the weather, the harvest, the fortunes and misfortunes, the trials and tribulations of everyday life, and of the very life itself.

The summer was in full swing: the second half of July, the weather warm with temperatures around 20 degrees Centigrade already by nine o'clock in the morning, and by early afternoon hovering around 30 degrees and rising. The townsfolk were out on the streets going about their business, or in front of their houses tending to their flowerbeds, or in the back, working in their opulent, lush gardens and proudly looking at the new, plentiful crops of vegetables. There were also many people just standing idly around on street corners or on the sidewalks in front of their houses, talking cheerfully to neighbors and friends with renewed hope, despite and oblivious to the ominous international and domestic news, incessantly proclaiming the world at the crossroads in the wake of massive social and political upheavals across the European continent and around the world.

Here, in this small town, life had its own pace, far removed from the worries of those who saw the latest, even the smallest developments as an existential threat to their rule, and just as equal, or perhaps far greater number of those who are ruled, the subservient, restless, working-class masses, who saw it as an opportunity for a much-anticipated change at last. The latest political developments were so far removed from the reality of their simple lives here in the peripheries, that their perception was quite often closely aligned with the official government position, whether out of conviction or for argument's sake, and still frequently seen around here as nothing more than a "foreign, hostile, bourgeois propaganda," although with a dose of skepticism, as with just about anything else in life, except the final judgment by the Almighty, whom they feared the most, and who undoubtedly presided over what would in the end be the ultimate equalizer, either the happiness of everlasting life, or eternal condemnation to the depths of hell, regardless of political convictions or social status.

The center of town at this time of the year was bustling with activity, mainly due to increased volume of people from the villages and other small towns, either on day shopping trips, visiting friends or relatives, or for entertainment, whatever little of it there was. The few cafés and restaurants along the long stretch of old, dilapidated two- and three-story adjacent concrete buildings of about three hundred meters long, or about three city blocks, were often packed with customers. The Town Hall offices were strategically located at one end, followed by variety of small stores, eating establishments, and, at the very far, opposite end of the row of buildings, also known as the "halls," was the police station. They were all in various stages of disrepair and neglect, most with patches of peeling paint or falling-off plaster. The halls were separated from the tree-lined main street by a wide green belt, which was one of the main features and attractions of the town, carefully tended to by a few seasonal landscapers. There were several different flowers planted in carefully arranged rows, starting with colorful tulips in the early spring, then later on daffodils, pansies, geraniums, carnations, mallows, at least three colors of narcissus, and few species of roses.

Close to the major street intersection in the geographical city center, right in the middle of the green belt, stood a large stone monument with a pointed top and crowned with a prominent, polished metal Soviet star, commemorating the town's liberation by the advancing Red Army from the German garrison stationed here in 1944. The front metal plaque, facing the sidewalk was engraved in Russian; and in the inaccessible back of the monument, there was a comparable plaque in Polish, the order of which was a contentious issue in itself.

On weekends, this area was coming alive, as young men and women from villages were arriving in groups by train, by bus, on motorcycles, bicycles, or even a few lucky ones in their own little cars, looking for entertainment, looking for fun. It wasn't long before minor disagreements with the local, easily irritable young men and women escalated into full-blown fistfights, spilling from the establishments onto the sidewalks. Those dust-ups between the locals and the villagers were always an integral part of town's tradition, and for many young men of both affiliations, a rite of passage, ascendency into real manhood, when honor is fiercely defended and respect is gained or just as easily lost, at least till next time. It was not uncommon to see men with bloodied noses or blood-splattered shirts stagger around, proudly displaying them like badges of honor, and walking back into the smoke-filled, packed restaurant, looking for some more action. The town's discreet bootlegger, Ivan Alkashov, or "Ivan the Terrible" as he was most commonly known, was always prepared for the "invasion," and kept his shack well stocked with his finest handcrafted "refreshments" for the after-hours crowd, those who never had enough.

It was Saturday, and a rare long weekend, culminating with a national holiday on Monday, July 22, commemorating the twenty-fourth anniversary of the Polish Committee of National Liberation, proclaiming the establishment of a new provisional government of Poland on the heels of the retreating German army and the advancing Soviet Army at the end of World War II. On special occasions such as this, usually associated with notable dates in the history of the socialist country, a live band was playing its best renditions of the most popular domestic and international pop hits, while drunken, sweaty patrons were shaking rhythmically on the dance floor, or in between the tables for lack of a better space, closer to the action, doing their best to impress their partners, or complete strangers who were too drunk to notice, or didn't give a shit anyway. The booze was cheap, but the selection was limited to three kinds of vodka; brandy and champagne from the Soviet republic of Georgia; two kinds of wine, red and white; and one kind of beer, always at a room temperature. Although the food menu suggested a reasonably good selection of dishes and appetizers, the patrons were quickly confronted with reality when the waitress in a well-rehearsed line and a facial expression of utmost innocence, convincingly assured the bewildered patrons, one after another, "I'm sorry, we've just run out of it."

In the end, it didn't really matter, as long as there was something, anything to eat at least; the booze was flowing uninterrupted, a package of cigarettes was always within easy reach, the band was playing, and the ladies were sending all the right signals: life was great for the moment, perhaps for the night. It was time to forget the politics, the glorious achievements of the country under the ever-vigilant United Workers' Party's, according to the government media, increasingly menacing veiled threats from the concerned Big Brother to the east, and the grueling everyday life in general, dispensing its own cruel, unforgiving dose of reality.

On evenings like these, Alek was usually out, pacing around the town center, or nearby, against his mother's best advice, fascinated by the rare display of its seedy side, however small it was, unlike the usually sleepy and uneventful days year round. He clearly kept within safe distance of all the commotion, on the other side of the wide, dividing green belt, just watching the local night life unfold, right in front of his eyes. There were times when he had to retreat, when the rowdies were getting to close for comfort, and looking for just anyone within the vicinity to unload their frustrations on.

13

THE WELL-KNOWN LOCAL hooker Anka, a familiar feature on a warm night like this, was also out, walking slowly in pair with her aspiring friend Elzbieta, or Ela for short, eager to learn the tricks of the trade from the pro herself. Anka wasn't a beauty in any sense of the word; she was worn out and with visible signs of neglect in appearance, but still in considerable demand, if the price was right, and it usually was. Ela was decidedly the much more desirable of the two, and still managed to maintain an aura of youthful innocence about her. Nevertheless, their services were in considerable demand, mostly among the sex-starved young studs of the local army unit, or the visiting village boys, whose only chance to see a piece of naked arse were the free-grazing cows in their natural environment of the green pastures. There was a saying around town: "In the absence of fish, even crab is a fish." Or "Any port is good in a storm." Both perfect metaphors for those two ladies of the night, especially the elder one, who from early adolescence decided that school was too tough, and there certainly must be an easier way, or quite possibly there was more to it than that.

Ela, being a relatively recent addition to the night trade, had dropped out of school just a few months into her second year at the local middle school. For Anka and Ela business on weekends, particularly on Saturday night was brisk, and Anka even managed over time to acquire some steady clientele. Rumor had it, even some prominent local public figures were seen with her, swiftly disappearing into a dark alley; but surprisingly, it was all viewed with a great deal of tolerance and understanding—all within acceptable limits, of course, as "Desperate times call for desperate measures" doctrine, at most a good topic for street corner conversations and gossip.

Some would argue with unshakable conviction: "I don't blame the man. Have you seen the hag he's married to?" The town's official slut and her faithful apprentice, Ela, over time became so indispensable that neither the mayor, Comrade Kutasiuk, nor the police commandant Sokolowski did anything about it; but it must be said for the two entrepreneurs of female gender: they worked hard at it. After all, in spite of all the communist rhetoric, it all came down to the old capitalist principle of supply and demand, and who in his right mind could argue with that?

Behind the row of buildings forming the so-called "halls," there was a small city park with a few tree-lined alleys and old wooden benches, almost completely drowned in darkness, except for a few light posts at the perimeter of the park casting feeble light over the treetops.

Some patrons used the park as a last resort to relieve themselves, or as a quick stop for any sexual activity due to lack of a better place in the vicinity, and it was absolutely free. Both ladies were seen to make a trip or two to the back and disappear into the darkness for at least half an hour at a time, and then mysteriously reappear, as if nothing happened. It didn't escape Alek's notice. He was watching it all from a distance, patiently waiting, and it hurt; but there was nothing he could do about it. After seeing Ela only, a couple of times before, Alek quickly developed a keen interest in her, an infatuation of sorts; and he made sure to be out on the town on those specific days during holidays, when the town was in such a celebratory mood despite the always-possible danger of running into a group of thugs. He was almost sixteen, but because of his height, the way he dressed, and his serious demeanor, he looked more like eighteen; and in September, he was set to go to the local middle school—that is, if the whole immigration business wouldn't work out. She was still very young, perhaps just a year or two at the most older than he was, possibly not even quite seventeen, was Alek's impression.

Anka was the well-seasoned whore in her late twenties, but if one was to judge by her appearance only, midthirties would most likely be her real age. Ela was blonde, slim, and rather tall, and also definitely the better-looking of the two, with proportional; shapely lower body, long legs; and delicate, thin arms. Alek was envious of all those times when she stood there smiling in the twilight of the evening, wearing her best summer dress with flowery pattern, standing in the shadow of a large leafy tree, or in the nook of a building, talking to a group of young men, few of them familiar local thugs, perhaps only a little older than him.

Alek watched from a distance, imagining himself being the object of her attention, just being in her presence, to feel her close, the way she stood close to, and touched the other men, with the sincerity and innocence of a young woman who still felt out of place in her new role, but most likely was there because she wanted to be, and just like the men she was courting, she wanted to be touched, she wanted to be noticed and loved, and who was there to judge her? Because for Ela, there was not much to go back home to.

Alek walked anxiously up and down the main stretch of sidewalk, trying to get a glimpse of coquettish Ela in the midst of young people in front of the restaurant, absorbed in a light conversation, frolicking, visibly delighted, as the sound of music spilled outside through the open windows of the restaurant into the warmth and stillness of a perfect summer night. There was an intense aroma all around, emanating from the multitude of flowers in full bloom in the nearby flowerbeds, mixed with the perfume of several young women standing outside, cigarette smoke, and alcohol, adding to the inimitable atmosphere and the enticing mystery of the night.

The cops were nowhere to be seen, conveniently absent, hidden away at the station, reluctant to get too involved, unless things got out of control and somebody rushed into the station screaming for immediate intervention. They preferred to stay out of sight for the most part, only occasionally venturing outside, making quick rounds, and going back in for a little celebration of their own.

Commandant Sokolowski was always restrained in his enthusiasm for excessive indulgence in alcoholic beverages on the job and kept his deputy, Kovaluk, an unrepentant boozer, and the two other brutes in uniform under his constant surveillance; but he did allow a couple of shots of vodka on special occasions.

Although it was quite late already, well past ten o'clock, and his mother was certainly worried, Alek just couldn't resist the allure of what was happening right in the center of town. After all, in just over a month, he was scheduled to attend the local middle school, crossing the once-unimaginable threshold to a totally different world of adulthood, something he's been waiting for with great anticipation for a long time. It was very seldom that he was still out past nightfall, even during the middle of summer vacation. Alek didn't want to go home, not just yet, not before she at least looked at him, or before she would somehow tell him she didn't care, and it was all in his imagination. Despite the fact she actually looked at him a few times before, for a second or two when on the streets, both going about their own business, he wanted to know if it meant anything, if she at least had noticed him, or was she just completely dismissive and indifferent like she was toward many young men he had seen vying for her attention?

Foolishly, for the temptation was too great, Alek moved closer and closer toward the restaurant, out in the open, within just several meters of the groups of young people, where he could be easily seen and recognized. It didn't take long before Alek was noticed, but not by Ela, but by a young man in his late teens, whom he recognized at once. He would never forget that face as long as he lived. It was one of the men who attacked him on that fateful day in September of the previous year, and the other hoodlum was with him too, but Sokolowski's son, Adam, was visibly absent. In fact, he had been since that time; Alek had never seen him out about town again. The two thugs were among a group of young men in their twenties, all clearly intoxicated, smoking cigarettes, flirting and obviously trying to hook up with the girls loitering around there on the sidewalk. The young man turned toward Alek standing several meters away in the hazy light of a nearby streetlamp, pointed and said, "Look, it's that Jew again."

Two other men and Ela immediately looked in his direction, staring back at them motionless, as if rooted to the spot. The man started slowly in Alek's direction, and was soon joined by a few others, including Ela, who seemed hesitant at first, but then followed nevertheless, swept by the group. The men surrounded Alek without any preconceived plan, just each one of them nonchalantly took his place in a circle, and the young women stayed a few steps behind, unconcerned, still with smiles on their faces, most likely curious as to what this was all about.

The man whose face was forever etched in Alek's memory, approached him slowly, as if dragging his feet, with the characteristic swagger of a typical punk, and stopped perhaps within just several centimeters of Alek, and looking straight into his eyes. Then with a derisive smirk, he blew a mouthful of cigarette smoke in his face.

Alek jerked his head backward, took a step back, and momentarily covered his eyes with one hand. The other men in the group burst into laughter. Alek was terrified. He was feeling trapped again, a feeling he was already well familiar with, and yet he didn't ask for it; all he wanted was to look at the people, listen to the music, enjoy the summer vacation, possibly to be noticed, and, if an opportunity shall arise, to readily extend his friendship to anyone who would take time to even notice him, or better yet to exchange a few words without having to take to the back streets and alleys in an endless struggle for day-to-day survival.

Suddenly he realized what a mistake it was to stay out so late. There were those who neither paid any attention to him nor cared to meet him, much less spend any time with him. The man stood right in front of Alek, and there were two of them behind him, a few on the sides, not in any particularly organized or intentional order but more as a result of curiosity-inspired following of the leader.

The man looked intently at Alek with an aura of superiority and the ever-present insidious smirk on his lips, and said, "Do you remember me?"

Alek didn't answer; he just looked back at him with anticipation, as did all the others gathered around them. The man grabbed Alek's arm with his left hand, squeezing it hard, and pulled him in closer with the same provocative attitude.

"So, you don't remember me…But I remember you quite well. What have you been doing here, sneaking around?"

"I'm sorry, I was just about to go home," uttered Alek

"I saw you standing around here for a long time. Were you waiting for somebody? What were you looking for?" the man persisted.

"Excuse me, I must go now. My mom is waiting," Alek said, trying to free himself by stepping backward and pulling his arm away.

However, the man held him back and squeezed even tighter, threw the still-smoldering cigarette butt down and said, "No, you're not going anywhere, not yet." And then turning to the others with the same derisive, contemptuous smirk, he added, "Did you hear this? The Jew wants to go back to his mommy. What should I do with him?"

There was no answer, no emotion; and the incident attracted little attention, beyond just from those gathered around Alek, despite the few other groups of young people standing around nearby, mingling, seemingly too absorbed to pay any attention.

"Please let me go. I'm sorry if I caused you any trouble, I didn't mean to," pleaded Alek in an increasingly desperate tone.

"You've been talking to the cops, Jew. What did you tell them?" asked the man with visible hostility.

"I didn't tell them anything. There must be a mistake," replied Alek.

"Don't lie to me. You were seen more than once going to the police station with your mother. It had to be for a reason. So, what was it all about?"

"Oh, it was nothing. Nothing to be concerned about, a private matter."

"A private matter with the cops, you say? How interesting. What would you possibly want to talk to them about?" the man persisted, getting increasingly agitated and suddenly sending a short, stiff jab into Alek's rib cage.

Alek yelped, let out a shrill cry of pain, bending his body forward under the brunt of the unexpected blow. He buried his face in his hands, as if expecting a barrage of punches to follow.

Ela, who was standing by silently, watching the whole scene unfold, immediately stepped forward and right in the middle of the unfolding drama.

"Tolek, what are you doing? What was that for? Leave him alone, do you hear? Leave him alone! What's the matter with you?" she said with disgust and grabbed the man's hands, forcefully separating him from Alek. Then she stepped right between them.

The man moved back, but was visibly stunned by the woman's reaction, and looked at her in disbelief. Then he turned sideways and looked at the other men, as if seeking support. There was no reaction, not a word was said; they all just stood there indifferently, reluctant to join in on either side.

Alek was still mortified and confused, but somewhat relieved by the sudden, unexpected turn of events. Ela was right there in front of him with her tantalizing presence, just several centimeters away, such as he'd never seen her before. Alek could literally smell them both, especially the man reeking of tobacco, alcohol, and perspiration mixed with the sweet smell of perfume emanating from Ela. He was repulsed by Tolek, but was strangely drawn to Ela, and prepared to endure even more indignities as long as she was within reach. Despite her well-known dissolute lifestyle and a distant and seemingly indifferent demeanor, or perhaps just well-concealed pretense, bound and restrained by a cruel, unforgiving, and unwritten, but commonly understood code of the street—"Thou shall not fall in love"—Alek was indiscriminately infatuated.

"You stay out of it," Tolek said to Ela.

"What was that all about? What has he done to you?" she asked.

"It's none of your business. I said stay out of it."

"It is my business. You just hit an innocent man for no reason at all."

"The Jew knows bloody well what he's done…he talks to the cops, and you don't talk to the cops. He should have kept his silence," Tolek said with increasing impatience and agitation.

"I don't understand. Talking about what? What does it have to do with you? How do you even know him?" Ela persisted.

"Listen, I know what I'm saying, and again, it's none of your business. Just stay out of it. Go and screw somebody."

"How dare you? You know, you're such an idiot. I thought you were a real man, but you're not. You're a coward, that's what you are. If you're looking for a fight, then go and find yourself somebody older." And she pointed to group of men standing near the entrance to the restaurant, and then continued with visible indignation, "Let him go, or I'll talk to the police myself."

"What are you talking about? Is there something going on between you two I should know about? Tell me, have you fucked him too?"

"Tolek, you're a sick man. There is nothing going on between us, but there might be, and it would be only my choice, not yours. You're drunk."

"Oh, I see what's going on…you've switched your interest to kids now? You want the first crack at his virginity, is that it?"

"You're such a fool you're embarrassing yourself. I don't want to talk to you, and I don't want anything to do with you. Yes, I'd rather talk to him anytime. He's probably more of a man than you'll ever be."

"Oh, how soon you forget, Ela. That's not what you were saying last night, remember? You're such a slut."

"Why don't you piss off and leave us alone? You're a total loser. Let me tell you something: at least I work for my money when I need to, and you're stealing and robbing people and waiting for somebody to buy you a drink—or better yet, threaten people to buy you a drink. That's the kind of man you are."

"I've had enough! Get the hell out of here and take your boy with you."

Alek was in shock at the unexpected turn of events. Never in his wildest dreams would he have anticipated this young woman whom he had barely seen fleetingly a few times on the streets to stand up for him, to come to his defense, and so bravely, against this well-known thug.

Ela looked defiantly right into Tolek's eyes for a few seconds and then slowly turned around to look at all the others assembled, his associates and mutual casual acquaintances, who were equally stunned by what had just happened.

Tolek stepped back two steps and with a characteristic derisive smirk on his lips, as if trying to show he was still firmly in control, awkwardly turned sideways, and looked at his friends triumphantly. They all stood in silence for a few seconds, but what seemed like minutes; only the muffled sound of music could be heard coming from the restaurant and the distant voices of some patrons standing near the front entrance.

Without hesitation, Ela took Alek by his right arm and, squeezing it gently, turned him around and shoved him along, out of the spot on the sidewalk he seemed rooted to, leaving the crowd behind. They walked briskly without a word for several meters, before Ela slowed down noticeably and looked back once, when she was certain they were within a safe range. They walked east, in the general direction of where Alek lived, as if she already knew, before she asked unexpectedly, "Where do you live? I'll walk you home."

"Oh, you don't need to do that. Don't worry about me, it's not very far."

"I don't even know your name, so what is your name?"

"Alek. Thank you for standing up for me."

"Oh, don't mention it…that was nothing at all. You know my name, of course. You've heard it many times just a while ago."

"Yes, I do. Nice name."

"So, tell me, what were you doing out so late? Isn't it past your bedtime?"

"Just hanging around. Summer vacation."

"I'm sure your parents are worried, Alek."

"It's my mom only. What were you doing out so late?"

"Same as you, and I'm sorry to hear that. So, you only live with your mom and no other relatives?"

"No, just the two of us."

"I'm curious, why?"

"It's a long story."

"How long?" Ela persisted, smiling.

"Oh, longer than the time we have."

"I understand. Maybe some other time."

"Maybe?"

"We'll see. I don't usually plan things far in advance."

"Do you know him well?"

"Know who?"

"Tolek."

"Why do you ask?"

"Just curious. It seemed like you've known each other quite well."

DOMINIK POLESKI

"Yeah, I've known him for about two years, maybe longer, but sometimes I wish I'd never met him."

"So why do you hang out with him?"

"It's complicated."

"I see. Tell me then, Ela, where do you live?"

"North, on Pulaski Street. Not very far from the center either, just different direction."

"You know, I've seen you a couple of times before," said Alek

"Don't be silly. I'm sure you have. This town is so small, everybody must have seen everybody here at least once before. I've probably seen you too—in fact, I'm almost sure I have."

"Yeah, you're right.

"How about your parents?"

"It's a long story."

They both burst out laughing. Alek slowly regained his confidence as they walked along the dimly lit sidewalk. The street was almost completely deserted; only occasionally, a hunched black figure moved swiftly, hurrying back home. The air turned colder by the minute, with sporadic light gusts of wind, and with them a few drops of summer rain falling gently and dotting the pavement.

Alek wanted to say something but couldn't find anything sensible to say, so as not to embarrass himself, and they walked in silence, arm in arm, so close to each other, and yet so far, engrossed in their own worlds. He glanced secretly at Ela's strangely sad face whenever they moved out of the shadow and into the range of each weak light cast by the tall streetlamps, spaced equally at long intervals along the street. At the next intersection, Alek turned left, and Ela followed into a dark narrow cobblestoned street emanating a surreal, eerie feeling, as if lost in the comfort of the perpetual abject poverty of the past decades, and forgotten by the world outside. There was a long row of old, decrepit communal housing apartment blocks drowned in total darkness, and only a few windows with sagging, nondescript linen curtains, behind which a stream of heavy yellow light betrayed any sign of life.

"I live over there," said Alek, pointing to one of the dark buildings just ahead. "I'll walk with you right to your door," said Ela.

"You don't have to."

"But I want to, do you mind?"

"No, I don't mind. My entrance is from the back of the courtyard, and it's completely dark there."

"So, is that a problem?, asked Ela.

"No, not a problem, but it's not a very nice place."

"Don't worry. Mine is not so nice either. My parents are not rich. Why do you think I stand there on the streets?"

"I don't know. I guess we both don't have much to brag about," said Alek. "At least we've got something in common."

Soon they were both in the back of the building, standing in front a single wooden door with a high, worn-out threshold.

"This is it. Once again, thank you for everything," said Alek in a low voice, almost a whisper, standing with his back close to the door.

"You know, I'm glad I've met you. You're a nice guy."

"Thanks. You're nice too. I'm happy to have met you too."

"I hope you don't mind me asking, but how old are you?

"I'm sorry, I forgot. Stress, you know…"

"Haha, yeah, I know all about it. Most of the time, I don't remember my age either, and who cares?"

"Right. Well, good night! I must go now. Thank you."

"Good night, Alek. Next time try to avoid that place I've met you at—this time of night anyway."

"I will, but where can I see you?"

"Why would you want to see me? You don't want to know somebody like me."

"Why not? I'd like to."

"I'm not sure. We'll see. Good night!"

"Be careful on your way back home, Ela."

"Don't worry about me, I'll be fine."

Ela leaned forward and gently touched Alek's right hand with the tips of her fingers, looking at him motionless for a few seconds. Then she turned around and slowly walked away into the darkness. Alek just stood there for several seconds, thinking about all that had just happened and listening to her departing steps until he couldn't hear them anymore.

DOMINIK POLESKI

14

T HE LETTER FROM the district passport office came in the mail in early August, as expected; and in two sentences, it changed the plans Mrs. Brodski and Alek had so carefully devised and nurtured in the past few months. It simply said:

> *We regret to inform you that, by decision of Regional Passport Bureau, in the name of and according to the laws of Polish People's Republic, your passport applications for the purpose of emigration have been denied. You may appeal the decision to the Ministry of the Interior, Warsaw, ul. Nowy Swiat 6, within 21 days from the date of this notification.*

The letter was sealed with an official stamp and Rakowski's signature. Mrs. Brodski had always harbored doubts about the whole undertaking, with little trust in the integrity and fairness of the system itself. If the bureaucrats expected and were so used to receiving bribes as indispensable part of the process, she would not conform, for she had nothing to give. She found it hard to comprehend how the fate of two harmless people from the peripheries of Eastern Poland could have an impact on the country such as this. By denying permission for a single mother and her son to leave the country for the destination of their choice, what was there to be achieved or gained by the vast, out-of-control communist bureaucracy? Was it all mandated from the top down, or was it all designed by overzealous local politicians at the provincial level with a vengeful streak and an insatiable appetite for power, left free to interpret the law as they saw it, and perhaps directly related to their level of political indoctrination in the communist ideology?

One other possible option, probably the most wicked of them all, was that it was solely the work of corrupt district passport authorities, local brazen opportunists far removed from any superior scrutiny and well entrenched in their beliefs that at least for a foreseeable future, they could extort the money with impunity.

Mrs. Brodski announced rather reluctantly, quite aware of the impact it might have on Alek, that they would not be appealing the decision of the Passport Bureau; she just didn't have the energy, time, or money to pursue what she thought was obviously a lost cause. They'd have to make the best of whatever life they had here; at least it was quite predictable with accompanying misery at times, but never a destitution, and added the reassurance as it played out within the boundaries of all-too-familiar surroundings, of knowing they were not alone, that most people here were not better off. It was a strange, unspoken understanding, and possibly the only common thread that bound them together more than anything—unity of people in misery.

Alek was inconsolable for a few days, as his hope for travel and adventure had been dashed, and with it his dreams of a new and better life in Israel, or somewhere, anywhere but here. It was difficult now to literally change the entire perspective on his future life, after all this time he had spent cultivating an imaginary splendid existence in an unknown dream world only he knew, where life was beautiful. He withdrew into solitude, didn't eat much, spent his days thinking, reading, flipping the pages of the geography atlas, listening to the music on their old, cabinet-style radio, writing something, or just lying on the sofa and looking aimlessly at the ceiling. Eventually, after about a week of soul-searching convalescence, without any pressure from his mother, Alek began to show some signs of interest in the world outside their home. Although still somewhat reluctantly, he agreed to go grocery shopping with his mother, under the pretext she needed help to carry it all in case they bought more than just bare necessities.

It was early afternoon on a Saturday when they stepped outside; the air was still, and the sun up high and not a single cloud to be seen

DOMINIK POLESKI

on a perfectly blue sky. On their way out from the courtyard, they greeted two women from the neighborhood who were standing there chattering while their small children were playing nearby. Alek had on a white short-sleeved cotton shirt and dark trousers, and a pair of the same worn black leather shoes, his favorite attire. Because of the way he looked, he was often mistaken for being dressed up for some special occasion, or celebration, that nobody else seemed to know about. But in fact, he was not; it was just his preference. Since the end of the school year, his black hair had grown much longer, now completely covering his collar; but he had not been paying any particular attention to it; and he was free of the constant nagging and harassment from teachers who supposedly were trying their best to enforce the imaginary, nonexistent school protocol, where short hair was a must. In fact, he had seen on a few occasions, but never experienced himself, the wrath of a particularly dedicated teacher trying to stop "bad influences" by pulling the poor pupil by the hair with such force as to almost lift him off the floor. One other popular form of punishment for overgrown hair was ear tweaking. Equally effective, and when properly applied, would often make the little recipient wet his pants. Such was the joy of education at the elementary school level, and for many little rascals, not to be forgotten anytime soon.

Alek and his mom walked leisurely toward the main street, enjoying every step of the way, and straight on to the town center, where most of the stores were located in relative proximity. It didn't take long before the sweltering heat and the sultry, stagnant air was becoming barely manageable, having a visible effect on the pace of life all around. The already-sleepy town became even more lethargic over time, with listless people moving sluggishly, apathetically, only if they had to go out at all, or others frantically looking for cover in the shadows of trees or in the nooks of buildings. People in these parts were accustomed to a rather cold climate for at least six months of any year, with a steady whiff of unforgiving, frigid air from the east, courtesy of the vast open spaces of the Soviet Union.

When summer finally came with its full intensity, and with it a sudden upward surge in temperatures, many people were naturally not prepared for the drastic change, running for cover and cursing Mother Nature. All those gathered in the vicinity of the town center, Alek and his mom included, could hear the distant sound of orchestra music, getting closer and closer with each passing second. There soon appeared a throng of several dozens of mostly black-clad people, marching slowly, right in the middle of the main street, with the orchestra up front, all dressed up in the characteristic black uniforms of railway workers, and with the rest of the people, family and friends, right behind them. The orchestra consisted almost entirely of brass-wind instruments, with a short, fat man in the middle of the first row with a large, round drum strapped at a skew over his torso. He was banging at it with regular intervals, and gasping for air.

The all-male band, and all on the brink of almost total exhaustion under the mercilessly burning sun, strenuously blowing and marching forward, and from time to time wiping off their foreheads with white handkerchiefs in between the notes. Only employees of certain positions, stature, or those with over twenty-five years of distinguished service were given the full honors of an official funeral. The resident Polish National Railways' band in traditional black garb accompanied the deceased on his last journey to the church, and then on to the cemetery, where he would be laid to eternal rest in a two-meter-deep pit. The funeral procession was a rare and somber event, and stirred the town's otherwise-uneventful days, with residents stopping to look and reflect on the life of the man who passed away that most of them knew, and on their own fragile existence, while still glad to be among the living. Right behind the orchestra, repeatedly playing few mournful renditions of the standard, classic funeral marches, followed four strained, heavily perspiring pallbearers carrying an ornate wooden casket on their shoulders. Then, closely behind them, the distraught wife of the deceased, wrapped in black lace veil, with their three grief-stricken adult children, with sullen faces and huddled together, staring down at the pavement under the burden of the sudden death of their beloved husband and father. Behind them, walking without any particular order, were members of his distant family, friends, neighbors, and just ordinary townsfolk feeling the need to pay their respects to the man they knew and respected.

Alek and his mom slowly followed the funeral procession while they were passing the town center, and on to the Catholic church under the patronage of His Holiness St. John about half a kilometer to the west. Along the way, Mrs. Brodski had a strange, nagging feeling to move closer to the front, to see the grieving family in the first row behind the casket. About fifty meters from the church, the band stopped playing, and the hunched old woman in the center briefly lifted the veil off her face to wipe the tears and perspiration.

Mrs. Brodski stopped in her tracks in shock, unable to move and utter a word. It was the dear woman, Maria Pavloska, slowly walking behind her husband's casket, with an expression of utter devastation. Her three children were all dressed in black, two daughters and a son walking together in the first row and holding her under both arms, with equally pained and grief-stricken faces. The four grandchildren, ages six to thirteen, were visibly distraught as they walked behind in the second row with their parents, either husbands of Pavloska's two daughters, or with Pavloska's daughter-in-law, the wife of her son, her eldest child. Mrs. Brodski motioned with her hand to stop a passerby and asked in absolute disbelief, "Is that Maria Pavloska?"

"Yes, it is," the passerby answered.

"And that is...," continued Mrs. Brodski, pointing to the casket without finishing her sentence.

"Yes, I'm afraid that is her husband, Stanislav Pavloski," answered the woman with a sigh. Then she asked, "Do you know them?"

"Yes, but not that well. What happened?"

"Heart attack, I'm told," the woman answered and then walked away.

Mrs. Brodski and Alek looked at each other, stunned; both were in total shock and lost for words. They took several small steps toward the church and watched the funeral procession from a distance for few more minutes, as it stopped at the wide entrance to the church courtyard.

The parish priest, Father Antoni, was already waiting, and after a few words exchanged with someone from the gathered crowd, bowed cordially and spread his arms in a most inviting, utmost sincere gesture, and asked them all to proceed to the church, without the band, of course.

Mrs. Brodski looked at the whole encounter with genuine interest, the way they all seemed to know each other, the way they understood the protocol, the procedures in the smallest detail, and the priest, like an old, much-revered friend, had always been there in their lives for better or worse. The truth be told, Father Antoni was always there, like an old trusted friend, an integral part of their lives: the baptisms, the first communions, confirmations, marriage vows, and funerals.

Mrs. Brodski and Alek were drawn closer to the courtyard entrance, which was marked by a massive concrete pillar on each side, each one connected further in opposing directions to almost two-meter-high thick, solid concrete wall surrounding the entire property in what seemed like a perfect square, with two narrow openings along the way, serving as additional exits and entrances. The whole structure, the church and the wall, was all white, freshly painted and glistening brightly in the intensity of the summer sun. The church dated back to the late nineteenth century, and was not an architectural marvel by any standard; rather, it was modest, unusually plain in its design inside and out. Along the perimeter wall, inside the courtyard were mature chestnut trees growing equally spaced, home to many species of birds.

After several more minutes, Alek couldn't quite understand his mother's prolonged interest in the funeral and all its activities, or whatever there was that caught her attention. He didn't like the strange curiosity and the mysterious look on her face, and soon showed his impatience; but nevertheless, he quietly waited and followed her every step.

The funeral procession disappeared inside the church, except for the band and a few other people, who for whatever reason opted to stay outside, in the shade of the large, leafy chestnut trees. There were a few wooden benches along the walls, in between the trees, perfectly located for all those who decided to rest, protected from the merciless sun for the duration of the funeral ceremony inside, or laid down their instruments while waiting.

Alek and his mom stood around the entrance for few more minutes, then slowly edged forward beyond the walls and inside the courtyard, without arousing any suspicion or attention among the several people loitering around the church grounds, looking for relief from the burning sun against the backdrop of a perfectly blue summer sky. They walked leisurely around the church, right to the back and then to the other side, along the west wall of this much-revered house of warship. They looked with utmost interest at the surroundings, and every detail of the church structure itself, including the roof and the bell tower. There was a profound sense of peace about the entire compound, an undisturbed atmosphere of a special, soul-soothing place, as if a sublime, unseen presence hovered above, wrapping its arms around it, and where even all the little earthly creatures were mostly silenced, for fear of disturbing what many believed to be sacred grounds.

15

AUGUST 20 WAS a day unlike any other since the end of the II World War. A day of unusual activity in the sky, with dozens of large Antonov transport planes streaking across the sky almost uninterrupted, one after another at regular intervals, in close formations, with a continuous drone throughout the day and overnight. They were all flying at very high altitudes and coming from the Soviet Union, headed southwest. People already out in the streets stopped, and many more came out of their homes and looked up at the sky in bewilderment, quietly speculating as to the meaning of the sudden, massive air force mobilization by the Big Brother to the east.

Alek couldn't satisfy his curiosity enough, and was outside a few times, well into the evening, to look at the airplanes passing overhead, until they couldn't be seen anymore as the night was setting in and only the distant roaring sound of their engines still reached the ground. He overheard the neighbors in the courtyard and across the dividing wooden fence feverishly discussing, and often arguing over, gravity and the significance of what they'd been witnessing. Whatever was behind it, the people were sure that nothing good would come out of it, and the prospect of yet another war, just over twenty-three years later, was frequently thrown around. The world was clearly at the crossroads— upheavals in the capital reshaping the whole political landscape, student protests across the country still freshly resonating, and similar uprisings across the continent giving rise to militant student activism, the Vietnam War still raging in spite of antiwar protests in America; civil rights movement and the assassination of Martin Luther King Jr., constant turmoil in the Middle East, the Cold War intensifying, and now what seemed like the beginning of a new major armed conflict .

The media were completely silent on the unusual events unfolding right in front of people's eyes, and didn't report anything out of the ordinary. As was always the case in times of uncertainty and abnormal activities, Radio Free Europe was always there to fill in the gaps, and although there was a renewed and intensified jamming of the waves, soon the announcement got through, transmitted incessantly with constant updates on the latest developments:

"On the night of August 20 and continued through the day of August 21, the army of the Soviet Union, supported by armies of three other Warsaw Pact countries—namely Bulgaria, Poland and Hungary—have invaded Czechoslovakia with an estimated 200,000 troops and about 2,000 tanks. It is suspected that Alexander Dubcek has been removed from power, and his fate is unknown at this time, but most likely placed temporarily under house arrest.

"There have been numerous independent reports of spontaneous uprisings of ordinary citizens of Prague against the invaders; however, nothing is known of any resistance by the regular Czechoslovak army, or its whereabouts. Numerous sources have confirmed several casualties, as well as acts of sabotage and peaceful resistance in the city, as well as other areas of the country to a lesser degree.

"The volatile situation is being closely monitored by the governments of major Western countries, who have publicly expressed their outrage and unequivocally condemned the invasion, demanding immediate explanation from Moscow. It is widely seen as a first implementation of the so-called Brezhnev doctrine, by which the Soviet Union reserves the right to intervene in a Warsaw Pact country to subordinate their national interest and hostile anti-socialist forces, to those of the Eastern Bloc as a whole and through military force, if necessary."

Mrs. Brodski was unusually quiet, although in good spirits, on Saturday afternoon, as the month of August and the summer were coming to an end, marking the fast approaching end of summer vacation and the beginning of a new school year. For most students, it was a much-dreaded time, when the looming end of freedom, as it was commonly perceived, was a time of such heightened anxiety that every passing hour brought them that much closer to the ultimate calamity—back to the classroom.

In the end, they resigned themselves to their unavoidable fate and spent the last days wasted on worries rather than on unhindered, lighthearted enjoyment, as was usually the case for most of the students, almost till the very end. The hardest hit were the children born into poverty, whose parents grew fruits and vegetables to supplement their meager income and had their offspring toil in the garden for hours each day, digging, planting, weeding out, picking the crops, and taking it to the market in town or the district capital. The sons and daughters in the surrounding farmlands and villages had it even worse, for their days were filled not only with never-ending hard labor from dusk till dawn, but also with working in the gardens and fields tending to the herds of farm animals and flocks of birds. Sadly, all that noble effort elicited very little sympathy among their peers; on the contrary, it evoked frequent scorn and contempt.

Mrs. Brodski was busy in the kitchen, hurriedly preparing food while humming some unknown, barely audible tune. She was all dressed up, as if going to attend a special event or an important meeting, with a subtle aura of secrecy, adding to the mystery of this fine early Saturday evening. At last, she looked at Alek with a prolonged and loving gaze and her familiar, serene smile and said, "I'll be back in not too long, son."

"Where are you going, Mom?"

"I'm meeting someone. No need to worry, just a social thing."

"Social? Is it he or she?" asked Alek with a hint of sarcasm.

"Why all those questions? You know I seldom go out, but this is one of those rare times. Just relax. Stay home, or go for a walk in the meantime."

"Is it he or she?"

"It's hard to say. It's rather two people that I'll be seeing tonight."

"Why can't you just say it? What's all this secrecy about?"

"Alek, I'll tell you all about it when I'm back. Nothing to be concerned about. As I said, a social kind of gathering, without any commitments."

"Mom, it's just weird, the way you're acting. What's the big deal?"

"It's not a big deal at all. Just drop it, son. You're tiring me."

"Does it have to do anything with me?"

"Maybe, we'll see. I'll let you know."

"Fine. You don't want to tell me, I don't want to know."

"I've got to go now, Alek. I'll be back later."

Mrs. Brodski looked at Alek with sign of exasperation on her face. She shook her head, but managed to smile one last time and then left home quickly, locking the front door behind her, and hurried west toward the main street. The weak rays of the setting sun, barely visible just above the horizon, pierced brightly through the few remaining vacant spaces between the low rooftops of adjacent houses and tree branches along the way, casting long, distorted shadows and then completely disappearing from sight with every passing minute.

There were already some groups of noisy young people gathering in front of the always-popular few night spots for the only entertainment in the town's center. They were standing there in the company of young local women, talking, laughing, and smoking cigarettes while waiting for the band to arrive and kick off the night with its already-well-known repertoire of pop hits of the last few years. The same band had been a familiar presence here with numerous appearances, but the patrons never seemed to tire of them or their music, and always gladly listened and danced to it, as if for the first time. From time to time, they added a song or two to their repertoire, and all those more devout followers of the female gender waited for it with great anticipation. In time, the four members of the band became well-respected local celebrities.

Mrs. Brodski passed the town's center without paying much attention to the locals and out-of-town revelers, moving few hundred meters west and only slowing down when she reached St. John's parish. She looked at the church with particular interest, from the bottom up to the bell tower, and the metal cross right at its peak. She stopped and hesitated for a moment, then proceeded cautiously, farther to the side of the church and on to its adjacent rectory. It was a gray single-story building with a wide wooden front door with a narrow stained-glass window at the top and two concrete steps leading to it. The front elevation had a few windows, all with the curtains drawn, but with no lights in any of the rooms with the windows, or any visible sign of life, except for a dim light in the corridor, just behind the front door, illuminating the stained-glass pane.

Mrs. Brodski walked up to the door and just stood there motionless for several seconds. She looked up once at the light coming though the colored glass, and then pressed the doorbell on the right side of the door frame, and waited. Only a prolonged period of silence followed, but no sign of life from inside the compound. She pressed the buzzer again, held it for a few seconds, and then released it and stepped back.

This time, after a while, she could hear a distant noise coming from somewhere deep inside, but approaching closer and closer, and finally, clearly audible footsteps just behind the front door. The soft, pleasant, and quite-youthful woman's voice behind the door asked, "Who is it?"

"Good evening, madam. I'm Mrs. Brodski. I was here a few days ago and had made arrangements to see Father Antoni, if you recall."

"Good evening! Oh yes, yes, I remember well, Mrs. Brodski." The woman inside, Ms. Klementyna, the cheerful parish maid, promptly opened the door and then stood to one side of the corridor, bowed, and, with a good-natured smile on her face, invited the guest in.

"Please come in. Father Antoni is in his study. He's been waiting for you. Please follow me."

"Thank you. I hope I'm not taking him away from some important matters."

"Oh no, no…as I said, he's been expecting you."

They walked in semidarkness to the end of the corridor, and then turned left into another corridor running in the opposite direction toward the back of the building. There was total undisturbed silence in the building. The air was stuffy, but of a rather pleasant smell—a rich combination of old antique furniture, floor polish, incense, and freshly extinguished or burning candle. At the end of this somewhat shorter but wider corridor, they came to a small vestibule with floor-length, dark and heavy curtains hanging on a semicircular metal rod suspended from the ceiling. Ms. Klementyna stopped in front of the curtain, and whispered, "Please wait here." She then slid the curtain open to one side and knocked gently on the door.

"Come in, please," answered a raspy, muffled voice from the inside.

Ms. Klementyna gently pressed on the door handle, pushed it slightly ajar, stuck her head in, and announced, "Mrs. Brodski is here to see you, Father."

"Come in, come in," the same male voice repeated.

Ms. Klementyna swung the door open and delicately pulled Mrs. Brodski by her arm, right behind her inside the spacious room, where Father Antoni was waiting. The priest was sitting at his desk, but got up and rushed toward the door to meet the guest. He crossed the distance in just a few long strides, and with a restrained smile and a cordial nod, he stretched out his right hand to greet Mrs. Brodski and introduce himself.

"Good evening, madame! I'm Father Antoni Pukalski."

"Zofia Brodski."

"I'm happy to see you. My good woman Ms. Klementyna told me you would be coming, so I was expecting you," said the priest, and then quickly measured her from head to toe with his lively eyes. He smiled mischievously at what he saw. Naturally, it didn't go unnoticed.

"I'm sorry for taking up your valuable time, Father."

"Oh, not at all, not at all…good that you came."

"Thank you. I'm so glad you agreed to meet me."

"My pleasure. If I can only be of help. Please sit down and make yourself comfortable, right here or there, my dear. Ms. Klementyna, would you be so kind as to bring us some tea and biscuits?"

"Yes, of course. I'll be back shortly," said the maid and left the room.

Father Antoni first pointed to one of the two chairs near the coffee table, then to a sofa on the other side. Mrs. Brodski chose the chair while Father Antoni waited and then started slowly pacing around, with his head down, looking at the floor, hands crossed behind his back. The priest, wearing a traditional long, black cassock, white clerical collar, and black leather shoes barely visible from under the robe seemed tense and uneasy, as if he'd rather be somewhere else. He was absorbed in his thoughts, obviously trying to find appropriate words to begin the conversation, or he was still under the impression of whatever he was preoccupied with before Mrs. Brodski came in.

She looked around the rather large room filled with interesting, eclectic collection of old furniture: a table with four chairs; a large oak desk with an ornate high-back chair; a bookcase filled with several rows of books of all sizes, neatly stacked, mostly in brown or dark-green hard covers; a three-seat gray fabric couch, a small coffee table, and two more wooden chairs with red cushions beside it—all in the same old, but comfortable and functional style. The spotless and perfectly polished wood floor was partially covered by two colorful and somewhat-worn area rags of Afghan or Persian style, most likely not original—one under the desk end extended beyond it on all sides, and the other, a smaller one, under the coffee table. The walls were decorated as could be expected—with three crosses in various places, and the iconic large picture of the Black Madonna, also known as Our Lady of Czestochowa. Also, as in every building of Catholic religious order, an ornately framed, medium-sized color photograph of Pope Paul VI. The other immediately noticeable decorative objects included two vases with freshly cut flowers, one on the table and a smaller one on the oak desk. Then a three-armed silver candelabra, with partially burned candles and, dripping, congealed wax, also prominently stood on the table.

One corner of the room was entirely taken up by a large, almost-up-to-the-ceiling exotic plant in a large brown clay pot. Undoubtedly, another curiosity and imagination-stirring object for any visitor was the glass enclosed middle section of the bookcase, filled with a variety of glasses and a few fine, cut-crystal wineglasses.

Mrs. Brodski couldn't resist the sudden but momentary nagging thought of what Commandant Sokolowski once told her about the break-in at Father Antoni's quarters, and the sofa frame full of money discovered and cleaned out by the thieves. She wondered if that was the actual sofa in front of her, and if so, had it been replenished with money? After a brief mental straggle, she abandoned the thoughts and tried to concentrate on the purpose of her visit. Except for the priest's steps, there was not a sound to be heard, either from the street or from inside the rectory; it was as if it was completely deserted.

"Mrs. Brodski," the priest said suddenly, "what is it that brings you here?"

"Oh, yes, it is rather hard to convey without being misunderstood. Actually, I've struggled with my conscience if I should have come here in the first place. I have thought about it for quite some time, actually."

Before the conversation went any farther, there was a gentle knock on the door, and without waiting for an answer, the radiantly smiling Ms. Klementyna walked in and announced herself. She carried a tray with a teapot, tea cups, two small porcelain desert plates, and a plate of butter biscuits. She quickly crossed the room and cheerfully set the tray on the coffee table. Then she removed all the contents, placed them on the table, bowed, excused herself,and just as quickly and quietly left the room, closing the door behind her.

Once the door closed, Father Antoni proceeded to sit on the sofa, close to the chair Mrs. Brodski was sitting on, and with his penetrating, lively eyes and a slight, but sly smile looked at his guest. At first Mrs. Brodski felt most uncomfortable under his steady gaze, his somewhat impatient and provocative demeanor, but quickly managed to regain her composure.

"Dear Mrs., you need not worry. I'm here to listen, and if there is anything I can help you with, I won't hesitate. Please tell me, what is it that brings you here?"

Before Mrs. Brodski was able to answer, Father Antoni poured the tea, and with naturally sincere gestures of his hands, invited her to taste the beverage.

"I've heard a lot of good things about you, Father, about the parish, the good work that you've been doing in the community, but I must admit I've never been to the church before. I'm not even sure if you know who I am."

"Let's just say I have a pretty good idea who you are, madam. Let's not forget, this is a small town, and sooner or later, word gets around."

"That makes it easier. I and my son, Aleksander, as far as I know, are the only Jewish family in this town. That's where the problem is. We don't go to church on Sundays like most people around here do, we don't celebrate the usual holidays like Christmas and Easter, or anything in between. God knows we've tried our best to assimilate, and on some occasions, yes, we celebrated with our neighbors, when invited. They're all very nice people, I cannot say enough, very nice people, and yet we struggle to be accepted here. It's either you're part of the Catholic diocese, or of the Eastern Orthodox at the other end of town. We're part of neither, but why should it be a problem living here in peace, side by side?"

"I see. I understand what you're saying. I sympathize with you, I truly do. We're all one in the eyes of God. We're all children of the Almighty, regardless of whether we're Pole, Russian or Ukrainian, I assure you. It is the people who make those differences and distinctions along ethnic, religious, and racial lines. The good God does not. In fact, God's message is universal for all the people regardless of their differences. You cannot find even one verse in the Bible to the contrary."

"Father, have you ever had people come to you, unbelievers in a sense, or the Orthodox, who wanted to join the church?"

"Oh yes, of course I have. You know, the war had displaced a lot of people and thrown many of us where we would otherwise never be, if we had a choice, and myself including. Are you thinking of joining the church?"

"No. I'm here about my son."

"Your son? Tell me about it."

"It's about Alek, not so much about me anymore. He's struggling at school, and wherever he goes, he has to look over his shoulder for fear of being assaulted one way or the other. They just won't leave him alone. I'm talking about the band of idle young hooligans roaming the streets, bullying and pushing around innocent people, even beating them up."

"Has your son fallen a victim of those attacks?"

"Yes, he has, a few times. Since Alek has really grown in the last two years, somehow he has become more visible in their eyes, and one of their targets. It seems as if they've been stalking him."

"I'm not sure there is any way I can help you with this, Mrs. Brodski. This is not something I deal with, as you well know. Have you talked to their parents or the school?"

"Yes, I've tried to find who their parents were, at least some of them. They are all busy working and don't know what's going on, or even care. They don't want to listen to this, and are quick to defend their children. I don't think that they actually have any influence on them anymore, even if they tried to intervene."

"Have you talked to the police?"

"Yes, I have. It was a waste of time. One of those hooligans was Sokolowski's son. Of course, the son and the father deny his involvement."

"Mrs. Brodski, it seems you've done whatever you could. It's really unfortunate. I sincerely sympathize with you. I'm sorry, but I just don't see there is anything more I could do for you."

"Father Antoni, I must say I've also been an object of some harassment in public places. The neighbors tend to avoid us too. There is very little interaction, so we just keep to ourselves. It's not easy for us to live in that old housing complex, with the constant feeling of isolation, being singled out for no apparent reason other than who we are. We are Jews, and always will be, and we don't have it written on our foreheads, and we don't behave differently than anybody else. We do look different. I never thought it would be such a problem, but obviously, I was wrong. In this small-town mentality, nothing escapes notice. I've been thinking for quite some time now. Please tell me, what would it take to have Alek baptized?"

The priest was visibly surprised by what he'd just heard and looked at Mrs. Brodski with disbelief and a hint of suspicion with that characteristic, penetrating gaze, as if trying to test her sincerity. "I must confess, I'm quite surprised by what you've just said. I've never dealt with such a case before. If I understand you well, you want Alek baptized in our church. You want him to become a Christian."

"Yes, that is our intention. I want him to have the same opportunities as everybody else. He has a whole life ahead of him and as long as we stay here in this town, I see that the only way forward is to take that step, to blend in. It seems to be a very important aspect of life around here, where much of it revolves around the church."

"Do you think that it will solve the problem? How about you, do you want to join the church?

"Yes, I think it might definitely help us to be become a part of this community in a way that everybody else is, if that's what is expected of us. I personally don't want to go through all this at my age. I'll live the rest my days just the way I am."

"Dear Mrs. Brodski, I must tell you, it is a serious matter and a lifelong commitment, a matter of faith, and it should not be taken lightly. I don't want to think that it is only about resolving personal issues by using the church as a means to do it, as part of some larger scheme. Do you realize the ramifications of such an undertaking? It's a life-altering experience, madam."

While saying this, the priest moved closer to the edge of the sofa, leaned forward, and gently laid his right hand on Mrs. Brodski's knee, as if trying to emphasize his point, or in a gesture of understanding and sympathy, looking straight into her eyes with a suspicious mixture of empathy, humility, and a hint of naughtiness on his pale, clean-shaven face.

She was momentarily startled by his unexpected bold gesture, stiffened and straightened her back, but kept her composure intact, and with just a quick glance at his right paw firmly on her left knee, without any obvious sign of disapproval, she continued, "Yes, I know, and I agree. As I said, I have thought about it for quite some time now—actually, ever since our applications for passports to emigrate were declined. I've talked to Alek about it in general terms a few times. He has expressed genuine interest in the church."

"You were planning to immigrate? Where to, and why?"

"Yes, a few months ago. We were thinking of Israel. I've heard there was an opportunity for us in all that political turmoil in the government. The doors appeared to be open for a time, if only briefly. Sometimes there are days that I realize there is nothing that keeps us here, and for Alek's sake, for his future, immigration would have been the best solution, I thought."

Father Antoni appeared to be taken by surprise by what he just heard. He briefly wiggled his fingers on Mrs. Brodski's knee and then took his hand back. He sighed, whispered a few incomprehensible words in what seemed like Latin, raised his eyebrows, took two sips of

DOMINIK POLESKI

tea, looked around the room, and then back again at his guest without saying a word for several seconds. Finally, he asked, "Does your son know you are here?"

"No, he doesn't, but he wouldn't object."

"Do you think we could meet and discuss this further? I'd like to hear from the young man himself. Of course, I expect that you would accompany him, in case some decisions will have to be made. Tentatively, I agree with your intentions, and I do not object personally."

"When is it convenient for you to see us, Father?

"How about if we all meet in a couple of weeks, in the evening, at six o'clock or so? It should give you some time to discuss and think this over. If you'll ever happen to be in the area, drop in and let us know exactly when you wish to come. There is no pressure. You must feel comfortable about it."

"Absolutely. We'll be here. Thank you so much for your generosity and understanding. I'm very grateful."

"Let me ask you, do you have the Bible at home? The New Testament?"

"No, I don't, but I'm somewhat familiar with its contents, as most people are. I do, however, have a copy of the Old Testament."

"Good, let me give you one," said Father Antoni as he sprang to his feet without hesitation. He went over to the bookshelf, looked over it up and down and then sideways, and then quickly noticed what he was looking for. He pulled the New Testament from one of the lower shelves, brought it back, and handed it to Mrs. Brodski. "Here it is, please take it. It's yours. This particular one is not entirely new, but it has not been used much, as far as I can see."

"Thank you. I certainly appreciate this. Let me pay for it," she said and began to open her purse, but Father Antoni immediately stopped her.

"Oh no, no, that's not necessary. It's a gift. We have many spare copies around here. I hope you'll find it most useful. Please look it over at home, and have your son study some parts that interest him, or he's not familiar with, before we meet next time. I'm certain this has the potential to open up many possibilities for the young man, a path toward the Almighty God and eternal salvation. Will it be something he would want to adopt for the rest of his life? It remains to be seen. Undoubtedly, it is a serious commitment, and should be taken seriously."

"Once again, thank you so much. I'm really so grateful for your generosity, and as a mother, I hope that you'll be able to help him, kind of like take him under your wings. Alek can be difficult at times, but he's a good boy. You know, it's that age when he questions everything, thinks he knows almost everything and doesn't seem to recognize any authority, but he's searching."

"I understand. Most of us went through all that once in our lives. I think we'll get along just fine. I'm looking forward to meeting your son."

Mrs. Brodski, visibly delighted with the outcome of the visit, got up from her chair and made a motion that she was ready to go toward the door. Father Antoni was already standing nearby, looking at her expectantly, with a slight smile of contentment and equally happy to be a host to such a refined dark-haired beauty. He too was ready to walk her to the door. One could only guess what tumultuous thoughts ran through the mind of this small-town parish priest with an insatiable appetite for temporal adventure, beyond the confines of strict Church doctrine. He considered himself a rather progressive messenger of the Word of God, and that of the Vatican, but felt at liberty to keep it somewhat open to personal interpretation, especially those parts vaguely related to spreading universal happiness.

He walked two or three steps behind Mrs. Brodski while admiring her tall and shapely figure. He just couldn't take his eyes of her bottom. She slowed down by the door, as Father Antoni leaped forward to open it and let the lady through. Without looking back, she proceeded hesitatingly along the long, dimly lit corridor toward the front exit door, and then stopped. The priest once again leaped from behind for the door handle and opened the door. Mrs. Brodski turned around to bid him good night, and the shrewd priest was right there, within a foot of her, smiling mischievously.

"Good night! It was a pleasure meeting you. Thank you for your time and the Bible," she said.

"Good night, Mrs. Pleasure was all mine. I'm glad I could be of help," said the priest, nodding his head.

She crossed the threshold and stepped outside into the perfect late-summer night. The air was still quite warm, with the strong aroma of chestnut trees surrounding the church compound, and a most pleasant mixture of flower scents carried over from the gardens of nearby residential dwellings.

"What a beautiful night! Please be careful…," Father Antoni exclaimed cheerfully, and with a genuine concern as he stood on the front steps for several more seconds, inhaling the fresh air and looking at the quickly departing silhouette of Mrs. Brodski.

16

THE SCHOOL YEAR began on Monday, September 2. It was mostly a sunny, but noticeably cooler, day, with temperature hovering around 16 degrees centigrade at its height, in the middle of the day. It was Alek's first day in middle school—a day of hope, but perhaps of equal amount of anxiety. If the elementary school was any indication, there was little to look forward to. Abuse from angry teachers and peers was prevalent, at least as far as he was concerned; and he'd seen many others fall victim to this senseless culture of power play at the expense of those they knew well would not challenge them, because they just couldn't.

Who could forget Mr. Fedoruk, the physics teacher, who seemed perpetually angry and ill-disposed to everything and everyone around him? He was often seen walking around the school with a sturdy oak pointer stick, and wielding it at the slightest sign of purported or imaginary transgression. Alek, too, on one occasion felt his unrestrained fury on the palm of his right hand, when Mr. Fedoruk decided to administer his brand of justice on Alek for accidentally running right in front of him and crossing his path. He considered it an intentional attempt to cause a collision and a premeditated effort to knock him off his feet. Alek took the punishment like a man and hid the swollen palm of his hand from his mother for a few days, and decided not to mention anything to her about it, for fear of her interference and further wrath from the cruel man.

Needless to say, Mr. Fedoruk's reputation quickly spilled beyond the confines of the school and became the subject of occasional derisive speculation as to the reasons behind his constantly sour mood and aggressive behavior. The story often repeated, which soon became the standard, and the only plausible explanation for his out-of-line conduct, was his sexual frustration. It had to be. It was said by those who claimed to know the subject well, that the man had failed after several nightly attempts to mount his unresponsive wife—brought to the brink of total exhaustion by the sheer load of housework, shopping, and their three children running around and causing mischief, so when the night came, she just lay down like a dead fish.

So it went on in perpetual circles for months on end, and months turned into years, and the desperate physics teacher was becoming more and more frustrated, looking for an outlet. It didn't take long before even the older kids picked up the story, embellished it a little, and repeated it often enough that when it eventually reached Fedoruk himself, he was literally beside himself, and vowed to catch the culprits, while administering his revenge indiscriminately and with renewed vigor. Alek's only hope was that at the new school, things would be different, and what happened in the elementary school was a thing of the past, never to be repeated; after all, he was a young man now, and he expected to be treated with the respect he deserved.

The highlight of the day was a general assembly of all the students and teachers in the large courtyard of the school, which started around ten o'clock in the morning. The students were assembled in orderly rows by classes, with the help of a few teachers walking around with sheets of paper in their hands, assigning students to their proper places. For many freshmen, it was the first opportunity to meet fellow classmates, size them up, strike up a conversation, and get the early feeling of a potential future friend, or foe. However, the first impressions were usually wrong, with a lot of posturing on all sides. As always, there were one or two pranksters in each class, vying for the early position of the class clown, and of course, a few more serious, somber types with annoying self-confidence, self-usurped leadership tendencies, perceived inherent right to scold and preach their wisdom to others without solicitation. Those were usually eager candidates for membership in the Polish Socialist Youth Association, the first-tier breeding nest and a springboard for future membership in the Party.

Alek was careful to not to draw attention to himself, and was not looking to engage anyone in a conversation either, but preferred to keep a low profile, quietly, unnoticed in the crowd, avoiding even the slightest overtures from those around him, as difficult as it was for about ninety minutes of this spectacle. The teachers, assistants, and administrators were proudly seated on wooden chairs assembled in a few rows, facing the students on the opposite side of the courtyard.

However, due to the large number of students, squeezed in a semicircle in rows and columns separated by classes, the closest were within about twenty meters of the school staff. The event began when the school director, Comrade Dymalski, dutifully called for a few minutes of silence, commemorating the twenty-ninth anniversary of the breakout of World War II, which began at four forty-five in the morning, when Germany treacherously attacked Poland on September 1, 1939. Then the silence was interrupted by the national anthem played through loudspeakers, as everyone stood at attention with sincerely sullen expressions on their faces. Then, after a minute or two of another period of brief silence, there followed a general informational session, and then finally, the assembly culminated with a lengthy, monotonous speech by Comrade Dymalski, a well-known bureaucrat, educator, and a notable Party member. As expected, he reminded all those gathered of the importance of good education; extolled the virtues of the socialist motherland, where for over twenty years now, people enjoyed free, unfettered access to all schools of their choice; introduced the teaching staff; and then praised the facility and newly acquired equipment; and, finally, went on a passionate rant about the ruling party's role and merits in the indisputable achievements of the socialist country:

"It is an unprecedented achievement of our country under the guidance of the Polish United Workers' Party and its infallible leadership, which made mass education its priority. It brought the country back from backwardness and the staggering rate of illiteracy under the previous bourgeois-dominated, class-divided society and the horrible destruction of World War II, to current highly educated population in a free and democratic country, with equal opportunity for all people regardless of ancestry or descent.

DOMINIK POLESKI

"Today, our socialist country has emerged as one of the leading countries among the progressive and fast-developing nations of the world. Illiteracy, which was a norm under the bourgeois and aristocracy, is now, as are they, a thing of the past, and, we can say with absolute conviction, have been successfully eradicated. We encourage our youth to study and work hard to follow in the footsteps of our great socialist leaders in science, industry, medicine, education, and politics. And when the time comes, to eventually take their places and continue the great revolutionary tradition of unparalleled achievements in all aspects of our lives, that we all can be proud of."

Later, after the official opening ceremony, the day was filled with mostly organizational matters, classroom assignment, weekly course schedule, supply list, buying and swapping books with students of higher grades eager to get rid of their old books and make some money in the process. Again, many opportunities presented themselves to mingle with other students and to get the overall feeling of potential for closer relationships, or even friendships.

Alek continued to stay clear of any engagement; in fact, he went out of his way to avoid any face-to-face contact, preferring his own comfort zone on the first day at the new school, although he noticed few students he had seen before, either at the elementary school or the streets. In the next day or two, as every year, it was expected to commemorate the beginning of World War II with a first class field trip to the grave of an unknown soldier on the outskirts of town. In the meantime, the corridors were alive, full of students, boys and girls from around town and the villages, walking around in different directions, standing around alone or in groups, engaging in lively conversations, laughing and telling stories of the past summer vacation, of the carefree world left behind. One could see teachers hurriedly crossing the corridors with intensity and seriousness on their faces, peeking inside the classrooms, paying little attention to the crowds of students loitering around. There was a different feeling to the middle school, not only the exterior of the building itself, the surrounding grounds with well-maintained landscaping, mature trees and shrubs, but inside as well; the floors, walls, doors, and windows, even the smell was different, as if aged with the school, trapped inside, and assimilated.

It was impossible not to notice the stark contrast in the actual interior appearance of the school to the one so admiringly described and praised by Director Dymalski in his opening speech. The long stretches of plain, worn-out PVC-tile flooring with cracks and missing pieces under the glare of dim, outdated, low-wattage incandescent lightbulbs. The dark-beige walls were long overdue for a fresh coat of paint, with clearly visible numerous chips, pen and pencil marks carved in little hearts and initials of unknown lovers, and crude attempts at mural art, or just signs of unloaded anger and frustration on the walls everywhere. Many wooden classroom and storage doors met with a similar fate and showed unmistakable signs of deliberate abuse besides their considerable age. Some sections of the walls displayed galleries of large framed black-and-white photographs of graduating classes from the years past, posing with their teachers, seated or standing in multiple rows, with sullen faces and looking ahead.

Alek looked at the old photographs with much interest when passing by, imagining his own class one day forever immortalized for future generations to see. One of the feature walls displayed a large red banner proclaiming the leading, indisputable role of the Socialist Party and the hope of the nation. He glanced at it quickly and moved along the main corridor, looking for his classroom according to the schedule he had received from the administration office. He recalled that fateful snowy December night when he stood outside beneath a windowsill, secretly peering into one of the rooms with the lights on when by chance he came upon a revealing, intimate encounter between Mr. Buzynski and the lovely Ms. Lubinska, the math teacher. He remembered it well. It was one of the first classrooms in the south end of the school, seemingly just like any other; but right across from it, on the east side of the courtyard, there was a windowless garden tool or equipment shed. It had double wooden doors facing that memorable window, and must certainly be seen from the inside now, through the classroom windows.

Alek quickly reached room number 103, hesitatingly pressed the door handle, and opened the door. The classroom was mostly filled with students, but with a few desks in the back still left unoccupied; and he was obviously late. The teacher, whom Alek did not recognize at first, was a middle-aged man. He was walking between the rows and talking, and did not immediately react to the sound of the door opening; but when several heads turned in the direction of the door, he too noticed Alek standing there, unsure of himself.

"Come in, come in, don't be afraid. Are you in the right class? Have you looked at your schedule?" asked the teacher.

"Yes, I think so. I'm sorry, I'm late", answered Alek.

"What's your name, young man?"

"Aleksander Brodski."

"Brodski? Let me see..." The teacher walked over to his desk in front of the class, took a sheet of paper in his right hand, and looked at it for a few seconds.

"Yes, Alek, you're at the right place, although late. But we won't be concerned about it today. Please take a seat in one of those vacant chairs in the back. By the way, as I've already told the rest of the class, I'll be your music teacher this year. Today we're just having a general information session, and it just happens that I'm here with you today. Tomorrow you'll start your regular classes according to the schedule. I know you're all eager to get out of here as soon as possible, so I won't keep you much longer."

Alek still felt out of place here, with an expression of awkward embarrassment on his face for being late, and now being the object of attention, as all eyes were on him for much too long to feel any comfort in the teacher's rather friendly and inviting overtures. He then walked toward the back and took a seat on a vacant creaky old wooden chair at one of the double wooden desks, supported by four wobbly metal legs, in the outside row parallel to the windows. There were two chairs to every desk, and both of them were vacant, as were a few other desks and chairs in the vicinity. All the furniture showed signs of age, and just like the walls and doors, and just about everything else in this school, displayed the legacy of previous generations and were covered with all sorts of pen and pencil markings and scratches, carved-out hearts, scrawled initials, a few little figures vaguely resembling intimate parts of the human anatomy, and engraved vocabulary not normally found in school curriculum, but an indispensable part of any student's repertoire.

The teacher started pacing again, and now was heading straight along the outside alley between two rows on desks, with his head held high, and talking about the challenges facing the school because of overpopulation and not enough space to accommodate all the students comfortably, hence the resulting large class sizes. Suddenly, Alek looked startled, as if he had seen a ghost, and looking at the teacher with all intensity as the man was walking in his direction, toward the end of the classroom. Alek uttered to himself, "Buzynski"

Yes, he was sure of it, the music teacher and a quite well-known local cultural celebrity, a man entrusted with the entertainment part of many official celebrations, either by his students, or himself playing the accordion or upright piano. Buzynski was best known among the students as Nightingale, dubbed quite appropriately so by someone several years ago, and the name had stuck ever since. He was certainly the man of that memorable night back in December, when perhaps for a few magical minutes for Alek, the time stood still. He lowered his head, pretending to look at his notebook, afraid to be recognized, although he was sure he couldn't have been seen outside the window, in the darkness of the winter night.

He couldn't quite understand what it was in that brief moment in a life of two people he didn't even know, although had seen them separately a couple of times, and the incident had stayed with him for all those months, and sure to remain in his memory perhaps for the rest of his life. What was the reason for that now seemingly insignificant event, which evoked in him such nostalgia and sorrow, and wouldn't let go? Why was he still strangely drawn to it when it had no meaningful effect on his life, and yet it remained a part of him? Why was it tormenting him after only a few minutes of a chance encounter, that related to an event in which he had no part but was merely an unintentional witness? Those questions Alek couldn't answer. He still vividly remembered Ms. Lubinska in a beautiful red dress, sitting on the desk with her legs crossed, as Mr. Buzynski stood in front of her and played the accordion with such devotion as he' never seen anyone play before. Their eyes were locked in a rare moment of pure loving embrace, and she was blushing. This picture, forever etched in Alek's memory for some inexplicable reason, always evoked a strange feeling of sadness and nostalgia in him, although with a lingering remorse of being an accidental witness to a private moment in two people's lives that he was not supposed to see.

Buzynski walked to the end of the classroom, without paying any particular attention to any of the students, rather, concentrating on his impromptu lecture and the floor beneath his feet. Then he turned around and walked slowly back to the front of the class. Alek looked outside the window, and there it was, about twenty meters away straight across—the toolshed he remembered well, when hiding below the windowsill over nine months ago, with his back against the cold concrete wall of the school, and he was sad...

17

S UNDAY, SEPTEMBER 8, marked a statutory national
holiday, and an annual harvest festival, celebrated throughout
the country in countless official celebrations with the participation
of the highest local and regional Party dignitaries, activists, and the
military. In the capital, the ceremony was held in the biggest sports
arena in the country, the 10th-Anniversary Stadium, opened in 1955
and commemorating ten years of the Polish People's Republic under
the rule of the Socialist Party, and ten years since the end of World War
II. The event was televised on national state television, transmitted by
the state-controlled radio, and was attended by the highest national
government dignitaries, ranking politicians, ruling Party bureaucrats,
highest-ranking army officers, and visiting guests from other communist
countries of the Soviet Bloc, but mainly from the Soviet Union. The
stadium was packed by about 100,000 spectators from Warsaw and
visitors from other cities, towns, and villages, as well as numerous
performers for the entertainment part of the whole spectacle.

The tragedy struck as the cameras were rolling, although few noticed
at first, or paid any close attention to the solitary black figure in flames
in the bleachers, amid the noise and commotion of the festivities in full
swing, thinking the self-immolation of the man was an integral part of
the entertainment. Soon, however, many people in the surrounding seats
recognized the human torch as a deliberate and premeditated act for
all to see; and they quickly dispersed and cleared the surrounding area.
A few threw themselves at the man, desperately trying to extinguish
the flames with their jackets, and rip the man's burning clothes off his
body. The police and security agents quickly moved in and cordoned

off the section and escorted the man down, before he collapsed and was rushed to the hospital.

In the following days and weeks, the state media were totally silent on the tragic story, and managed to effectively suppress it; but it quickly spread nevertheless, at least to some parts across the country, as Radio Free Europe, in spite of the incessant jamming of the waves by state security apparatus, filled the gaps and details of the event with periodic updates as more facts were coming in from family and friends of the man in the stadium, which in part read,

> *Ryszard Siwiec, a 60-year old accountant, husband and father of five children from south-eastern city of Przemysl, and the former member of the resistance in the Home Army during World War II, had poured inflammable liquid over his body at the Harvest Festival in Warsaw on September 8, and lit himself on fire. The tragic act of self-immolation in the presence of almost 100,000 spectators and highest government officials in the stands, including the first secretary of the Polish United Workers' Party, Vladyslav Gomulka, Prime Minister Jozef Cyrankiewicz, ministers, regional Party secretaries, all high-ranking army officers and foreign guests. The details of his sacrifice were apparently well planned in advance, and done in protest of the recent invasion of Czechoslovakia by the Warsaw Pact countries, including Poland, and against the Polish communist government. He was rushed to Warsaw Hospital, where he received a brief visit from his wife, but died four days later, on September 12, from his injuries.*

***

Mrs. Brodski, with Alek by her side, stood on the same steps in front of the door to the church rectory, pressed the doorbell, and waited. There was no sound coming from the inside, just undisturbed, total silence surrounded by the wall of the compound, lined with chestnut trees all around, gently waving their branches with a delicate rustle of leaves already changing colors, and glistening in the low setting sun. This time Alek pressed the doorbell twice in succession, and they waited. After several seconds, they heard the sound of footsteps fast approaching, and finally the familiar cheerful voice of Ms. Klementyna.

"Good evening! May I help you?"

"Good evening, miss! I'm Zofia Brodski, with my son, Alek, here to see Father Antoni."

"Oh yes, of course. Please wait a second." Then the sound of a brief struggle with a slowly turning key inside the old lock followed, and the door opened. Ms. Klementyna stood at the threshold with a radiant and inviting smile.

"Please come in. I'm happy to see you again, Mrs. Zofia. It's been few weeks, but I'm really glad you decided to come back. Your son, such a handsome young man. You must be proud of him. Father Antoni will be delighted to see you both. Please follow me."

"Thank you for your kind words, miss. I'm also happy to see you."

They all walked in single file along the familiar dimly lit corridor to the back of the building, with the same characteristic smell of antique furniture, incense, burning candle, and fresh wood floor polish. Finally, at the end of the second, shorter corridor, Ms. Klementyna stopped at a small vestibule, at a door shielded with a long, dark curtain suspended from a semicircular metal rod, parted the curtains, and knocked on the door.

"Please come in," responded the priest almost immediately.

Ms. Klementyna swung the door open, took few steps inside, and Mrs. Brodski and Alek followed right behind. Father Antoni, as before, lifted his head from behind the large oak desk, sprang to his feet, and, in a few strides, crossed the room to greet them. In a most cordial manner, he then bowed his head slightly and stretched out his right arm in a sincere gesture, but with a somewhat restrained smile to Mrs. Brodski.

"Good evening, Mrs. I'm happy to see you again, and glad that both of you could come here tonight. You look lovely this evening, and a very nice dress you've got on you, I must say."

"Good evening, Father. Thank you. This is my son, Aleksander," she said, feeling uneasy right after hearing those rather unexpected compliments coming from a parish priest.

Father Antoni nodded and shook Alek's hand with a genuine expression of interest and satisfaction that the young man managed to come, despite his doubts.

"I'm glad I can finally get to meet you, young man. Your mother told me good things about you. Please do not feel intimidated in any way."

"Good evening, Father," Alek answered politely, but timidly, looking into Father Antoni's eyes, but visibly moved and unsure of himself despite the priest's friendly, inviting manner.

"Let us have a seat, please," said the priest, pointing to the couch and chairs around a coffee table. Then, turning to Ms. Klementyna, he added, "Could you bring us something to drink? I think it's about teatime for me."

"Yes, of course. I'll be back shortly."

Mrs. Brodski seated herself on the couch this time, and Alek took a seat on one of the two chairs around the coffee table. Father Antoni also took a seat on the sofa, but at the other end, and looked at his guests for a few seconds with a penetrating gaze, as if trying to guess at their thoughts. They sat silently and looked at him with anticipation. The parish priest then mentioned something about being extremely busy, his very hectic schedule, frequent trips to the villages, families in great need and distress, and the overall pessimism in the country and abroad.

It wasn't long before Ms. Klementyna was back with a tray of teapot, cups, butter biscuits, desert plates, and napkins. She smiled, bowed, and left the room drenched in the dim light of a desk lamp and the weak light beaming above from a few small bulbs in an old four-armed chandelier hanging from the middle of the ceiling. Alek curiously looked around the room, and it seemed as though everything in it was quite interesting, emanating a feeling of comfort and serenity, as if there was a certain mysterious meaning to all the objects around, which had been in their original places for ages and could not be anywhere else. Although the interior of the room itself, the walls, the floors, the windows, and the furniture clearly showed all the characteristics of advanced age, as if from a different era, they were all nicely restored and maintained, and were most likely destined to serve well for many more years. Everything here seemed to convey a feeling of durability and permanence, like the church itself, which had withstood the test of time; but only the people had come and gone for generations.

Father Antoni, like a good host, poured the tea and then got right down to business.

"Please try some tea and the biscuits. They're both splendid. As I said before, I'm glad both of you are here, and that's good news. The fact that you've returned, tells me that you've given the matter some thought and are here to tell me all about it, otherwise you would not have bothered to come at all. Am I right?"

"Yes, you're right. We've talked about it indeed," said Mrs. Brodski "Are you ready to join the church, then?" asked Father Antoni.

"As I said during my first visit, it is only for Alek. I'll live out my life just the way I am. Alek has his whole life ahead of him, and it is his future I'm mostly concerned about."

"Alek, let me ask you directly, are you ready to be baptized and accept Jesus Christ as your Lord and the Son of God?"

"Yes, I am," Alek answered without hesitation.

"That's good, that's really good. The sacrament of baptism is the most important decision in one's life, young man. You probably know this holy ceremony is usually done at infancy, but as they say, better late than never."

"Yes, I know."

"I assume you realize that it all comes with certain responsibilities. The baptism is just the beginning. Next comes the first communion, then the confirmation, then possibly marriage, and so on. That's not all. In between there are numerous holidays, religious celebrations, and periods of special prayers leading up to important dates in the calendar year, which the church dutifully observes, and as a good Christian and Catholic, you'll be expected to attend many of those. Not to mention, you'll need to study the catechism and also attend our weekly classes for young people like yourself, here in one of the two rooms adjacent to this building."

"That sounds like a lot, but I think I'll manage. Actually, I'm looking forward to this new life."

"That's good to hear, Alek. There are some technical issues as well. Frankly, I've never had to deal with a situation like this before, where a parent is not a Christian, nor is anyone else in the immediate family, I suppose. I will have to consult our diocese's bishop, Modlinski. Mrs. Brodski, I'd like you to leave me your names and your address before you go. I don't see any obstacles, but we must follow proper procedures. It might take a few weeks."

"We understand, that's not a problem. We've waited this long, we can wait a little longer. It is rather an unusual situation, I must admit, when a Jew comes in and says of his own free will, that he wants to be baptized in a Catholic church by a priest," said Mrs. Brodski with a big smile.

Father Antoni burst out laughing, got up from the sofa, and walked over to his desk, where he picked up a pad of lined paper and a pen, and then quickly returned to his seat, handing the paper to Mrs. Brodski.

"Please write down your full names and address for me," he said. "Of course, I'll be happy to. I hope we'll hear from you soon."

"I promise, as soon as I hear something, I'll let you know. It will be just a formality. I do not anticipate any problems. It is always good when new faces want to join our growing congregation. As they say, the more, the merrier."

Suddenly and unexpectedly, the engaging conversation was interrupted, as the old wooden entrance door creaked and slowly moved ajar. Quite surprised, the three of them instantly turned their heads in the direction of the door, but it took at least a few seconds before a male figure appeared, leaning inside halfway through the door. The intruder instinctively looked toward the sofa, chairs, and the coffee table where they all sat, and then with a reserved but slightly mischievous smile, he waved his right hand and said, "Good night, Antoni. I must be going now. Take care, my friend, and see you soon. Good night, madam, and you, young man. Please don't get up. I'll find my way out."

Father Antoni immediately jumped to his feet, but had barely managed to take few steps around the table and toward the man peering inside, when the door closed and, without even waiting for the answer, the man quickly disappeared. Only the receding sound of each step could be heard behind the wall separating the corridor and leading outside. Father Antoni took two more short steps toward the door, but stopped in his tracks with an expression of faint disappointment.

"Good night, Vladimir," he said quietly, as if to himself, and then slowly turned around and returned to the sofa. Again, he looked at his guests with that characteristic penetrating and scrutinizing stare, as if probing for the secrets of their thoughts. Once satisfied with what he managed to observe, and there was nothing to be concerned about, he made a few unfamiliar, undefinable facial expressions, sighed, and smiled with a delicate, good-natured smile, as if signaling the end of momentary disruption.

"That was my good friend Vladimir from the Orthodox Church, as you may have noticed. He was just visiting briefly. Have you met him before?"

Alek just shrugged his shoulders indifferently, silently, without a hint of awareness of who he was, but the question certainly caught Mrs. Brodski's attention.

"Yes, I've seen him before here and there, and I've heard about him, but I've never met him personally. It's such a small town…," she said.

"I'm curious, what have you heard about Father Vladimir?" the priest pursued with continued interest.

"Nothing in particular, I think. Otherwise I would have remembered it quite well, but since I can't really remember anything of significance, then I guess it was just that, nothing in particular," she answered evasively.

"I see. I've heard rumors around town, but regardless of what you've heard, let me assure you, those are just rumors. There is absolutely no truth to them whatsoever. Father Vladimir is the most decent man and God-fearing apostle of Christ you'll ever meet. But let us go back to our business, shall we? Tell me, Mrs., from what I understand, there are just the two of you, right?"

"Yes, family of two. My husband, Jakub, died several years ago, after a lengthy illness. Ever since, we've been on our own—and struggling, I must say. We don't have any close family in Poland that I know of, only distant cousins on both sides of the family in the old eastern territories. Now it's all Soviet Union. Quite possibly, a few who somehow survived World War II could have immigrated to Israel or the United States, but it's just my speculation. The rest died during the war as far as I know. Sobibor, Belzec."

"I'm sorry to hear that, it breaks my heart. That's really tragic. I sympathize with your plight, Mrs. Brodski. I feel your pain. I meet a lot of people, and trust me, there are many who struggle under the current system with personal tragedies, in most unfortunate circumstances. What happened during the war was horrible, whole communities wiped out, most families affected…We've been living in peace now for over twenty years, but it's not a paradise either. We all know that, regardless of what they tell us."

Father Antoni leaned over, reached over to Mrs. Brodski at the other end of the old sofa, and with what seemed like genuine concern and empathy, touched her hand and held it for several seconds, as if trying to soothe her pain. She didn't shy away or resist the priest's gesture, but seemed rather comforted and relieved. Alek didn't make much of it either, but found the priest's actions to be sincere and reassuring; after all, he was a man of God, well known and respected by most.

"Thank you so much, Father, for understanding. We really appreciate your kindness and support," said Mrs. Brodski in a rare moment of revealing personal confession. It was more than she wanted to say, and said in a long time to a man she hardly knew, a small-town Catholic priest. The thought that it would stay with him forever, never to be passed on any further, was reassuring and enough to convince her this was a man she could trust. After all, he was bound by secrecy.

"Dear madam, it is my pleasure. You can always count on me. I'm a priest, but I know what's happening in this country. Frankly, I don't see much prospect for drastic improvement in the quality of life here anytime soon. I'd argue that there is no hope at all. I understand, and

I don't blame you for looking at ways to improve your situation. It's only natural."

"I think I told you before, during my first visit, that we tried emigration. After all, nothing really keeps us here, at least not much. We were advised by someone knowledgeable and of considerable authority around here, that particularly the Jews were allowed to leave the country—whoever wanted to, of course. Unfortunately, we were turned down. I don't even know on what grounds, but whatever it was, now it forces us to make the best of the situation we're in right now, and in this town."

"Without getting too much into politics, which is not my specialty obviously, from what I know, the emigration policy is aimed primarily at the elites of this country, those in politics at the highest levels, academia, mass media, and possibly judiciary, but not ordinary people, Mrs. Brodski."

"Well, at least we've tried, and should things change, we'll be ready to try again. In the meantime, we'd like to really become part of this community, as opposed to being the outsiders we feel to be now."

"I understand. I think you've made the right decision, and the first step toward your goal by coming here. Before I'll get a reply to my inquiry from the bishop in the meantime, you could give more thought to Alek's baptism, do some planning, make preliminary preparations, like choosing your godmother and godfather, would be a good start. I also think that it would be beneficial for the young man to familiarize himself with the New Testament even further."

"That's what I intend to do," said Alek.

"Good. It might prepare you for what's ahead in terms of our church activities and celebrations throughout the year. I have no doubt it'll have a positive effect on both of your lives. It'll set you on a new path, it'll add meaning to your lives, you'll meet new people, might even find new friends, and you'll gain acceptance. It will change your life, believe me. Let me ask you, Alek, do you have any personal interests or hobbies? What do you do in your spare time?"

"I read, listen to the radio, and sometimes draw and write."

"What do you read, if I may ask?"

"Anything really—books, newspapers, magazines. The public library is about a hundred meters from our home."

"That's very interesting. I'm curious. What do you draw?"

"Mostly ordinary people, with pencil, ballpoint pen, or fountain pen."

"I'm impressed. Now you've got me really interested. How about writing, what do you write?"

"I should say, I'm trying to write poetry and short stories, but I know I'm not that good at it. It's not anywhere near to what I read," said Alek shyly.

"That's wonderful. I'm really impressed. What an outstanding young man you are. Mrs. Brodski, you must be proud of your son."

"Yes, I am, although he spends so much time by himself it troubles me. I wish he'd go out sometimes and interact with his peers, but he's just not close enough with anyone to keep in touch after school. This is one of the reasons we're here—we'd like to change all that, to get him involved with other things."

"Alek, I hope it's not too much to ask, but could you recite one of your poems to me? That is, if you remember it by heart. I must admit, I'm really interested. Literature is something that I myself immerse in. You're a very creative young man."

"I'd rather not. It's not worthy of your time, Father."

"How do you know? Don't worry, Alek. I have a feeling it is really good."

"I'm not so sure, but I like doing it. I still have a lot to learn."

"Alek, if you remember one of your recent poems, please recite it. Don't let Father Antoni keep asking you," his mother interfered.

"Listen to your mother," added the priest.

Alek's options ran out; he didn't expect such turn of events. He was asked to recite one of his poems—in fact, to reveal his innermost thoughts in the process, which he was guarding so meticulously. He looked at them, as if pleading for mercy, but there was none to be found. His mother only smiled with a look of pride in her only child, and Father Antoni was looking at him with anticipation.

"Fine, it won't be long, but don't laugh. I'm warning you, it's not any good," said Alek. He got up from his chair, stepped back from the table a few short paces, hunched over, and then, looking at an unknown, distant point in front of him with a sullen, almost-mournful expression on his pale face, began:

Speak to me

Speak to me, Father of All
Devine voice, touch my soul
Your strong, merciful hand
Lift me up above despair.
Years of shattered dreams
Grief-stained path impressed
Tear-soaked ground beneath
Will you bury me?
I've walked for years alone
Eternal truth has eluded me
Quest for reason ran its course
Only faint hope still remains.
In the ravaged body's shell
My life-scarred, naked heart
With relentless throbbing pain
Aches for your healing voice.
Hear its agony's sacred cries
Speak to me, Father of All.

When Alek finished the recitation, he seemed visibly moved and exhausted, and just stood there for a few seconds amid total silence. He then slowly returned to his chair, with his head down, and quietly waited for a response.

Father Antoni looked at him with astonishment, and his mother seemed equally bewildered and truly concerned about her son's very personal confession through his writing, and how little she actually knew about his state of mind.

"I must say, I'm pleasantly surprised at the quality and maturity of your poem, Alek. Next time, I'd like to see a few of your drawings too. The poem was very revealing, a personal plea to God to hear you out and to speak to you, unlike anything I've ever heard before from someone of your age, or anyone for that matter. I'm beginning to understand better your decision to come to know God through Jesus Christ."

"It is still hard for me to understand that being somewhat different would be a reason to feel so isolated and ostracized in this town. It never occurred to me that Alek had suffered to such a degree, although I always thought we had a good, close relationship," said Mrs. Brodski

"You must understand, my dear, it's all this small-town mentality. Cultural divisions, and even ethnic differences, come to surface from time to time, despite the impression of peace and tranquility. One common thread is Christianity—besides the widespread misery, of course—whether Roman Catholic or Eastern Orthodox, but it binds these people together. It gives them hope. To tell you the truth, some Party bureaucrats are trying to discourage people from going to church. Yes, even in this small town, they're quoting that old, worn-out phrase of Marx: 'Religion is the opium of the people.' You would be surprised by the rampant hypocrisy. Quite often, the same people who preach that communist propaganda, come secretly at night to have their children baptized, or to make arrangements for their loved ones with the last rites, or to have someone perform Christian burial. I've seen it all."

"How interesting. I would have never thought. I think under the circumstances, people do whatever it takes to get ahead, and I guess for some, the church and Marx can get along. We all know what life is like around here."

"Let me tell you something about Commandant Sokolowski. Just between us, something I just can't get over, something quite disturbing. Few weeks ago, it was brought to my attention that the captain was shooting at birds here, around the church with a small-caliber KBKS rifle. As you know, lots of birds, mostly crows, nestle in those tall chestnut trees around the compound, and he just stood there on the west side behind the concrete wall separating us from the adjacent empty lot, and was target-practicing. Apparently, a lot of children gathered and witnessed the whole incident, as he was shooting unceremoniously for what seemed like an hour, and many of them were naturally horrified. I was told that the disturbed birds were circling around in flocks, and many sat on the cross on top of bell tower, and even there, Sokolowski showed no respect. The lead hit the cross several times according to the witnesses. He killed several crows. Some fell on top of the metal roof, and some on the ground below. Many were badly injured, and imagine all those poor helpless creatures had to be picked up later and disposed of. Horrible, absolutely horrible!"

"I'm shocked. As you say, absolutely horrible. Who would have thought? To me, Commandant Sokolowski seemed like a relatively decent, reasonable man doing whatever he had to do as part of the responsibilities of his job. I've never sensed in him any deviations or extreme tendencies. On the contrary, he seemed like a levelheaded, rather helpful man, whatever his motives were—at least in my dealings with him," said Mrs. Brodski

"I'm sorry for straying from the subject with this terrible story, but it has affected me deeply, I must say. When you would least suspect, people you think you know and respect show their true colors in the most unlikely circumstances. I'm happy to have met you and know both of you. I know you're both good people who found themselves in this often-inhospitable town and are struggling to survive. I assure you, you've made the right decision. It will help you, and in time, you'll meet many good people like yourselves."

"You've convinced us, Father. We'll certainly wait with anticipation for news from the bishop. As you suggest, we'll start preparations, but we must be going now. Thank you so much for your time, generosity, and support," said Mrs. Brodski as she rose from the sofa with a visible expression of satisfaction and newly found inspiration. The priest and Alek, rejuvenated in his decision to become a Christian, sprang to their feet almost at the same time, and all of them headed for the door. Father Antoni again walked behind them with a mischievous smile on his face, in his compulsive habit of admiring his female guest's shapely, slim figure.

They stopped just outside and into a twilight of September evening, in a gentle, cool breeze bringing with it the distinct smell of changing season, the unmistakable scent of approaching autumn. They looked at each other for several seconds, as the parish priest, in a fatherly, sincere gesture of kindness, put his arms around their shoulders and said, "I truly believe that there is more to life than this temporal existential misery, and beyond it, there is life everlasting."

Father Antoni bowed cordially with a warm smile, bid farewell to his quests, shook their hands, and promised to be in touch either by mail or through his indispensable assistant, Father Feliks, or he wouldn't even mind if Mrs. Brodski just dropped in, in a couple of weeks. And then they all parted with a good feeling of mutual respect and appreciation.

18

T HE SECONDARY SCHOOL under the patronage of Roza Luksemburg was not exactly what Alek had expected, although there were a few noticeable differences, and the distance from his home was about the same as that to the elementary school he had gone to for the previous eight years. He noticed that initially, the teachers treated the students with much more respect. In fact, some teachers, mostly male, made a point of occasionally referring to students as Mr. and Ms., followed by their family name. It wasn't always taken seriously; however, sooner or later, the sarcasm became plainly apparent once the usual problems came into play, like the first poor marks on tests and essays, homework not done, habitual tardiness or disruptions in the classroom. One thing was certain: there were never any overtly aggressive verbal outbursts, name calling, or threats from the teachers, as was often the case in the previous school.

Alek did not fall into any of those categories to invite a public scolding; he was consciously always on time, had his homework done, was reasonably well prepared for the tests, although his first marks were rather low despite being in the passing range, and he never participated in any discussions or interactions as much as he could. Generally, he preferred to keep a low profile, unless specifically asked or challenged by the teacher, or by one of his peers—something he could not avoid.

One of the negative aspects of the new school was the frequent changing of classrooms. There was a physics lab, chemistry lab, biology lab, one for both geography and history classrooms, one and the same for mathematics, the Polish and Russian language, and of course, the gymnasium, perhaps his most disliked place in the entire school. Alek did not like sports, particularly in the setting of this decrepit old gym in urgent need of repairs, and in it, any of the individual exercises or group games, like volleyball, basketball or indoor football. Not only that, the gym needed renovations; but it was badly lit and relatively small for what it was designed to be, with a visibly reduced basketball court, small and cramped change rooms, making it the perfect place for those few students whose only purpose in life, it seemed, was to make it miserable and most unpleasant for others.

There were two gym classes a week, the last hour of the school day on Tuesday and the last hour on Friday. The Friday session was exceptionally stressful; it was joined with a different class, with all the male students from the second year. All of them were older, and for Alek, it was a dreaded, torturous experience. The horrible commotion, shouting, running around, pushing, and shoving; the ball flying in different directions; the piercing whistle of the teacher; and before long, he could hear somebody's voice calling, "Get him! Get him!" Which for those special few in the class was enough to send the ball flying at great speed in his direction, or bump into him with full force and knock him down, and then laugh uncontrollably, as if it were the most hilarious thing in the world.

Another place in school that required special attention and vigilance was the school cafeteria, and it too wasn't planned for future expansion, and could not receive the volume of students descending here for the lunch break. Just like most of the school facilities, it had been allowed to deteriorate for far too long over the years, either due to lack of funds or mismanagement; regardless, it was not the most inviting environment for a meal. Around noon, a single-file line of noisy, restless students stretched from the front counter to almost half the length of the cafeteria. There was the usual pushing, jumping the queue, and general disruptions from the usual few older underachievers who commanded the most attention, ready to unleash their brute force if challenged. Over time, it became an accepted fact, just the way things were; and most learned to live with it rather quickly, without provoking anything more serious beyond the occasional verbal insults.

Behind the counter, two sluggish, middle-aged female servers, who looked like they would rather be anywhere else but here, only added to the problem. Although the cost of food was just a nominal amount, the cafeteria had little to offer, just a few bare basics, like ham-and-cheese sandwiches, or plain Swiss cheese sandwiches, cheese buns, tea biscuits, and, of course, tea, a hot liquid product known as grain coffee, and one kind of soda. Many students usually brought their own food and used the cafeteria to sit down and interact with their friends.

Alek seldom ventured into the school cafeteria; he usually had his own lunch brought from home, unless on one of those rare occasions he didn't have anything with him, or one of his classmates insisted he should go to keep them company, and that it would be beneficial for his own sake to show affiliation and loyalty to the class rather than roam the corridors alone in the meantime. Once inside the cafeteria, however, Alek still tended to stay aloof from the biggest crowds, patiently waiting, or rather slouching, in line for a cup of tepid grain coffee, looking ahead, seldom sideways, so as not to invite unnecessary stares. He wore his customary white dress shirt, baggy black trousers, and old, worn-out black shoes.

In this school, his attire didn't attract as much attention as it did in the elementary school, where all those little brats running around noticed even the slightest peculiarities about everything and everyone. Here it was different; not many cared. A much more serious attitude prevailed; the curriculum was more serious, something to contend with, and not to be dismissed lightly. And the teachers were bloody serious about it too.

Alek eventually joined a hardly occupied two tables pulled together, in a far corner, with two loners like himself. They never received any attention, except occasionally for all the wrong reasons, when eventually noticed by one of those burly underachieving types looking for cheap entertainment at their expense. Isolation, however, was a sure way to lose a popularity contest among the girls, who tended to group around the more outspoken, athletic, and seemingly constantly joking types, whose main mission was to be the center of attention at all cost. The quiet, withdrawn smaller groups were perceived as a bunch of boring losers, generally treated with disdain, and who permanently resigned

DOMINIK POLESKI

to the fact that none of the school beauties would send as much as an accidental glance in their direction.

For Alek, it was an infrequent chance to interact with a few like-minded colleagues, share some stories like anyone his age would, at times even ordinarily silly things, and yet in their own way much more. From current and recent events, or impressions of the latest music hits from Western European and American charts, to the latest and most-talked-about foreign and domestic films, to opinions on books; they shared some interesting stories from other people and, of course, occasionally even talk about God.

Rarely, Alek had a nagging need to elaborate on his newly attained conclusions, after hours of thinking and pondering the meaning of temporal life itself, the sense of human existence, often late at night, lying in bed, blindly looking at the ceiling in the total darkness of the room, and asking, "Why am I here? What does it all mean? Why is life such a struggle, even for those who seem to have it all, who cannot buy themselves out of the inevitable death, and neither can take their riches with them? If good, virtuous lives are to be rewarded, why is there so much misery, disproportionately more, among the downtrodden, poor but earnestly religious, God-worshipping people than among the well-to-do, immoral, and wicked, at least so it seems?"

Alek, recently being strongly under the influence of the Bible he had received from Father Antoni, was further thrown into doubt and confusion. He thought that if Jesus Christ's horrific death was the ultimate price paid as redemption for humanity's sins and its ultimate salvation, then it was certainly a waste of a good man. Not only were the people not redeemed and delivered from evil, if anything, the world had gradually gotten much worse, and the three decades between 1914 and 1945, encompassing the two world wars were the best testimony to all that. That evil triumphed on such unimaginable scale, that all the previous centuries from the death of the Son of God, was just the beginning, like a gathering storm, slowly increasing in intensity, and culminating without precedence in such mass destruction and loss of human life, the magnitude of which had no equal in the history of the human race. Barely out of the ruins and ashes of the Second World

War, the specter of communism descended on Europe like a plague, to draw more blood and tears, to sow more misery, especially among those nations who suffered the most in the previous conflict.

Alek's mom did not always openly agree with all his gloomy and pessimistic views, but she expressed her skepticism about the contents of the Bible often enough that it only added to his own internal struggles. Although at times their conversations turned into bitter arguments, he was just as exasperated by her reluctance to even engage in those exchanges, her condescending tone, her outbursts of laughter, and ultimately giving up too easily. On the other hand, Alek's few new colleagues who dared to delve into the subject when confronted with his unexpected digression into matters of philosophical nature, trying to explain all that is going on in the framework of religious beliefs, for the most part, had a much simpler view of the world around them, or simply didn't know what the hell he was talking about.

Although he had heard it in the past numerous times, all evil in the world was somehow always easily explained by the church, and then repeated endlessly by those who listened and believed, as God's retribution for people's sins. Regardless, it all didn't make sense to Alek at all, because if that was the case, then God in his insatiable lust for vengeance, craving for blood, perpetuated the never-ending cycle of violence and misery. It must be true, then, that "man was made in the image of God." They were all the same, equally vicious, bloodthirsty entities.

To Alek, it seemed only natural to question why during the war, when all those helpless people by the millions must have prayed earnestly for their lives, for a miracle when they saw German soldier's gun pointed at their head, nothing happened. Then in a split second, the gun went off as the soldier pulled the trigger with typical German efficiency and then moved on to the next, and the next, and the next, as bodies were falling into the ditch previously dug up by the victims themselves, while the good, merciful God was looking on. Nevertheless, Alek was certain he was right, especially after he had given so much thought to it. The arguments were plainly obvious and irrefutable, he insisted, and the Bible wasn't his only source. After all, the town's library was about a hundred meters away from his home. He must have already read a sizable portion of its contents, and increasingly more and more serious literature that others of his age would not even consider.

The new course at school, called "Introduction to Marxism and Leninism"—which rejected all the supernatural and blamed much of humanity's ailments on the religious beliefs imposed for centuries by the influential Church enforcers—added to the confusion.

The Marxist realism proclaimed the new truth and was here to enlighten the masses that were enslaved in religious dogma, and help them break the shackles that had kept them in bondage for centuries, empower them, and set them free. Rational as the new school curriculum seemed to Alek, in reality, it had not convinced him. In fact, he could not recall a single person he knew who could say anything positive about life under the supposedly benevolent "dictatorship of the proletariat"; even Father Antoni himself was highly critical of the new communist reality.

On the other hand, the church did not offer a tangible alternative either. If the common tenets of religious beliefs postulated the fatalistic, predetermined nature of life being the central part of the Christian doctrine, then what good was a prayer if it wouldn't change the outcome anyway? Naturally, it would seem completely useless, futile, even an utterly foolish practice. Even more problematic to him was the Catholic certainty of the Holy Trinity—the Father, the Son, and the Holy Spirit—which seemed to defy logic completely, and that was something even his mom agreed on. But as usual, with the characteristic condescending tone or suspicious smiles.

Alek reasoned, "Since Christ died on the cross, then who actually died? Only the Son, or the three of them at once? Is God dead? What father would sacrifice his only son in the name of some elaborate scheme to save the people, his own imperfect creation? He certainly could have done a better job in the first place, and no wonder, when the time of need comes for God's immediate, decisive intervention, he cannot be relied upon. Was this plot devised only to save the Israelites and a few other nations in the neighborhood, because in all the rest of the world, people didn't know anything about it, and missed out on the offer and till this day have no regrets?"

The one thing Alek dared not share with anyone was his decision, and his mother's idea, originally suggested by her old friend Maria Pavloska, to be baptized in the local church. The closer he was to the set date of Saturday, November 2, the day after All Saints Day, mutually agreed upon with Father Antoni following a rather prompt and positive response from the bishop, the more apprehensive and withdrawn Alek was becoming. His doubts and increasingly frequent regrets had intensified, turning into an obsession, taking up most of his time, incessantly occupying his fragile mind, and relentlessly tormenting him. *What have I done? How did I get myself into this? What's wrong with me?* he asked himself repeatedly. At times he felt like calling off the whole arrangement; after all, nobody could force him into something full of contradictions, something he was not sure about, and, most likely, didn't even want, at least most of the time, except on the increasingly rare occasions when suddenly, out of nowhere, he had a renewed surge of longing and hope for that mysterious something of which Father Antoni said with such profound conviction, "It will change your life."

19

E LA, THE PRETTY girl Alek met the past summer at night in front of the restaurant, who so courageously saved him from inevitable beating, appeared suddenly and totally unexpectedly. The crowded school cafeteria was the last place he expected to see her again; after all, she had her life well planned out at the time, and the street was to be her life, at least for the foreseeable future, since things were not going well with her habitually drunk father. Apparently, she dropped out of the second year of school the year before and was not planning to return anytime soon; but here she was, standing near the entrance, just inside and looking around. She was wearing a tight navy-blue skirt, significantly above her knees, borderline acceptable, or possibly even beyond acceptable school limit; a light-blue blouse with a large collar; and a gray cardigan. From a distance, she seemed anxious and out of place, although evidently looking for someone; otherwise she would not have come here, or join the queue.

Ela didn't recognize Alek, but he, ever so vigilant, with his eyes often on the entrance door, noticed her immediately.

"I know her," he said to his companions and pointed with a quick movement of his head in the direction of the door. They both looked up, startled, and immediately turned in her direction.

"No, you don't," said one with absolute conviction.

"I don't believe you," said the other with a dismissive smile.

"You want to see? Just watch me," said Alek, jumping to his feet and quickly striding across the room; and within seconds, he was right beside Ela, who had already turned around as if ready to leave the cafeteria.

"Hello, Ela!" said Alek, standing two paces behind her.

She slowly turned toward him and looked at the young man in front of her with bewilderment, which quickly dissipated and was replaced by a smile on her face. She looked at Alek intently for a few seconds, and then said, "Oh, hello, Alek. What a surprise!"

"I'm just as surprised as you are."

"I didn't expect to find you here."

"Neither did I. Were you looking for me?" said Alek with a playful smile.

"I mean, I knew you were coming to this school, you told me, remember? Still, somehow I didn't connect."

"Yeah, I remember well that I told you. What are you doing here? Are you back in school now?"

"Surprise! Yes, I am. Decided to come back. Let's move away from here. There is just too much noise in here. Do you want to go for a walk?" said Ela.

"Yes, of course. Let's walk around the corridors, shall we?"

"You haven't changed. You're just like the day I met you."

"Is that good or bad?

"Of course it's good."

"You look great, Ela, I must say."

"Thank you. I'm happy to see you."

"I'm so happy to see you too. I've been thinking about you."

"I don't believe you," said Ela with a radiant, coquettish smile as they slowly walked down the long stretch of main-floor corridor.

"Would I lie to you? Look at me, could these eyes lie?"

"No, not your eyes, for sure, but your mouth probably could." And she burst out laughing.

"So, tell me, Ela, why did you decide to come back? What year are you in now? If I'm not mistaken, you dropped out in the beginning of your second year, right?"

"Yes, you're absolutely right, so I'm back in the second now."

"Why?

What do you mean, why? I wanted to learn how to read and write a bit better, you know…a literate hooker. Sounds better, doesn't it?"

"What? Don't say that. Wasn't that supposed to be long behind us, like grade 3 or 4, at the latest? I didn't know you somehow slipped through the cracks so long ago, but as they say, better late than never."

"Hey, hey, don't be so nasty."

"I'm just kidding, you know that."

"Of course I do. Don't be so serious. So, do you want to know the real reason I came back here?"

"I'm dying to hear. Surprise me, please."

Ela, looking at Alek with a mischievously wily smile, slowed down the pace, looked around, and said, "The real reason I'm back at school is...because I knew you'd be here. I wanted to see you, and as often as I can. To hell with education."

"Oh, now that's a good reason. Finally, you're making some sense. Ela, do you really think I'm so naïve? Now, try again."

"I just told you. That's the truth, Alek. Now, you look me in the eyes...that's the truth, but please don't make me repeat it, or I might change my mind."

"No, no, I believe you, I do. I'm sorry, just wanted to make sure."

"Forgiven, but only the part about education wasn't entirely true. I'm in here for more than just improving my reading and writing. I started late, two weeks into the year. Problems with admission. They did me a favor, I guess. That's what the director said, but it's behind me now, and I'm glad to be here."

"You know, somehow I've always known that you are here for more than just reading and writing. You're much more than that," said Alek with a big smile, truly amused by the conversation.

"Well, Alek Brodski, I wish I could talk to you longer, but I must be going back to class now. Math. That's not something I'm looking forward to. By the way, how is your math?"

"Sorry, can't help you with that, if that's what you mean. I'm struggling myself. For me, it's history now."

"So, what's your thing? Anything you're good at?"

"Oh yes, you can count on me with Polish, all the required reading, Russian, history, geography, biology, introduction to you know what, and art. Count me out with chemistry, physics, and math, of course."

"Oh good, I might find you useful after all."

"Yes, I'll be at your service. Is there anything I can count on in return?"

"Of course, a lot, but what do you have in mind?"

"Oh my god...What a day! I can't believe it, it's a dream...A beautiful woman is offering me her services. I knew I could count on you. You've proven it once before by saving my life," said Alek, completely at ease and laughing.

"Now, I must go. As much as I'd like to stay and talk to you, I must go," said Ela, equally delighted.

"So, till tomorrow?"

"Till tomorrow."

Alek stood in the corridor, by the wall, looking at Ela departing quickly, navigating between students rushing back to their classes. She turned around once, looked at him one last time, and then disappeared behind a corner. Alek waited for a few more minutes for much of the foot traffic to pass, and he was sad. He was strongly under the impression of what had just happened, and couldn't quite get over the effect Ela had just made on him, when least expected, right here in this school, where he'd spend almost the next four years. This girl was something else, unlike anyone he'd met before. It all seemed too good to be true.

What was it? There had to be something he didn't understand; he didn't quite get it. Why did she stand up in his defense back there on the street last summer? Why did she really get enrolled in this school? Was it really true what she was saying, that she wanted to see him? Did she give up what she was doing? At the same time, Alek couldn't help but think that when he talked to her, he was a changed young man from a quiet, shy, and withdrawn teen. With Ela, he was completely transformed, at ease and confident, as if he had known her for at least a few years, as if she was his sister, his soul mate.

Is this just a passing dream, or is it real? How long will it last? Will she eventually get bored and move on? What about that crowd she was hanging out with? She couldn't just give up and cut off all her connections. They wouldn't let her even if she tried, Alek thought. But she had shown to be most determined, if she wanted to be. He was definitely impressed by Ela's fearless attitude, unlike his own, which he could not control in the face of adversity, real or imagined danger. A year before, he was confronted with exactly that: the danger was real, and he could not stand up to the thugs, did nothing to fend them off, or even attempt to defend himself. The old woman Pavloska, who happened to walk by, showed instant, unrestrained courage and saved him from most likely more verbal, humiliating insults, tousling around, and a beating.

20

TUESDAY, OCTOBER 1, at sundown, and the tenth day of the month Tishri marked the beginning of the holiest day in the Hebrew lunar calendar, Yom Kippur, the Day of Atonement, preceded by a period called the Ten days of Awe, Rosh Hashanah. The holy days since September 12 leading to Yom Kippur were not particularly celebrated by Alek and his mom; and as for the personal reflection, self-examination, and repentance, they thought they'd done it year round, and possibly even too much of it, anyway.

However, on the day of Yom Kippur, Alek took a day off school, as did Mrs. Brodski a day off work, and they just stayed home, especially since it was such a miserable day outside; and they fasted for most of the day at least. Alek spent many hours thinking about his decision to convert to Christianity, struggled with it, prayed earnestly, and asked God for forgiveness, in case he committed a serious transgression, begging for guidance, hoping all would be eventually exonerated and the upcoming year would be, indeed, a turning point in his life. After all, God was one, Jesus Christ was a Jew, and his actions were seeking the glory of God, his own ultimate salvation and, in the meantime, a place in community he felt excluded from.

Alek and his mother didn't talk much throughout the day but mostly kept to themselves. However, by the end of the day, in the evening, she occupied herself with light household chores, and Alek tried to catch up on his homework.

The school as the time went on, and well into the autumn, was increasingly becoming a fight for survival. Many teachers, who initially displayed a well-maintained composure, civility, and restraint, dropped their facades; and by November, just like the change of seasons, had shown their true colors. It seemed that for many, teaching through terror, threats, and intimidation was the norm. They relished the unconstrained power and tolerated no dissent, just because they could, knowing well they wouldn't be challenged, and that was how the system had always worked, from the top down. For many students, the unreasonably heavy load of school subjects—and with them lab classes; experiments on the old, outdated equipment; and then the amount of homework, assignments, group projects, required reading, followed by periodic quizzes and tests—was the end of any positive notions of the middle school they had. Those who since early childhood harbored noble dreams and hopes for a better future, as most of them did, had to abandon them along the way, adapt, and bury them deeply in their severely strained minds, and quickly realize it was mostly about day-to-day survival. By now, relatively closely guarded friendships, networks of support groups, and cliques of like-minded students were well formed.

Alek found himself mostly on the sidelines, increasingly isolated, except for occasional interactions with a few generally perceived misfits for their total lack of any athletic abilities, unappealing physical looks, their attire, or just their general tendencies toward scholastic achievement, despite the highly regimented and often brutally unforgiving program, than about popularity among the students or personal favors from the mostly miserable teachers.

Ela became Alek's most frequent and faithful companion, although he met her few times a week in the cafeteria, or the corridors of school, and occasionally walking back a short distance from school before she turned off in different direction and headed back home. It didn't go unnoticed, and became just another added reason for resentment and harassment by the popular school "elites," or the tough guys, who were setting the tone, the general, prevailing atmosphere and governing conduct besides the official rules set out and strictly enforced by the school administrators. Just to be seen in the crowd with an attractive girl like Ela, for a few of those "strong but stupid types" was more than they could take, and invited fits of jealousy and the most incredulous comments: "Have you seen who that Jew is going out with? Can you believe that?" they would say, thinking they themselves had to settle for second best when compared to Ela. No, they wouldn't miss an opportunity to let their resentment be known through intimidating, disdainful stares, vulgarities. They would block Alek's path, or "accidentally" bump into him from time to time, when their frustration boiled over, assuming, and rightly so, that Alek would not defend himself. Yes, he just stood there, looking and waiting with bewilderment, unable to move, expecting the worst, which never came, because something always happened. The traffic flowed, the bell rang, someone intervened, or teachers approached and they would all scatter in different directions.

The weather was increasingly and noticeably colder by the day, with gusts of chilly air and a mixture of freezing rain and early snow from across the border, the vast flatlands of the Soviet Union, and as always, inviting the familiar sarcastic remark from the locals: "Nothing good has ever come to us from the east."

The school became even more inhospitable with its dim lighting, dingy, decrepit, poorly heated classrooms and corridors, with old, outdated radiator heating system fed by coal or metallurgical coke shipped from the southern mills, a pile of which was a permanent feature in the back of the school, by the small rectangular windows set just above the ground, with direct access to the basement boiler room. The fuel was shoveled inside through the low windows with broken glass, by the boiler room operator, an older man who was well known to all. He was always in tattered clothing, with blackened stringy hands and arms smeared with ash and coal dust, and a tired face covered with wrinkles. He had been around the school for as long as anybody could remember.

Mr. Anastazy Kotlinski was a good-natured chap, a widower who kept to himself but had much sympathy and understanding for the students striving to gain education against all odds, under the most unfavorable conditions, because he himself had very little and was clearly ashamed of that. It was a common practice by the school administrators and many teachers, as a punishment for most infractions, to send male students, "the rotten apples," to help the old Kotlinski shovel the coal.

DOMINIK POLESKI

Anastazy was delighted to be relieved of the most arduous task of his thankless and lonely job, when eager equally delighted young men, only too happy to get away from the stress of the classroom, dropped in unexpectedly from time to time to give him a hand, keep him company, and smoke a cheap cigarette that the boiler attendant generously shared with them during a well-deserved break from the heavy shovel. At regular intervals, although infrequent, Anastazy didn't show up for work, as if reminding all those student ingrates and teachers alike not to take him for granted, that he deserved respect regardless of the rampant, angry speculation that the previous night he was simply self-medicating again, got sloshed, and couldn't drag himself out of bed.

The school, without the heat, was freezing: with fogged-up windows, unbearably cold chairs and desks one would not dare to sit on. The students and teachers would rather stand or pace around, wearing their coats, the girls huddling together, gnashing their teeth, surrounded by clouds of vapor, and panic slowly setting in, before word came from the school director, Comrade Dymalski, that the classes shall be dismissed for the rest of the day. The well-known expression commonly used around town, "It is cold like an old whore's heart," was often repeated by mostly male students, who thought it was a perfect metaphor for the chilly and miserable days like these. It was a rare opportunity for Alek to spend more time with Ela and walk her home, which she didn't object to this time, unlike his few previous attempts, citing a variety of often-trivial reasons to cool off his enthusiasm, just in case he expected to be invited inside the house at the end of the journey.

Despite the dreary day, they were both quite excited about having most of the school day off, a rare opportunity, but something they both strongly agreed on, perhaps for different reasons, that particular school was not a place they enjoyed spending their time in. It was Saturday, the sixth day of the week; and it meant all schools, offices, and government businesses worked till one o'clock in the afternoon, which was generally recognized as one of those few tangible achievements of socialism.

The Party never failed to remind the populace and frequently promote this, as their benevolent gesture for the benefit of the working classes, while reminding them that on the other side of the Iron Curtain, they were still all stuck in the age not much different from that of the Industrial Revolution, when a twelve-hour work day was the norm and child labor was as common as child education nowadays.

Alek and Ela walked slowly, enjoying every moment, paying little attention to the light, cold drizzle mixed with the swirling sparse snowflakes quickly melting midair and then disappearing before reaching the ground. As much as Alek tried not to think about possibly being invited inside Ela's home, he was increasingly apprehensive. What would he say? How would he behave as she introduced him to her parents?

"What are you planning to do for the rest of the day?" asked Alek along the way, trying to test her intentions.

"I'm behind with my studies—in fact, with almost everything—and you're going to help me', she said without hesitation.

"Am I?" asked Alek, caught off guard.

"Yes, you will, won't you?"

"Oh yes, of course."

"I'm glad to hear that, or you'd regret it."

"I would? What would I regret, if I may ask?"

"You would regret all the missed rewards expecting you."

"Now you're making things interesting. I can't wait."

"Another good trait you have that I like…you're so agreeable."

"You're too kind, my dear," Alek said and finally burst out laughing.

"Don't laugh, Mr. Brodski. You must understand, in the end, a woman always gets what she wants."

"How prophetic, and what is it that you want?

"In the immediate future, my homework done, tons of it. And as for the rest, we'll see. It will depend on the academic results first. You mentioned on a few occasions in the past that literature and history are your passions, and apparently, you've already read most required books till the end of the fourth year. Well, you're just who I need right now, because as you well know, literature is not something I'm crazy about. I have other worthwhile, less consuming, and more pleasurable passions."

"My understanding is, you desire my invaluable services with writing essays, summarizing books of prose and poetry, conveying to you what

DOMINIK POLESKI

they're all about, and preparing you for the tests so you don't have to spend too much of your precious time on those tedious tasks, right?"

"Right, very nicely said. I knew you were the perfect man for the job."

"It looks to me that our cooperation will undoubtedly flourish, under the circumstances, and let me assure you, I'm committed, but let me just go over the details of our agreement one more time, madam. What's in there for me?"

"Oh, my dear prince wasn't paying attention…I thought I made myself abundantly clear."

"Not so, not so. Please repeat it, princess, if you don't mind."

"Not at all, I'll be happy to. Tell me, when you're with me, what's really on your mind? What is it that you want most? What's your greatest desire?"

"Oh my god, are you reading my mind? It's a deal."

"The question is, are you up to it, Alek? I just might test your commitment sooner than you think."

"Don't worry about me. Just make sure you don't renege on your end of the bargain, my dear."

"Alek, I'm not sure what's really on your mind, but don't get carried away. Aren't you more concerned about winning all those wars you've been waging with your toy soldiers?"

"Ela, for your information, all the wars have been won a long time ago. Now it's time for consolidation of powers that come with the territories and to collect the spoils of the wars."

"Let me just ask you, seriously now; does your mom know about me?"

"Yes, she does."

"What did you tell her?"

"You have no reason to be concerned. Actually, I told her about you the day after that night near the restaurant last summer. I didn't tell her everything, of course, but enough to know that you're someone special."

"Could you be more specific?" Ela continued with her usual playfulness.

"Well, she knows you're my friend, and that you've got guts, you're witty, sweet, fun to be with, and, of course, pretty," replied Alek, taking on a more serious demeanor and emphasizing each word.

"That's all?"

"What do you mean, that's all? I told Mom all she needs to know from me. The rest you can tell her yourself."

"It sounds like an invitation to me. So, when will I meet your mom?"

"Actually, it's up to you. No pressure. I'm open to suggestions. Whenever is convenient for you is fine with me, or should I say for us."

"I'll let you know."

They were both unusually at ease and happy, walking slowly and laughing, as if nothing else around them mattered, or even existed, and time was at a standstill; and they didn't mind, in spite of the heavy, overcast, and gloomy weather. They were fast approaching Ela's home in an old and poor neighborhood, just like almost any other, on the outskirts but still relatively close to the town's center—a long walking distance, one could say. They passed a few ordinary people on their way, going about their business in both directions, without paying any attention to the world around them, just scurrying along the wet sidewalks with their heads down, as if shielding themselves from the biting, cold drizzle.

Alek and Ela were already almost completely drenched, bent over, dragging along their dripping bags full of books and school supplies they carried with them every day, and it all didn't matter, at least not for a few precious hours, even under the gray, heavy sky. Before they reached the door of Ela's house, she had already pulled a key from her navy-blue trench coat pocket and, without hesitation, opened the door and pulled Alek right behind her before he even had a chance to utter a word, still thinking about the conversation they had along the way.

Once they were inside, she quickly took her coat off, hung it on a freestanding wooden coat hanger in the foyer just inside, behind the front door, took her wet shoes off, and literally ordered Alek to do the same. She pulled on the sleeves of his heavy black overcoat, one by one, while he struggled to free himself from it, and then once off, he threw it on top of the already-overloaded hanger, and his wet hat even higher. He left his schoolbag on the floor, by the wall, right beside the coat hanger. Alek didn't even have time to think, say anything, or resist when he was pulled by the arm from the foyer and into the kitchen, leaving a wet trail behind him.

Ela's mother stood just inside the kitchen and seemed rather startled and uncomfortable seeing Alek right behind her daughter—something she was obviously not prepared for.

"Mom, I want you to meet my friend Alek," Ela said without hesitation.

Mrs. Nowak stretched out her hand to greet Alek, but their eyes met only for a split second, as she almost instantly lowered her head and turned sideways; but it was still long enough for Alek to notice what seemed like bruises and a black eye on her pale face.

"Mom, the classes were dismissed for the rest of the day. There was no heat in school. It was freezing, so we came home. I invited Alek to help me with some studies and homework. He's really good at many things."

"It's probably an exaggeration to say I'm good at many things, but I try," said Alek, equally uncomfortable in the strange surroundings.

"Don't mind me, do what you have to. Please go right inside the living room," Mrs. Nowak said dismissively, with her back to them.

"Good. Follow me, Alek," said Ela, pulling him behind her to the next room.

Once they were in the living room, Alek couldn't resist the temptation to look around, although he tried to do it most discreetly. It was only on a few occasions that he had an opportunity to be in other people's homes in his entire life; he and his mom just never went anywhere. It was extremely seldom that anyone invited them, and even if they were invited on rare occasions, his mother usually turned down the invitation, using all possible excuses she could come up with.

Ela's living room was of average, middle size, but crammed with all kinds of old, outdated furniture accumulated over the years, and which probably had its purpose. One thing was certain: it definitely was not a household of affluence; on the contrary, it was of rather modest means, to say the least, and like most families in town, the Nowaks were caught up in the never-ending cycle of grinding poverty and misery, which there seemed to be no way out of. Although the room had two windows, it was relatively dark, which Ela, immediately remedied by turning on the light switch near the entrance door frame. The three-bulb chandelier, centered on the ceiling above, lit up the room, casting a weak yellow light over the entire area.

"Have a seat, Alek, wherever you want," said Ela.

"Thanks," he said and sat on the sofa, up against one of the gray walls.

"You must be cold. It's not very warm in here either, but at least it's not as cold as the school. How about if I make some tea?

"That would be nice."

"Wait then. Feel at home. I'll be back shortly," Ela said and then hastily left the room. Alek, while waiting, looked around with genuine interest, further exploring the room, its every corner, the floor, and every piece of furniture and decoration there was. There was no luxury here, just simple basics all around, which withstood the test of time. Even the smell inside the room seemed old, as if well established, but delicate and pleasant, an integral part of the surroundings, not at all offensive to a new visitor unaccustomed to the strange home. Although his first impression upon entering was that of a very old, cluttered, and disorganized mess, he came to realize on a second look, that it was actually quite functional; everything had its place and purpose, and above all, the place was tidy and clean.

Ela was back soon with a blue towel over her shoulder, two mugs already filled with fresh tea, a sugar bowl with a spoon in it, and two napkins. She set the drinks on the table. Her hair was already ruffled up and dried with the same towel that she handed to Alek.

"Here, dry yourself up," she said.

"Thanks," he said and rubbed the towel quickly and vigorously over his head, face, and neck.

"Let's sit at the table, Alek."

"Sure, is everything all right?"

"Yes, of course. Why do you ask?"

"Maybe this is not the best time for a visit?"

"Oh no, it's just as good as any."

"Doesn't your mom mind? She seemed unwell. I had a feeling she was distraught."

"No, she doesn't mind at all. She knows about you. You've noticed she was upset? What else have you noticed?" inquired Ela.

It was obvious to Alek that she was referring to the clearly visible bruises on her mother's face, and decided to avoid the subject.

"What did you tell your mom about me?"

"Don't worry, nothing bad. I mean, just look at you—you're a walking virtue."

"What? That means you don't know me at all."

"I know you well enough, Alek. I think you're a good, smart man, unspoiled by the world around us yet. You seem so innocent, almost like someone from a different planet."

"Well, my dear, that's all very interesting how you see me, but I wouldn't entirely agree with your assessment, and neither would my own mother, I assure you. Anything negative about me?"

"Yes, but I'm not sure it can be called negative. I get the impression you're a little naïve at times, that you believe in a world which doesn't exist. You think following the Ten Commandments will guarantee your success."

"Naïve? You must be joking. I disagree, again, with your opinion. How about my looks? My hair, my eyes, my dark complexion, which all seem to be a problem for some people. I look different, unlike the people around here."

"What looks? Don't be silly. If anything, you're rather good-looking, I must say, but don't let it go to your head."

"I'm a Jew, and I look like a Jew. Everybody knows that."

"So…it's not written on your forehead that you're a Jew. It shouldn't make any difference, certainly not to me."

"I never told you this, but just over a year ago, I got beaten up pretty badly in the alley, just off the main street. I think exactly for that reason."

"That's horrible! What happened?"

"I'm sorry, Ela, but I'd rather not talk about it. It's all behind me now."

"Why won't you tell me? Who did this to you?"

"Really, I don't want to talk about it, or my whole day will be ruined."

"No problem. But at least tell me, who was it? Anybody I know?"

"Believe it or not, it was Commandant Sokolowski's son, with two others you must have seen here and there. An old woman, Pavloska, who happened to walk by, saved my arse."

"Did you report it to the police? Did you tell Sokolowski the elder about it?"

"Yes, my mom went to the station, and then both of us, but as expected, it was a total waste of time. Sokolowski said he conducted an investigation and denied his son had anything to do with it."

"Of course he will deny it, that bloody bastard. I hate them. They all think they're above the law. They're all crooked. They've been taking kickbacks from my friend Anka, whom you must have seen on the street last summer, just so they'd leave her alone. I won't even mention what else they want from her, but you can imagine. Of course, they've been hustling that old man Ivan for years and years. They want a cut from the liquor he sells. Everybody knows they buy from him too, especially that fat boozer Kovaluk, Sokolowski's deputy."

"I didn't know all that," said Alek.

"Now you know. How are you supposed to know if you're stuck in the house most of the time with your mom?"

"Those kinds of things wouldn't interest me anyway. That's something I don't even want to know."

"Fair enough. So, how did it all end with Sokolowski's son and the assault?"

"Nothing came of it. He denied everything. My mom didn't want Pavloska, who witnessed it all, to get involved any further, and of course, Sokolowski didn't want to do anything about it either. That's all in the past, so let's not talk about it anymore."

"Right, let's talk about homework, shall we. I need an essay done on Renaissance. Jan Kochanowski and his literary works."

"Have you borrowed the book of his poetry from the library?"

"Yes, I have."

"Have you read it?"

"Not all of it, only about two-thirds."

"And what do you think about it? What do you have problems with?"

"I don't understand a lot from his writings. It's all written in this old sixteenth-century Polish that I don't get, much less any profound messages or ideas he's trying to convey."

Ela pulled out the book of poetry, and some notebooks and pens from her schoolbag. She spread it on the table and looked at Alek with anticipation. He glanced at her and at all her school supplies on the table, smiled, and slowly took a sip of tea, as if gathering his thoughts. They both sat in silence for two or three minutes, visibly enjoying each other's company, as if time was of no essence, and the more it dragged on, the happier they seemed to be.

Alek momentarily had the impression he'd known her for a long time, as if they'd always belonged to each other but were waiting only for the right moment to finally meet. What happened on the street the past summer had to be a destiny fulfilled, although under rather dramatic circumstances. Occasionally, Alek caught himself being carried away by his excessive imagination and silly, youthful notions of a future life together, joy, happiness, and possibly even family life. The fact that Ela wasn't fond of literature or history didn't bother him at all; on the contrary, he found it that much more interesting, an opportunity for him to shine. Ela, undoubtedly, had other positive qualities and attributes he found most compelling: she was bright, quick witted, courageous, mature well beyond her years, loyal, ambitious, and pretty. Despite her young age, she already had a past not to be proud of, and for a time until quite recently, had an enviable reputation in the town's night life circles.

Nevertheless, Alek felt that to be seen with Ela, one would not be compromised, but most certainly, it could be a reason to provoke jealousy, possibly leading to something more serious. She had the admirable looks, wits, charm, and manners like no one else he'd ever seen or been around. To him she was irresistible, even knowing her past, at times he was overwhelmed with a persistent, nagging question: "Why me?"

Alek took the book of poetry by Kochanowski into his hands and slowly flipped several pages, pausing from time to time, and reading a few verses with a barely audible murmur, while Ela watched his every move with genuine curiosity. Soon Alek stopped scanning the pages, took one of Ela's notebooks with lined pages, turned it to the back with an obvious gesture of attempting to tear out a few clean sheets, and asked, "May I?"

"Be my guest," she answered.

"I will write a general outline, analyzing his major pieces, what the author is trying to convey, their impact and place in Polish literature, because those will be the only ones most likely discussed in class. Jan Kochanowski's poetry is unique in a sense that it introduced new forms of writing never before produced in our literature, and now are considered indispensable classics. Probably his best-known works are the threnodies, a series of elegies he wrote after the death of his beloved two-and-a-half-year-old little daughter, Ursula. His other highly regarded works are the epigrams. I'll write for you also some general conclusions that the teacher will probably place particular importance on, and you can expand it in your own words. I think you have to read the book too, and if you'll read it more than once, you might find the old Polish quite comprehensible. You should also read the introduction in the beginning of the book, if you haven't already. It practically covers everything. Promise me you'll read it."

"I promise," Ela said with a big grin.

Alek begun to write, quickly filling the page, occasionally making some verbal comments and referring back to the book, then filling in the second blank page of paper in much the same fashion. Then he stopped halfway through the third page, lifted his head, and looked at Ela, satisfied with his accomplishment.

"I was only going to write an outline, but it turned out to be almost the whole essay. As I said, you've got to read this thing, it's not that much. You could probably read it in a few hours, I'm sure. I went through some of his most popular works already in the eighth grade, so not that long ago. We had to memorize one of his poems, and recite it in front of the class."

"So, which one did you recite?"

"Threnody number 7, a rather short piece. How about you?"

"I'm impressed. We had the same thing in our class, but I'm sorry to tell you I have nothing to brag about. I can't remember a thing."

A distinct, muffled sound of doors being slammed reached them in the living room, followed by a commotion in the corridor, which seemed to have moved quickly into the kitchen, and then a hostile exchange between a male and a female, who was most certainly Ela's mother. Alek sat motionless and looked at Ela with profound concern as her demeanor suddenly changed. She too sat and listened intently, without uttering a word, waiting for the incident in the kitchen to unfold, or just die down on its own, without further escalation or need for intervention. The male voice turned into incoherent shouts, interspersed with only a few brief conciliatory words in a much more subdued tone from the female.

"My dad is back from work', said Ela with tears welling up in her eyes.

"Should I leave now?" asked Alek.

"No, please stay."

"I'm sorry for asking, but is there a problem?"

"Yes, there is a problem, almost every time he comes back from work."

"I know it's none of my business, and I feel sorry for you and your mom, but what is it about?"

"He comes back drunk, that's what it is all about. And if he's not, he comes back with a bottle of vodka and starts drinking."

"How long has this been going on?"

"Almost as long as I can remember…"

"I'm really sorry to hear that. Is he getting violent?"

"Of course. You've seen the marks on my mom's face, haven't you?"

"Yes, unfortunately. That's so sad. I feel for both of you, but I think I should be going, just in case things get out of control."

"No, please stay, Alek, exactly for that reason. I want him to realize that other people know what's going on too."

The sounds from the kitchen were getting louder and louder by the minute. Unmistakably, there was an all-out argument, with Ela's mother no longer in a pleading, subservient tone, but unceremoniously confronting her husband. Ela got up from her chair and started to move haltingly toward the living room door, when came the sound of objects shoved around, followed by a loud bang, and the piercing noise of shattered glass. Ela grabbed the door handle and stormed out of the room, leaving the door ajar, apparently without trying to conceal what was happening.

"Let go of my arm! Let go of me!" shouted Mrs. Nowak.

"Dad, please let go of Mom," said Ela.

"You shut up! Don't interfere!" Mr. Nowak shot back in a slurred speech.

"No, I won't shut up. You should be ashamed of yourself," continued Ela.

"You get out of here! It's none of your business!" shouted her father.

"It is my business. I won't let you hit Mom again. I'm not afraid of you anymore."

"Just look at you, you have no shame. You're completely wasted," said Mrs. Nowak in a contemptuous voice.

"I said shut up, both of you! I'll do whatever the hell I want!" Mr. Nowak shouted again.

"Oh no, you won't anymore. Get out of the house, you hopeless drunkard!" added Mrs. Nowak.

"What did you say? Get out of my way, you bitch, or I'll…I'll…"

"If you ever lift your hand at Mom again, I swear to God, I'll kill you!" shouted Ela.

"What did you just say, you little whore? Get out of here, both of you get out! Get out of my house!" shouted Mr. Nowak, struggling to pronounce the words.

"For your information, it is as much our house as it is yours, if not more, in case you haven't noticed, being drunk all the time," said Mrs. Nowak.

"I make the real money around here, and you two spend it," said Mr. Nowak.

"You've lost your mind. What is there to spend? Most of the money you make, you spend on booze. You have no clue what we do here to put food on the table and to pay the bills," said Mrs. Nowak.

"You both have no clue what I do, how hard I work, what stress I go through to make some money, and it's never enough. What the hell am I supposed to do? Steal? There is no hope in this fucking country, no hope in this bloody system that was supposed to take care of its working class. It's all a big lie, it's a fraud! I can't expect any help from you, so I may as well drink and forget."

"Where is any logic to that? To drink and forget? Do you ever think about your wife and your daughter? Do you ever think how we pay for food, fuel, and electricity? Do you, you pitiful drunkard, know that the last time I bought something for myself was probably three years ago?" Ela's mother continued with a trembling voice.

"I've heard enough! Clean up the broken glass, you useless sluts!" shouted Mr. Nowak, swaying on his wobbly legs.

"You broke it, you clean it up," said Ela.

Mr. Nowak began to pace around the kitchen with his head down, shattered glass crackling under his feet, slowly moving toward the door and then to the living room, glancing back at his wife and his daughter with his fogged-up eyes and a disdainful sneer on his lips.

"Don't go there!" shouted Ela with a hint of panic in her voice.

He didn't react, but he barged noisily into the living room and, just as fast, stopped in his tracks once he noticed Alek standing next to the table, looking frightened, as if expecting a storm to unleash its fury.

"Who the hell are you?" asked Mr. Nowak

Ela and her mother, who followed him into the living room, quickly moved in between them to prevent any escalation, or should matters get out of control, they were ready to react in what seemed like a well-rehearsed maneuver.

"He's my friend, just visiting us," explained Ela.

"What is he doing in my house?" asked her father, pointing at Alek, visibly surprised by his presence.

"As I said, he's visiting. We were doing some homework," replied Ela.

"Why is he in my living room? What's going on here?" continued Mr. Nowak with increasing agitation.

"You leave him alone. This nice young man is Ela's good friend from school. They were studying, that's all. Just leave him alone and get out of here," said Ela's mom forcefully.

"I want him out of my house!" shouted Mr. Nowak, taking two steps toward Alek.

Both women immediately moved in, one on each side; grabbed him decisively by his arms; and blocked him from going any farther. He was swaying on his legs, breathing heavily, and staring menacingly at the young man in front of him. Suddenly, in a most strenuous effort to free himself, he twisted his body to the right, swung his right arm above his shoulder and pulling his wife with it, trying to loosen the restraint, while Ela still held on to his left arm.

Alek, in a split second, decided it was time for him to leave. He leaped to the side and out of the way, and then hurriedly retreated into the corridor leading in a straight line to the exit door. Without hesitation, he jumped into his wet boots, threw on his heavy damp coat and hat, bent over and grabbed his packed schoolbag, looked back one last time, and then pressed the door handle.

Ela rushed out of the living room and with tears in her eyes, threw her arms around Alek's neck. "I'm so sorry about this," she said trembling.

"Don't worry about me, I understand. I'm sorry for you and your mom," he said with sadness in his voice, looking straight into her tears-filled blue eyes.

"Thank you for your help. I wouldn't be able to do it myself."

"I'm happy to be of help. I'll see you on Monday. If anything happens, you can always come to my home. You know where I live," said Alek

"Thank you. See you," said Ela with sincere gratitude.

They stood there motionless, embracing, and without saying a word for several seconds. Then renewed commotion coming from the living

DOMINIK POLESKI

room told them it was time to go. Alek slowly opened the door, as if trying not to disturb Ela's father any more than he already was. They were hit by a strong gust of wind with droplets of cold rain swirling around and stirring the surrounding trees. Alek stepped outside, turned around, and looked one last time at Ela standing in the doorway, with a feeble, yellowish light in the corridor of her house behind her. She waved delicately, and he responded with his own slight hand gesture. Then he turned with his head down, nestled between the large upright collar of his coat, and his sagging schoolbag in his right hand, and he quickly departed.

21

ALL SAINTS' DAY, November 1, 1968, was a day of much increased activity in town, just like the weekly open market day, except it was a day free of school and work, and like a national holiday, it was celebrated across the country. It was a chilly, overcast day with gray, shifting clouds stretching right across the sky; and as expected, there were no breaks in sight for a foreseeable future. Sporadic gusts of wind brought with it cold showers, adding to the gloomy, unpleasant atmosphere and somber mood, which, like a dark veil, shrouded the town.

Despite the dismal weather, hundreds of visitors descended for the yearly commemoration, filling the streets, the church, a few restaurants, and the cemeteries alongside the locals out in force. The Catholic cemetery was by far the largest, covering a wooded area of irregular shape, surrounded by a white concrete wall, located in the northwestern part, a considerable walking distance from the town's center. The cemetery was well organized, with several alleys crossing the grounds in different directions, and rows upon rows of graves marked by simple crosses, gravestones, tombstones of different sizes, or more elaborate large monuments bearing inscriptions of the name, date of birth and death of the deceased person, and an epitaph in memory of the loved one.

At the wide entrance gate, a few vendors, always in search of ways to make some extra cash, were peddling their homemade stick candles, or the more popular ones in small and thick, colored glass containers for those who didn't get around to buy them in advance at the local store, now closed for the day. Two older women, just inside the gates, were selling a few varieties of cut-flower bouquets and flowers in brown terra cotta clay pots at very reasonable prices.

The Eastern Orthodox cemetery was much smaller, surrounded by an old, rusty chain-link fence, but nicely settled near a picturesque, secluded pond overgrown with mature trees and evergreen shrubs in the vicinity of the Orthodox Church. Next to the Orthodox cemetery, on an even smaller plot, was the Jewish cemetery, surrounded by its own remnants of broken and rusted chain-link fence; and at the entrance, at the end of a narrow, old dirt-and-gravel pathway, equally badly damaged, was a permanently wide open iron gate made of long, two-meter-high square rods welded up together with cross bars. The cemetery contained perhaps few dozen upright tombstones, scattered over most of the area, without any particular order, many of them leaning, as the ground around them eroded over time. Almost all the tombstones were severely weathered and blackened, a few crumbling by the effects of changing weather over years and decades, surrounded by high, dense grass and bent weeds discolored by the fast-changing season.

Alek and his mother took advantage of the solemn occasion and the official day off to visit the grave of Jakub Brodski, their husband and father. In the early afternoon, they got dressed in their best autumn attire and walked several blocks to the site of his grave. The tombstone of Jakub Brodski, made by a local mason, was only one of three relatively new ones, and they had no idea who they belonged to; they didn't recognize the names. Most of them were buried there before World War II, a few during the war, and a few in the years since.

The little plot that included the tombstone of Jakub was the best maintained of them all; in fact, it was the only one that had signs of regular upkeep. The other two more recent graves, possibly erected sometime in the last decade, seemed to have been visited at least several months before, suggesting that the family of the deceased were not local residents but lived out of town, but for reasons that would never be known, buried their loved ones here, in this small town, near the border with the Soviet Union. The rest of the tombstones had been abandoned, forgotten, and eventually overgrown, without any recognizable path leading to any of them.

Alek and his mom each placed a candle in a small, blue glass container, as was a common practice on this particular day. They also laid a pebble that each had picked up on the road to the cemetery on both sides of the arched top of the headstone with a Star of David in the center, and which turned into symmetrical flat stone shelves. They stood in silence, looked at the familiar simple inscription in Polish and the dates that meant only one thing: he died too early, he died too young:

Jakub Brodski
Beloved Husband and Father
17.4.1924–28.10.1961

They prayed earnestly in silence, standing close together with their heads bowed for several minutes before they noticed an elderly man in a long gray trench coat tending to one of the graves, pulling at the weeds and flattening the old, dry grass and invading withered branches of low shrubs on all sides. They looked at the man working with considerable exertion, care, and dedication around the grave of his loved one, and reflected on their own lives, full of loneliness, uncertainty, pain, and grief. On this day, they both, in their own ways, missed Jakub more than ever, and were again cruelly reminded how life was unfair, for some more so than others.

It was futile to endlessly speculate, as many had before them for generations, on the mystery of life and try to make sense of it all. For Alek, every year set him apart even farther from the cherished memory of his father, and increasingly he had to make an even greater effort to cling to whatever was left of it, to the remaining scattered, precious pieces in his fragile mind. In the corner of his eye, to the left, Alek noticed his mom pulling a white handkerchief from her purse and, with a delicate touch, dried her eyes. Soon he couldn't resist the tears rolling down his eyes, and could barely control his pent-up emotions and try not to sob openly in the wake of increasingly surging feeling of unbearable grief.

The gloomy weather, the surrounding eerie silence with infrequent, indiscernible voices coming from the adjacent Eastern Orthodox cemetery, and occasional gusts of wind bringing with it the smells of autumn leaves mixed with the distinct, stirring-the-senses smells of burning candles, evoked a strange feeling of despair and hopelessness and distant memories. The dark, low-hanging and shifting clouds above the town and this patch of wooded area, with candles flickering through the swinging low branches and skeletons of bushes swaying gently in the wind, magnified the somber mood of the occasion commemorating and honoring the deceased, who lay there with their secrets, undisturbed in eternal sleep.

Alek's mother, without looking, sensed his internal struggle to control his emotions. She moved closer and placed her right arm around his shoulders. Alek, who could barely maintain his placid composure, shivered momentarily from her unexpected loving, motherly gesture, and under the weight of her embrace. Reassured, yet holding back tears, he slowly moved closer and leaned his head to the side, toward his mother, and he was sad.

22

ECEMBER 6, AS every year marked St. Nicholas Day, happened to be Friday, and not celebrated in any meaningful way in the Brodski household, although Alek was very much under the influence of schoolmates and the activities of the closest neighbors, who celebrated in their own ways, or not at all. Alek and his mom were all consumed with preparations for Saturday, the fateful day they'd been waiting for, for a long time, the day which, according to Father Antoni, was supposed to change his life—the baptism.

All the arrangements were already in place after two additional trips to the rectory of St. John's church, during which the ever-consummate priest was by then completely charmed by Mrs. Brodski, and it became impossible to tell whether his seemingly selfless support and unmitigated enthusiasm was for Alek's baptism, for or his apparent infatuation with his mother. Nevertheless, Father Antoni was impressed and pleasantly surprised by Alek's overall progress in the knowledge of the Bible, his maturity, and renewed commitment to life as a Christian in the near future. He no longer questioned their decision to have Alek baptized and to take that fateful step to become a member of the congregation, but accepted their initial explanation as a sufficient and justified reason to become fully integrated in the local community for years to come.

It was universally understood that life in these parts was hard and centered around work, seemingly never-ending chores, and the daily struggle for basic necessities. The Church gave people hope that there was something better awaiting them in heaven, an eternal joy and happiness, a paradise and life everlasting, as proclaimed by Jesus Christ, the Son of God. To get to the Promised Land, all one had to do was to believe, to follow the Ten Commandments, and diligently practice a weekly generous offering, preferably a tenth of one's income, when the collection basket came around during Sunday Mass. All those who were deprived, wronged, abused, and mistreated in their temporal life here on earth would be abundantly rewarded by the Father in heaven, and their tormentors would be condemned to the eternal fires of hell, for death is the great equalizer and God is just. In Luke 18:25 Jesus said: "For it is easier for a camel to go through the eye of a needle, than for a rich man to enter the kingdom of God." And further, according to the gospel of Luke 9:48 "Whoever is the least among you all, is the greatest." For most people those words were the ultimate consolation; after all, who to believe if not the town's highest moral authority, the parish priest and its undisputed messenger of God.

It was already dark outside, with a light snow falling from the sky and reflected in the dim light cast from the tall lampposts lining the main street on the north side, slowly adding to the already-thin layer of the powder covering the streets and sidewalks, with few freshly impressed tire tracks in both directions and scattered footprints of various shapes and sizes, quickly disappearing under new white snow.

The temperature was already hovering around -13C, and as expected, at this time of the year in these parts, perhaps colder than in most other areas of the country, being heavily influenced by the unforgiving, bleak weather patterns of the neighboring vast, flat stretches of the Byelorussian Republic of the Soviet Union to the east. It was almost six o'clock in the evening, and Alek and his mother were running late, but they walked slowly, hunched together and mostly in silence toward St. John's church, taking cautious steps so as not to slip and fall. They were both wrapped in their heavy overcoats, with collars turned up, looking down below at the slippery path in front of them, Mrs. Brodski holding tightly on to Alek's right arm as they trudged along the almost-empty main street with just a few lost souls along the way, scurrying for cover. They passed rows of familiar old, dark houses drenched in darkness, except for scant yellow lights, as if framed in the small rectangular windows, trapped behind shabby, sagging curtains, as the only visible signs of life, sheltered from the inhospitable, desolate world outside.

Alek recalled all those times in the past when late in the evenings, he had a habit of taking lonely excursions around town, along the streets he felt were safe enough to roam undetected, approaching the houses and peering inside through the first-floor windows. Many homes still had the curtains drawn apart, with unsuspecting dwellers clearly visible from the outside, going about their lives under the glare of weak incandescent lightbulbs, inadvertently revealing the secrets of their lives. On a few occasions, he felt guilty about being a witness of things he didn't want to see, but he was still mysteriously drawn to his strange habit of inconspicuously looking into people's homes. He had seen abject poverty, people at their best, in the most intimate situations, and at their worst; households dominated by violence and brutality administered against helpless wife and children, whose screams could be clearly heard outside, all at the mercy of a usually drunken and out-of-control husband and father.

They entered the church from the back, left side door and right into a cold vestibule, which was almost completely dark, except for a solitary short but thick candle flickering in a metal holder affixed to the wall under a painting of the Virgin Mary and the baby Jesus. Another heavy, wooden door led to the inside of the main church area, just barely warmer and filled with rows of benches, split in the middle by a walkway, starting a few meters from the back and right up to the front.

The entire floor was covered by beige-and-black ceramic tiles, except the wide, cascading steps from the altar, which were covered by red a carpet, and which ended about three meters before the first pews. The altar was dominated by a golden tabernacle right in the center and a large cross with a life-sized figure of Jesus Christ affixed to the back wall. On the left-side wall in the front of the church was a wooden pulpit, embellished with meticulously carved decorative elements and a dome over it, also adorned with symbolic religious components raised high above the floor, with narrow steps leading to it.

On each side of the church, closer to the back, was a meticulously ornamented confession booth. The high concrete walls of the church contained five large stained-glass windows on both sides. The most prominent features on both side walls, however, were the Stations of the Cross, a series of framed three-dimensional statues of Christ on the day of his crucifixion, imitating Via Dolorosa in Jerusalem, believed to be the path Jesus walked to Mount Calvary on that fateful day almost two thousand years before. Only the front of the church was lit up by a large crystal chandelier suspended from the ceiling with several small lightbulbs and two burning long and thick candles set in tall, heavy wooden holders, one on each side of the wide steps leading to the altar, casting weak rays onto the first few pews on both sides and the small group of people already seated there in anticipation of the ceremony about to begin.

Alek and his mother quickly joined the group, and were very happy they all came, and excited to see them since they didn't know many people in town, and probably the only person they could call a true friend was a recent widow, Maria Pavloska, despite their significant age difference. Two of her three children with families also delighted Alek and his mom with their presence for this special occasion, and all, just like their beloved mother, Maria, were good-natured and most pious people.

Also present was Mr. Kaminski, who was with his wife. He was the poor tailor who lived on the other side of the dividing fence, in the adjacent cluster of decrepit communal housing homes. Over the years, they had both expressed many friendly gestures of support and understanding toward the Brodskis, and even offered a few good deeds, selflessly, without expecting anything in return. They led a rather private life with little interaction with the neighbors on both sides of the wooden fence, beyond the daily preoccupation with constant stream of small sewing jobs for people from the surrounding neighborhoods. They both worked side by side, out of their living room, with his wife assisting with the less demanding and complicated sewing tasks.

Unfortunately, sometimes in the end, it turned out the customers had no money to pay, or had just a portion of it, and in return offered their own labor, or to share something they could spare out of what little they had. Sitting quietly in the second pew were two invited neighbors from the same building. Both were middle-aged women of struggling working-class families, who occasionally visited Alek's mother for tea or coffee, friendly gossip, or just to share and comfort each other in the miseries of their lives. More than once, the women sought temporary shelter from their husbands on a drunken rampage; if only they managed to take the children and escaped in time, and then shivering inside with fear and the children crying as the men went door to door, staggering, looking for them, shouting obscenities, pounding madly with fists and threatening to break the doors down if the occupants didn't open them immediately.

Thus, still relatively loose neighborly bonds were formed over time, out of necessity rather than anything in common, sadly perhaps misery being the only exception. They all waited, sitting close together, Alek and some of them shivering wrapped in heavy winter coats in the semidarkness of the dimly lit, cold church, mostly in silence out of respect for the House of God, as was the custom; but also, the low, freezing temperature made it impossible to talk without a considerable effort. The payment for performing the baptism had already been made well in advance; the parish priest wouldn't have it any other way, and although it was a significant amount by any measure, about a half month's salary, he preferred to call it a "donation."

Father Antoni was late now, but they all could hear distant noises and subdued voices coming from the sacristy. Finally, he emerged in his black frock with a white cape over it, with the Bible in his left hand, in the company of his assistant, Father Feliks, and a teenage altar boy with a silver tray in his hands, carrying two glass containers, the larger one filled with Holy Water and the other with Sacred Chrism, made of olive oil and sweet perfume, and a neatly folded bright white cloth. He and Father Feliks approached the pews, looking at all the gathered and greeted them cheerfully.

They all got up when he was still a few meters away and, almost in unison, answered, "Good evening!" And a few, who were familiar with the church protocol, added, "Praise be to God."

Father Antoni looked at all of them again, from left to right; bowed cordially; and, with a gentle smile, replied, "Praise the Lord Jesus Christ!"

He then approached the first pew and extended his hand to each and every one of them, with particular emphasis on Alek, whom he greeted especially warmly, and his evidently happy mother. Then he leaned over to the guests in the second row, and they all, one by one, leaned forward and met him halfway, extending their hands to the priest, smiling sincerely. He seemed to be in a particularly good mood, full of energy, jovial and smiling, as if a good, old friend met again. Father Feliks, in a well-rehearsed manner, followed a similar routine and greeted everyone cordially, and then moved to the side, to allow Father Antoni to take the center stage, who promptly began with a short introductory speech.

"I'm happy to see you all tonight, on this cold but special day. And because it is already close to Christmas, it makes it even more special. We're gathered here in this small group of family and friends to celebrate the sacrament of initiation—Alek's special day, his baptism, a day that will leave an indelible mark on his entire future life from this day forward. We will welcome him to our Christian family, which undoubtedly will be a turning point of his life and a fulfillment of his dreams, as related to me over the course of many months, during which I got to know him and his beloved mother quite well. Although small, but what a wonderful family they are. From this day on, Alek will be free from the power of darkness and cleansed of the stain of humanity's original sin, and will have access to God's gift of salvation, bountiful grace, his limitless generosity, and his profound, unconditional love. I know that Alek is already quite familiar with the New Testament and the catechism of the Catholic Church, which we've talked about in the past. While we're standing, I'd like to propose that we all say the Lord's Prayer, shall we?"

Alek seemed quite uneasy about the absence of his friend Ela, although she assured him she would definitely come; and he was somewhat intimidated by all this attention, even his name being pronounced among the group of people he hardly knew, except perhaps for Pavloska, for whom he had a special affinity and whom he considered a family friend. By extension, her grown-up children seemed somehow close to him, although he didn't know them well at all, having met them only twice before at their mother's house, when he was there with his mom visiting Maria.

Father Antoni once again looked at them with a delicate smile on his lips, and when satisfied, he began the prayer, and they all followed him in reciting the Lord's Prayer.

After finishing the recitation of the Lord's Prayer, Father Antoni again looked over at the guests, Father Feliks, and his altar boy, and then asked the guests to sit down. He then turned his attention for a few seconds to something out in the distance, at the end of the church, gathering his thoughts. He then announced that he would like to say a few more words before the actual ceremony of baptism, and that he was aware of how anxious they were to start and get it over with, but that he felt obligated nevertheless to fulfill his pastoral duty, and touch on few related things, so vital to the ritual of baptism itself.

"I'd like to add what the catechism of the Catholic Church says on the subject, which summarizes it quite well. The sacrament of holy baptism imprints on the soul an indelible spiritual sign, and is the basis of the whole Christian life, the gateway to life in the Spirit. Through baptism, we are freed from the sin and reborn as sons of God. We become members of Christ. Baptism is the sacrament of regeneration through water in the word, and renewal by the Holy Spirit. It derives from the Greek word *baptizein,* which means to "plunge" or "immerse." Our Lord Jesus Christ gave himself to be baptized by Saint John the Baptist in the Jordan River. I'd like to read to you now a passage from the New Testament, which Jesus said after his resurrection."

The priest slowly flipped the pages of the Bible he held in his left hand to the gospel of Matthew 28:19. He then looked again at the gathered guests from left to right, with a more solemn expression on his face, and began to read in a deliberate, steady tone, emphasizing each word, "Go therefore and make disciples of all nations, baptizing them in the name of the Father and the Son and of the Holy Spirit, teaching them to observe all that I have commanded you."

"Now, I'd like to invite our fine young man Aleksander Brodski to come forward and stand about here, in the center, facing the altar and the light, and his mother, Mrs. Brodski, to stand to his left, and both godparents slightly behind Alek. Please, please, come forward, and let us begin."

With some hesitation, Alek took off his coat, left it on the bench, and slowly, with obvious uneasiness, came forward, as commanded by Father Antoni. He was wearing an oversized black suit, a white dress shirt, a black tie, and nicely polished black shoes. His mom followed him right behind, keeping an eye on her nervous son, and put a hand on his shoulder once he reached the designated spot.

His godparents, Maria Pavloska and Mr. Kaminski, with some initial difficulty shedding their heavy overcoats and getting out of the narrow pews, joined them a few seconds later and took their places behind Alek and Mrs. Brodski.

The priest quickly joined the group too, standing with his back to the altar. He looked at them all intently for a few seconds, as if trying to read their thoughts, and then beckoned to the altar boy to move closer to his left side. He turned to Alek, standing just over a meter in front of him, towering above them all, and then he also acknowledged Mrs. Brodski and the godparents, each holding a hand on Alek's shoulder, and then with a nod of his head, and without further delay, he read out from a large hardcover book bound in dark-brown leather held out by Father Feliks, who was standing on his right side. Alek looked back hesitantly once again and noticed Ela, who came in late and was just settling in alone, farther back, away from the main group, in an empty pew somewhere in the middle of the church, as the priest spoke in a calm but resounding voice, placing particular emphasis on key words.

"Let us renew the promises of the holy baptism, by which we renounce Satan and his works and promise to serve God in the Holy Catholic Church, so I ask you, do you reject Satan?"

"I do," said Alek.

"And all his works?"

"I do," he professed again.

"And all his empty promises?"

"I do."

"Do you reject sin, so as to live in the freedom of God's children?"

"I do."

"Do you believe in God, the Father Almighty, Creator of heaven and earth?"

"I do."

"Do you believe in Jesus Christ, his only Son, our Lord, who was born of the Virgin Mary, was crucified, died, and was buried, rose from the dead, and now is seated at the right hand of the Father?"

"I do."

"Do you believe in the Holy Spirit, the Holy Catholic Church, the communion of saints, the forgiveness of sins, the resurrection of the body and life everlasting?"

"I do," came the reply again.

"God, the all-powerful Father of our Lord Jesus Christ has given us a new birth by water and the Holy Spirit, and forgiven all our sins. May he also keep us faithful to our Lord Jesus Christ forever and ever."

"Amen," they all said in unison.

Father Antoni put his hands together and with utmost concentration and intensity in his voice, pronounced a few incomprehensible sentences in Latin; and when he finished, he made the sign of the cross, with his right hand directed toward Alek. He then turned to the altar boy standing to his right and took from the tray he was holding the transparent glass flask filled with holy water, approached Alek, and gently laid his left hand on top of his head, and with a slight push downward, he inclined him to bow down, due to his considerable height.

Once again, he looked at his mother and the godparents standing near him, and then back to Alek, with the most serene, sincere, and saintly expression on his face, and uttered, "Aleksander Jakub, I now baptize you in the name of the Father." And the priest carefully, but skillfully, poured the first of the holy water over the top front of Alek's head and continued emphasizing each word, "And of the Son…" He poured the second small part of the water and added, "And of the Holy Spirit…" And he poured the third and last part of the water over the top of Alek's head. A faint smile appeared on the priest's face as he placed the glass carafe with about half of the holy water left in it back onto the tray held by the altar boy.

DOMINIK POLESKI

Alek slowly lifted his head up, looked at Father Antoni with genuine gratitude, and then at his mother, and smiled; and in his whole demeanor, there was an unmistakable appearance of satisfaction and great relief, for he seemed a changed man, indeed. The priest, without a word, handed him a folded white linen cloth from the tray, which Alek immediately understood was to dry his wet hair and face. Then with just a slight, agile movement of the fingers of his right hand, he hastily fixed his ruffled hair.

Father Antoni once again turned to the altar boy standing to his right and dipped his thumb in the other open small glass container with the sacred chrism, perfumed olive oil consecrated by the bishop, and anointed Alek's forehead with a sign of the cross, bowed his head, and whispered something in Latin.

Unexpectedly and suddenly, the light in the back of the church high above the balcony housing the pipe organ lit up, and someone invisible from the floor started to play the most profoundly pure and beautiful heavenly music, but gently, quietly, and with such lightness, as if barely touching the keys, and yet touching the souls of all those listening.

They all turned around; looked up in the direction of the sublime, sweet sound; and they were stunned by the beauty, listening motionless, seemingly mesmerized. Unmistakably, it was the resident organist, the town's well-known and well-respected musical genius, Mr. Kopytko, at his best.

He lived just outside the walls of the church compound, in a little old wooden cottage, surviving modestly on a meager pension allotted by the church, the ever-frugal Father Antoni, and giving piano lessons to a few students, often musically deaf but coming from families with higher expectations, who had money to spare, and wanted their children to go beyond just the regular school curriculum.

He was a rather short and chubby fellow, but a kind and pious man, with the most agreeable and gentle disposition, and would most likely play for free if asked, just for the love of music. He was known to deviate on occasion, possibly only a few times a year, from the religious repertoire, especially after the late-night Mass, and with uninhibited enthusiasm, delve into the classics, like Bach, Mozart, or Beethoven.

Sadly, very few in town recognized his skills, much less what he was actually playing.

Father Antoni was very proud of his services, or as he rather called it, his mission, and considered him absolutely indispensable, despite the fact this older man lived in poverty and the church coffers were full. However, the parish priest found it particularly hard to part with money, but somehow collection came to him naturally. He stood there with the rest of the baptismal guests, with clearly apparent contentment, and listened attentively to his virtuoso, Mr. Kopytko. The priest, without attracting any attention, approached Alek, patted him on the back, shook his hand, congratulated him warmly, wished him well in his new life as a Christian, and expressed his sincere hopes that they would be seeing each other more often from now on. Alek was visibly emotional, with tears in his eyes; and his usually hunched-over, lanky figure was now fully upright with pride, and newly found great upsurge in self-esteem.

Father Antoni then moved on to his mother and congratulated her on her son's life-altering experience, and told her how proud she should be of her son, and expressed his hopes to see her more often, although, of course, not in the church on her knees in the front pew but, rather, in a more informal setting, "to get to know each other better." After all, he was a self-professed connoisseur of beauty and fine things in life, and she was both—a beautiful and a fine woman. He spent little time on the godparents, Mrs. Pavloska and Mr. Kaminski, just a quick handshake, "Keep warm," "Sleep well," "Thank you for coming," and "Good night." Then unceremoniously moving on to the rest of the guests standing near the benches, he ran through them all even faster, with even quicker handshakes. "Thank you for coming," and "Good night."

Father Feliks followed suit and cordially shook everyone's hand, bowed, extended his best wishes, especially to Alek, and said his good-byes with a sincere smile. No one paid much attention to the altar boy, and his presence would have been completely forgotten had it not been for Mrs. Brodski, who turned around amid the whole commotion and noticed him just standing there, exactly on the spot where they all left after the ceremony.

DOMINIK POLESKI

She approached the teenager and said farewell, also on behalf of Alek, who was preoccupied with the quests, who showered him with attention and best wishes. Of course, they were all invited well in advance to the Brodski household for an official reception, and now the invitations were enthusiastically reaffirmed once again.

Alek did his best to maintain a respectful façade, furtively looking at Ela; and she looked back at him with a sad, withdrawn expression. The inspiring baptismal experience unquestionably had a positive effect on the spirits of the entire main group, despite the cold temperature inside and outside of the old St. John's church, they all became quite animated, almost exuberant as they were slowly edging toward the exit through the dimly lit church, along the main aisle in the middle, and as the organ virtuoso, Mr. Kopytko, played his heart out, adding to the feeling this was a momentous occasion.

Alek suddenly stopped by the pew Ela was sitting in and uncertainly sat beside her, at the edge of the bench, and looked her in the eyes. All the guests turned around and stared at the young couple in bewilderment.

"I'm sorry for being late," she said with unmistakable sadness.

"Don't worry, it's all right. I'm glad you came," said Alek.

"Congratulations!"

"Thank you."

"You must go now."

"Not without you."

"I can't go."

"Why not?"

"Some of those people know me. They know what I had done. I don't think they'll like me being there."

"I don't care what they think. I'd like you to come to my house, please."

"You know I can't. Besides, I'm not in a good mood tonight. I don't want to spoil the celebration. You must go now, Alek."

"Promise me you will come later. They probably won't stay long because of the children."

"We'll see, I can't promise. Go now."

Alek looked at Ela, at her beautiful face; she had tears in her eyes and quickly lowered her head, as if embarrassed or trying to conceal something. He touched her clasped, trembling hands and then got up and hurried to join the group of guests, leaving her behind. In the back of the church, just before leaving, almost all of them turned around one last time, looked at the well-lit altar in the distance, crossed themselves, some kneeling down in reverence, paying homage to the Almighty God, Creator of heaven and earth. The entrance vestibule was drenched in the twilight of two candles burning on opposing walls, one near a clay, lifelike figure of Christ on the cross with his nailed feet low enough above the tiled floor as to become over decades a revered shrine for the throngs of faithful on their way in or out, to stop for a quick prayer, and a fearful glance at his horrific wounds, his head tilted to one side with his closed eyes, and his sad face, his crown of thorns, and perhaps to plant a kiss on Christ's pierced, bloodstained, cold feet.

Nearby, within easy reach, affixed to the wall, was a carved-out stone basin filled with holy water for the patrons to solemnly immerse the tips of their hands, make the sign of the cross, and utter, "In the name of the Father, and of the Son, and of the Holy Ghost. Amen." Then they stepped outside. The guests, except the children, all lined up dutifully to perform this long-held tradition, and then slowly left the church into the darkness of the night, to be immediately struck again by the cold air of the fast-approaching winter, which in these parts, as expected, always advanced from the east, with its merciless fury, and perhaps sooner than anywhere else.

The weak light from the inside shone through the tall, colorful stained-glass windows, casting feeble rays in the immediate vicinity of the church, barely illuminating the perimeter of the building. They could still hear the music as they descended down the prominent, wide but slippery stone steps of the main church entrance, thinly covered by a layer of fresh snow, and walked through the wide-open gate marked by two massive concrete pillars, one on each side, and onto the sidewalk of Warynski Street, named after the famed, late notorious nineteenth-century socialist revolutionary Ludwik Warynski.

They all walked slowly along the almost completely deserted main street, crossing dark and empty side streets drenched in strangely soothing silence and the mystery of the special night, leaving a trail of shoemarks imprinted in the fresh layer of snow. The group moved in a loose column, led by Mrs. Brodski alongside Alek, with her right hand under his left arm, followed by the rest of the guests huddled together, without any particular order. Some engaged in lighthearted conversation along the way, exchanging their admiration for Alek, his tireless, loving mother and their friend Zofia. They were still deeply moved and still under the impressions of the baptism ceremony and its participants—Father Antoni Pukalski, Father Feliks, the altar boy, and, finally, the always-dependable and irreplaceable organist, Mr. Kopytko, whose heart-warming, inspiring music still resonated in their minds. The guests, being witness to this most soul-enriching ceremony, had a profound feeling of spiritual renewal, a feeling of inexplicable lightness, as if they too reaffirmed their Christian vows, and committed their lives again to the timeless teachings of Jesus Christ.

Alek thought of Ela when passing the deserted familiar streets lined with the leafless, ghostly skeletons of trees and scarcely lit old houses, the long stretch of the central shopping plaza, known as the halls, with all the lights already out and the stores boarded up for the night, the memorable restaurant, and farther down the road another one, the only places with visible signs of life; and with a gentle, light snow falling, it all evoked in him a surreal feeling of nostalgia and loneliness. They soon reached the house, stomped their feet just inside the foyer to shake off any traces of snow off their boots, and then one by one, they all went inside, hastened by Mrs. Brodski.

The hostess led them through the kitchen to the living room, which also served as a bedroom for them, and asked them to take off their coats, keep their shoes on, and sit wherever they could. It was already quite chilly inside, although before they left, the large tiled stove in the corner of the room was filled with fresh coal; they were hoping it would still retain the heat when they got back. Alek looked inside the pit and threw a few scoops onto the almost-burned-out but still-glowing few remaining little lumps of coal.

Soon after, the guests showered Alek with attention again, presented him with an array of practical gifts, mostly envelopes with wish cards accompanied by modest amounts of bank notes in various denominations, a few books, a new, elegant fountain pen, and a sketchbook with a charcoal pencil set. Again, a renewed flood of best wishes followed, handshaking, hugs, and pats on the back, making him most uncomfortable, awkwardly trying to maintain his best composure, reciprocating kindly with gratitude for their generosity, and smiling shyly as best as he could, and when expected.

Mrs. Brodski threw herself into serving the food and drinks with the help of Mrs. Pavloska and Mrs. Kaminski. All was ready in advance; in fact, she had worked on this for the past three days, running to the stores a few times for missing ingredients, which were not always available, or exactly what she was looking for; and eventually, as a last resort, he had to borrow a few things from her closest neighbors, or modify some recipes to suit what she had, or even giving up on some of the planned dishes altogether.

It didn't take long before all began to arrive on the fully expanded living room table covered with a white tablecloth. Two additional chairs were brought in from the kitchen and squeezed between all the others. The plates, cutlery, and glasses were already there, set before they left for the church, and now just moved around to make space for two more sets. The children were planned to sit on the sofa and eat with plates held on their laps. There were traditional, most common hot dishes, cold snacks, and a variety of cold cuts with a generous supply of vodka to wash it all down with, or soda for the children or those who abstained from drinking alcohol. Later, tea was served with a few choices of pastry, and more vodka flowed with frequent exclamations "Na zdrowie," literally, "to health," and all along, a lively conversation accompanied the feast.

Alek struggled to maintain his interest in the topics discussed, most of little substance to him, anything from bits and pieces of the country's politics and recent international events, as related by the government media and compared to what supposedly Radio Free Europe was broadcasting. Also figured prominently around the table discussion were the local news; Christianity and its essential role in the society; the local church and its most visible representative, Father Antoni; and, of course, the widespread gossip surrounding his alleged "wild side."

The priest's friendship with Father Vladimir, the well-known parish priest from the Eastern Orthodox Church, whose presumptive double life was now legendary in the entire county, also came under scrutiny. It was duly established, with much friendly deliberation and laughter, that the friendship between the two clerics was no accident. Throughout the ordeal, Alek hoped that they would just leave him alone, because even if he tried to excuse himself from the dinner table, there was nowhere to go, nowhere to hide. He thought about Ela. She seemed to be in obvious distress in the church, and although she didn't categorically turn down another invitation to attend the post-baptism reception in his house, he was sure she had no intention of coming. He had a nagging, persistent thought that something grievous must have happened to her, most likely another violent confrontation with her father, and how everything else was now secondary.

Even the baptism itself seemed of little importance, especially when he had those momentary, inexplicable flashbacks to the time just several hours before, when he was free of all the additional burden, free of doubts that were tearing him apart, and like a swarm of stinging bees, invading his mind and wreaking havoc in their wake. The whole sumptuous feast was becoming a suffocating nuisance, a burden full of unbearable regrets weighing heavily upon his conscience for his lack of gratitude to his mother, for her unwavering dedication, all the hard work she put into preparation of this reception with what little she had, to make this day truly memorable for him. It wasn't meant to be, but what he dreaded most eventually happened: his restlessness was noticed.

"Alek, tell me, what do you want to be when you finish your school?" he was asked unexpectedly.

"I'd like to continue my studies at university, preferably Warsaw or Krakow," he answered politely.

"What would you like to study there?"

"I'm not sure yet, but possibly art or literature."

"Oh...is that so? Do you want to be an artist, like a painter, or a writer?"

"I'm not sure, but possibly."

"It all sounds interesting, but how are you going to support yourself?"

"Exactly by that, painting or working for some national newspaper or magazine."

"Very good. Good luck with that. So, you're already planning to leave this town in the not-too-distant future, right?"

"No, not so soon. But if everything goes well, in about four years."

"You're not thinking of leaving your mother behind you, are you?"

"It might be necessary, but only for a few years."

"Then what?"

"Once I'll finish my studies and get a good job in one of those cities, she would join me, of course."

"Sounds like you've got it all figured out, down to the last detail."

"Not quite, but I hope to start a new life eventually, somewhere else."

"Alek, you've never shared those plans with me before," interrupted his mother, visibly surprised by her son's decisive answers.

"No, Mom, I have not, and I'm sorry, but these are only plans, just my imagination, too distant to be taken seriously at this time."

"All right, fair enough, but I'd like to be informed in advance what my only son is planning. Is that too much to ask?"

"Of course not. I promise I will, when the time comes."

"Who was that young woman in the church, Alek?" asked Pavloska's son, who was already quite intoxicated and becoming a nuisance to all with his intrusive questions and confrontational behavior.

"That was my friend Elzbieta form school. She was invited too, but unfortunately, she was late, and couldn't come to dinner tonight. She had some important family matters to attend to," Alek answered evasively.

"Are you sure? It seemed to me she was more than just a friend from school," he continued.

"As I said, a good friend from school. Sometimes we do homework together."

"Alek, I'm just asking. In church, it looked like there was more in common between you two than just homework."

"I'd rather not talk about it," said Alek.

"You wouldn't want to be like that Jesus Christ's apostle Peter, who denied him three times, would you?"

"I'm not denying anything. I just don't want to talk about it."

"You know, I have a feeling I've seen that young woman before. In fact, I'm almost sure I have," persisted the young Pavloski.

"This is a small town. I wouldn't be surprised if you've seen her somewhere at least once," countered Alek.

"What I mean is, I've seen her working the streets."

"Marek, I think you've had too much to drink to say such a thing. Please leave Alek alone," Maria Pavloska interfered sternly in Alek's defense.

"All I'm saying is that the young man is not telling us the truth," continued her son with the same derisive tone and sarcastic smirk.

"Marek, I'm asking you to stop this nonsense right now and leave. Just take your wife and daughter, and go home. You've had too much to drink, and you are embarrassing me, your family, and making a fool of yourself," added Pavloska with even greater passion.

"Yes, Mom is right, Marek. We must go now," added his wife, Krystyna.

It was almost ten o'clock when Marek took another shot of vodka, looked at the people seated around the table, murmured something to himself, and then grudgingly got up and walked slowly over to the coat hanger near the kitchen door. He put on his heavy winter coat and said, "I'm ready. Shall we go, then?"

Before he stepped out the door, prompted by his wife, he offered Alek what sounded like an apathetic apology, to which Alek didn't respond at all; he was just glad Marek Pavloski was leaving.

Shortly after ten, Pavloska's daughter, with her husband and their two exhausted children, also moved toward the door, escorted by Mrs. Brodski and an equally worn-out Alek. It wasn't long before Mr. Kaminski, Alek's godfather, and his wife Amelia, decided it was time to head home. Although the tailor didn't miss a round of frequently replenished vodka glasses, he hung in there remarkably well, was exceedingly well mannered and polite to the very end, and even offered to walk Maria Pavloska home. She promptly accepted his offer, and soon the three of them were standing at the door, all bundled up, hugging and kissing as the best of friends, promising to get together in the near future, since Christmas was just around the corner, giving plenty of opportunity to forge even closer bonds, and once again offering Alek their best wishes.

The two female neighbors from the same housing complex were the last to leave, since they didn't have far to go, just on the other side of the same old building, with entrances from a common corridor on the north side just off the street. They left their children in the company of their husbands, under the care of older siblings, and felt it was a rare opportunity to leave it all behind, even if it was only for a few hours.

Alek was by then completely tired, couldn't sit straight after a long and exhausting day full of unprecedented events and drama. He got up and moved to the sofa with obvious signs of irritation. The women were still in no hurry to leave, overstaying the hospitality of the hosts, risking the wrath of their husbands, as long as Mrs. Brodski was listening to their stories of misery, how life had dealt them the wrong cards, and how there was no way out but to carry the cross. Each one had an appalling story of mistreatment at the hands of her often-drunk husband on regular missions of dispensing his brand of discipline and justice at will, to "set her straight" whenever he felt she "stepped out of line."

Finally, they too left reluctantly, and it seemed they would rather have stayed even longer, but must have finally realized it was time to go, so as not to make matters even worse. They said their farewells with teary eyes, but were grateful for the honor of being invited to the baptism ceremony and the reception. They hugged Mrs. Brodski and then once again passed on their best wishes to Alek, and then finally left.

Profound silence befell their home, almost eerie, uncomfortable, as if some invisible but deeply felt soul had left the room with the guests, the essence of the celebration which was supposed to mark Alek's new beginning, a turning point, promising new and joyous life as a Christian and his mother with him. Mrs. Brodski was tired, but soon begun to clean up the table and take things back to the kitchen, making several trips back and forth, while Alek sat impassively on the sofa, in a strangely pensive mood, and he was sad.

23

D ESPITE THE HIGH hopes for dramatic changes in his daily existence, not much had changed in Alek's life, and soon almost everything went back to normal, as things used to be, except for the added responsibility of attending the church every Sunday morning, a schedule which with time became rather impossible to maintain, eventually turning into a more feasible arrangement, every second Sunday, and then the practically obligatory, regular New Testament indoctrination, known as "religion classes." Those were held regularly, once a week on Thursdays, in one of the specially converted bleak, poorly heated, and badly lit rooms at the church rectory, with several rows of wooden desks and chairs similar to those in his school.

Alek continued to see Ela, mostly at school, usually during lunch breaks, which raised suspicions, unwanted attention and occasionally, resentment. Sometimes they met after school if the end of their classes happened to coincide, and walked home together as far as they could. They parted just before the town's center, and walked the last stretch of their way home in different directions. Even less frequently they met to study or do the homework together, since Ela's father, Mr. Nowak, was regularly intoxicated and continued to display hostility towards his wife and daughter, Alek, and just about everybody else who happened to visit them. In turn, Ela was reluctant to visit Alek's home, despite his repeated invitations. She didn't feel comfortable in his mother's presence for fear of being asked about things in her past or her family life she'd rather not talk about. Alek was especially concerned, when Ela unexpectedly didn't come to school for a few days in a row, every few weeks, or showed reluctance to meet on weekends without any prior warning or explanation. Once she came back and resumed regular attendance, she brushed off Alek's inquiries and his displays of genuine concern. Those were times when he began to suspect Ela of having relapses into her old lifestyle, the allure of nightlife, perhaps out of necessity.

Christianity—it was the beginning of a new experience, a long and winding road toward Alek's first communion, reception of the Eucharist, and the third of seven sacraments, immediately preceded by the second sacrament, the sacrament of penance, his first confession. When it finally arrived, Alek again felt out of place in a group of about thirty mostly second-grade children and their parents involved in all the activities of their little pupils, constantly showering them with unwanted attention; but he was all alone throughout it all, and he preferred it that way, away from his mother's prying eyes and uncomfortable meddling.

Alek attended all the preparatory sessions leading to the scheduled ceremony on Sunday, May 18, 1969, all by himself. A trip to the district town was necessary to buy the customary white suit and matching shoes, a required part of a standard attire to symbolize purity.

Alek found the first confession to be the biggest challenge, and he couldn't imagine standing in a long line up to the confession booth among the restless little children, so they had a prior arrangement made with Father Antoni for a separate session just for him. It still posed a problem of honestly confessing his sins to the priest he always had reservations about. In the end, he decided on a much-scaled-down version list of his sins whispered to the ear of Father Antoni, just enough to sound credible. Alek knew well in advance from his school friends, especially those who continued to confess regularly into their teens, what the intrusive priest wanted to hear. One of the first questions was often about the "first experience," which only meant one thing and for whatever reason the cunning priest wanted to hear all the sordid details from a terrified teenager. However, if there was little to confess in that respect, the priest felt obligated to continue the interrogation, and drill the young man about the next best thing on the list of grave sins—masturbation.

"When?", "Where?", or "How many times?", the priest wanted to know, and then in a spirit of compassion and understanding, graciously

DOMINIK POLESKI

assigned penance, but just came short of condemning outright the "sinful" and "unhealthy" practice.

The weather was exceptionally nice and sunny on Sunday, with spring in full bloom. It was a warm and windless day, perfectly coinciding with the church's special Mass full of people, the participants, the parents, extended family, guests, and unrelated churchgoers who just happened to be there, or who thought there would be greater value in the first communion Mass. It was all that and more; in fact, one could hardly imagine a more ceremonial, festive, and celebratory event, exceeding Alek's and his mother's expectations.

Following the official reception of the Eucharist, the Body of Christ, the concluding prayers and hymns with lively accompaniment of the indispensable organist, Mr. Kopytko, the whole group spilled out of the church and assembled on the prominent front steps, with Father Antoni taking the central position in the back row, just in front of the wide-open, massive double church door. The children were carefully organized in descending rows on the wide granite stone steps by Father Feliks and an official photographer hired by the church to document the occasion.

Alek stood next to the priest, towering above all, with a serene and confident expression on his face despite the rather awkward assembly among the much younger children, holding an official framed religious picture with the church seal, date, and the parish priest's signature in one hand and a candle in the other.

Mrs. Brodski stood in the back of the crowd, near the entrance to the church courtyard, by one of the large concrete pillars, looking proudly at her son standing on the top landing in the center, next to the priest.

A few meters away, surrounded by a large throng of gathered people, in no particular order, stood Ela looking on, although barely visible, as if determined to feel inconspicuous, as if she didn't know him at all, just a coincidental observer. Outside the church courtyard, along the wide, tiled sidewalk, a teenager was passing by in a hurry on his way to the train station, quite oblivious to the ceremony in progress. Then he suddenly looked sideways, noticed the large celebratory occasion, and stopped frozen in midstride.

Unknowingly, without any preconceived idea, as if by an inexplicable stroke of fate that was meant to be, he looked at the group of communicants on the church steps and noticed Alek Brodski standing right in the middle, and their eyes met briefly, mutually recognized each other, apparently in a gesture of inherent understanding, as all those times in the past, seemingly by coincidence and in the most unexpected places.

Alek immediately recognized in the teenager the same boy he had seen a few times before, who was curiously watching him from a distance, without any particular reason, but with a sense of strange, heartfelt concern and sympathy, and yet as if detached and afraid of something. The teenager then let his gaze travel farther to the side and noticed Mrs. Brodski standing by the pillar, smiling warmly, looking around, as if eagerly seeking any sign of approval and recognition, a trace of appreciation, but no one seemed to notice or care. Their eyes too met for a split second, as all those years ago, when just a child, through the hole in a wooden fence, with mutual affinity, and as if they had always known each other.

The boy smiled back timidly, and then quickly resumed walking to the train station, with renewed vigor and haste, to catch the next train to the provincial capital Lublin, leaving the town behind, and never to come back.

THE END

DOMINIK POLESKI

CPSIA information can be obtained
at www.ICGtesting.com
Printed in the USA
LVOW03s1518230418
574530LV00002B/523/P

9 781524 583088